Also by Phil Mizen

Young People, Training and the State: In and Against the Training State

Hidden Hands: International Perspectives on Children's Work and Labour
(*with C. Pole and A. Bolton*)

The Changing State of Youth

Phil Mizen

palgrave
macmillan

First published 2004 by
PALGRAVE MACMILLAN
Houndmills, Basingstoke, Hampshire RG21 6XS and
175 Fifth Avenue, New York, N.Y. 10010
Companies and representatives throughout the world

PALGRAVE MACMILLAN is the global academic imprint of the Palgrave
Macmillan division of St. Martin's Press, LLC and of Palgrave Macmillan Ltd.
Macmillan® is a registered trademark in the United States, United Kingdom
and other countries. Palgrave is a registered trademark in the European
Union and other countries.

ISBN 0–333–73949–3 hardback
ISBN 0–333–73950–7 paperback

This book is printed on paper suitable for recycling and made from fully
managed and sustained forest sources.

A catalogue record for this book is available from the British Library.

A catalog record for this book is available from the Library of Congress.

10 9 8 7 6 5 4 3 2 1
13 12 11 10 09 08 07 06 05 04

Printed in China

For my sister, Cas

Contents

List of Tables

Abbreviations

APS	Assisted Places Scheme
BCS	British Crime Survey
CB	Child Benefit
CJA	Criminal Justice Act
CJPO	Criminal Justice and Public Order Act
CP	Community Programme
CTC	City Technology College
CYPA	Children and Young Person's Act
EAZ	Education Action Zone
EPA	Education Priority Areas
ERA	Education Reform Act
ET	Employment Training
FEFC	Further Education Funding Council
GCSE	General Certificate of Secondary Education
GDP	Gross Domestic Product
GM	Grant Maintained
ILO	International Labour Office
IS	Income Support
IT	Intermediate Treatment
JSA	Jobseekers Allowance
LEA	Local Education Authority
LMS	Local Management of Schools
MApps	Modern Apprenticeships
MSC	Manpower Services Commission
NA	National Assistance
NDLP	New Deal for Lone Parents
NDPU	New Deal for Partners of the Unemployed
NDYP	New Deal for Young People
NEET	Neither in Employment, Education or Training
NVQ	National Vocational Qualification
NMW	National Minimum Wage
OECD	Organisation for Economic Co-operation and Development
OFSTED	Office for Standards in Education

ORF   Output Related Funding
SAT   Standard Assessment Task
SB   Supplementary Benefit
SEU   Social Exclusion Unit
TEC   Training and Enterprise Council
TfW   Training for Work
TUC   Trades Union Congress
TVEI Technical and Vocational Education Initiative
UB   Unemployment Benefit
WEP   Work Experience Programme
YOP   Youth Opportunities Programme
YT   Youth Training
YTS   Youth Training Scheme

Introduction

The twin concerns of this book are well expressed by its title. To begin with, it is a book about youth as a political construct and how what we have come to recognise as youth is very much a product of state and government. In this respect it may appear to traverse a terrain already familiar to anyone who takes more than a passing interest in the plight of the young and their significance to the political and social processes of modern society. There is, of course, a long-standing fascination with how youth's representation in official discourse continues to orbit around a tenacious dialectic between the extremities of menace and desire, threat and renewal. What Davies (1986) has termed 'threatening youth' provides an especially powerful weapon in an extensive and sophisticated state armoury geared towards the imposition of its own version of events as a means to effect desired 'solutions'. The approach taken here, however, is somewhat different. For sure, the need to reveal these hidden agendas and deconstruct the coercive practices they contain is a clear and pressing one. But the argument pursued throughout this book is informed by a concern with youth's material and institutional existence; with youth as the product of the concrete activities of state and government; with how the crisis of the state that unfolded during the final quarter of the twentieth century was simultaneously expressed in terms of a crisis of youth; and with how the ideological representations of 'problem youth' contain an element of practical truth, however distorted, if only because the young have been forced to pay a heavy price in the 'resolution' of this crisis.

In considering youth's political construction this book gives considerable importance to the practical importance of age. In the years in which I have been researching and writing about youth, it has become apparent to me that an understanding of age is necessary to the appreciation of youth's social and political significance. It is primarily on the basis of age that young people's lives are organised, as states have developed complex and sophisticated networks of regulation for the young structured by criteria of chronological age. It is by reference to age that young people find themselves placed into a more or less common relationship to the central institutions of modern society. And it is on the basis of age that young people find themselves physically divided from families, communities and friends. Strangely this basic fact finds little place in a now extensive literature on youth. Sociologists and others have rightly attested to the continuing power of class, gender and ethnicity in shaping the contours of youth and delineating its limits and possibilities, but little comment has been offered as to why age in youth has assumed such an importance to the activity of modern states.

To make sense of the political importance of age and youth this book therefore offers a dissenting voice in what may be loosely, if somewhat awkwardly, termed 'youth studies'. It does so by presenting an argument that, if it possesses any originality, stems from the unapologetic focus it gives to the political importance attached to age in youth, and to the considerable practical implications that flow from this. More specifically, the argument developed here seeks to derive the importance of age and youth from the form of the modern state. Age, it is claimed, has a number of important political dimensions. It allows states to foster divisions, more often than not arbitrary ones, on the societies that they seek to manage by projecting certain forms of activity on the day-to-day organisation of social life. At the same time, the degree of real universalism that states attribute to age provides one means through which more traditional sources of division can be reproduced and, in recent times, reanimated. And most important to the purpose of this book, age also provides the means to effect young people's (re)integration into the broader political strategies that governments adopt in their endeavours to manage the contradictory development of capitalist social relations.

This last point takes us to the second major theme of this book: the changing cost of being young. It is often remarked upon how youth constitutes the best days of one's life and there is without doubt more than a grain of truth to this. Whatever else it may involve, youth certainly remains a time of relative freedom. Yet the simple 'state' of being young has always exacted a price and for some this has invariably been greater than for others. For it is a central argument of this book that in recent times the consequence of government policy for young people has been felt in terms of the reconstitution of youth into a more costly 'state' to be, as governments have set about eroding young people's access to and claims upon key sources of support. For some this claim will undoubtedly run against the grain of common sense since after all, youth today has never been such a time of plenty. It is indeed the case that for a notable minority the increased cost of being young pales against an unprecedented expansion in their freedoms and opportunities. The contention here, however, is that for most young people the fact of possessing a certain chronological age has become the basis for their reintegration into a relatively more demanding 'state' of youth and one that can exact a demanding price.

Responsibility for this is in no small way directly attributable to the political reconstruction of youth and to the substance of government policies. The time frame of this book is the last 25 to 30 years of the twentieth century and there are clear reasons for giving special attention to this period. Historical interest aside, it is a time when the post-war world came adrift from those moorings which, for a while at least, had seemed to offer some possibility for stability and security. It is a time when custom and practice were quite literally turned upside down. It is a time of crisis, austerity and change. It is also a time when the promise held out by the political commitment to a society managed in ways that would foster inclusion, concession and conciliation gave way to a new era of austerity as governments brought market forces, money and the rule of law to the fore. For as we shall see, the political crisis that swept over and then engulfed the social democratic state from the middle of the 1970s onwards, was also played out in terms of a crisis of youth. Whereas age and youth had been elevated into one of the defining principles of the social democratic commitment to inclusion, with the turn to monetarism this relationship was reversed and governments actively sought to construct a new and increasingly exclusionary condition of being young.

For these reasons, this changing state of youth has not always been well received. While it is not my intention here to explore those 'senseless acts of beauty' (McKay 1996) that young people have both directed and staged in the face of this new austerity, their agency is an ever-present dimension. An important sub-theme of this book is the continuing and active presence of the young in shaping the events examined here, although not so much in terms of organised or public displays of defiance. It is indeed the case that a precondition for the political reconstitution of youth examined here, was the defeat of those organised sources of support and resistance that underpinned more politically inclusive times. Nevertheless, far from being passive observers of the recasting of their lives, one of the major problems faced by successive governments has been the refusal of large numbers of young people to take at face value the new institutions and practices constructed in their name. Precisely because the thrust of government policy has led to a new austerity – as jobs have been lost, education commodified, welfare withdrawn, resources eroded, leisure criminalised, punishment extended and so on – this reconstituted state of youth has not been accepted lightly. Underneath the sporadic displays of public defiance, there have been a set of far less visible but still endemic active responses on the part of the young that have ranged from apathy and resignation on the one hand, through to opposition, defiance and resistance on the other, and coloured with varying shades of cynicism, suspicion, destructiveness and simple bloody-mindedness in between. One of the defining characteristics of this new state of youth has been the remarkable tenacity of young people to push at the boundaries that now delineate their lives and to step outside of the new institutional barriers designed to fence them in.

These themes find a fuller elaboration in Chapter 1. The purpose here is to provide a robust and coherent framework within which the practical details of the changing state of youth can be more fully comprehended. This is followed in Chapters 2 to 6 by an examination of specific areas of state activity that are central to the political reconstruction of youth. Beginning with the deepening crisis of the mid-1970s and ending with the defeat of the Conservatives at the 1997 General Election, each chapter gives attention to how the crisis of the state and its 'resolution' on terms expressed by monetarism, also involved the methodical destruction of the more inclusive forms of youth that had been a hallmark of the Keynesian welfare state. In doing so, each chapter also explores how this process of monetarist restructuring has brought about the reorganisation of young people's lives along more exclusive lines. Not only was youth politically reconstituted into a more costly 'state' to be across this period, but each chapter also pays particular attention to how in turning to the politics of exclusion, to austerity, money and the market, governments have reanimated sources of division between the young. Read separately these individual chapters are intended to provide a detailed introduction to particular areas of state activity and government policy that have been pivotal in reshaping the lives of the young. When taken together the focus on education and schooling, work, unemployment and government training schemes, social security, the family and the welfare state, and crime, delinquency and youth justice, should allow the reader an expansive, although by no means exhaustive, analysis of the changing state of youth in the last quarter of the twentieth century.

For those who find themselves asking 'what about Blair?', Chapter 7 considers the implications of the first New Labour government (1997–2001). New Labour's election victory that year is often interpreted as marking a significant shift in the mode of government and politics in the United Kingdom and some have already begun to explore the implications of this for young people. Whether or not there exists a 'Third Way' for youth that eschews both neo-liberalism and markets on the one hand and the state and social democracy on the other remains a moot point, however, and the purpose of this chapter is to contribute to these debates. This is particularly important because during Tony Blair's first government New Labour certainly set in motion a number of crucial developments that focused on the lives of the young. Ostensibly the most 'youthful' political party ever, New Labour came to power promising the literal rejuvenation of a tired country and a 'new deal' for Britain's world-weary youth. Unfortunately, the analysis developed here is not so sanguine. Beyond doubt, New Labour has given to 'youth policy' a measure of importance probably not witnessed in living memory, but it is argued here that the significance of this is strictly limited. If no simple facsimile of the strategies pursued by previous Conservative governments, it nevertheless appears to be the case that the substance of New Labour's 'youthfulness' during the first term of government involved a marked, if somewhat distinctive, extension of the strategy of austerity already established.

In tackling the changing state of youth, this book limits itself in the main to developments in England and Wales. From the outset, it needs to be made clear that this limitation is in no way a product of any chauvinism on the part of the author, but should be taken as more a mark of respect. It is from a recognition that the politics of youth and age takes distinctive forms and contains particular national characteristics, that some judgements and interpretations on the changing state of youth in other areas of the United Kingdom have been left to those far better qualified to make them.

Finally, this book has taken shape across a number of years and many have contributed to its conclusion. Not least in this has been the patience, encouragement and support provided by Catherine Gray, Jo Digby and Kate Wallis at Palgrave. Thanks must go to: John Harris, Sharon Wright and Andrew Parker who read and provided valuable comment on one or more chapters; to Nathan Hughes and Alison Rolfe for allowing me to draw upon their own investigations; to

Mick Carpenter who had the good grace, not to mention considerable fortitude, to listen to and debate many of the ideas and themes contained herein; and to Jane McAllister, whose interest and support seems to know no boundaries. This book has undoubtedly benefited from these contributions but needless to say responsibility for any failings are solely my own.

CHAPTER 1

The Changing State of Youth

Last year we wrote a pamphlet ... urging a policy of child-centredness for the New Labour Party of Great Britain. To introduce it we asked Gallup to survey opinion among those aged 16 and over on the future prospects of children. 'Do you think that children today have a better future in front of them than you had when you were a child, a worse future, or about the same?' The overall response result was: Better 8 per cent, Worse 63 per cent, Same 15 per cent, Don't Know 4 per cent.

(Halsey and Young 1997)

Such sentiments stand in stark contrast to a time not much more than a generation ago when a British Prime Minister, Harold Macmillan, famously remarked that the British had never had it so good. Undoubtedly a rare rhetorical flourish from a politician better known for his sobriety, viewed from the vantage point of half a century later it now has a certain ring of truth. In what the historian Eric Hobsbawm describes as the 'golden years' of twentieth-century capitalism stretching for almost 30 years after the Second World War, 'the world, particularly the world of developed capitalism, had passed through an altogether exceptional phase of its history: perhaps a unique one' (1994: 257–8). The post-war reconstruction of a society ravaged by war, privation and loss had brought with it full employment and a rising standard of living which, together with the growth in democratic institutions and an unprecedented expansion of social rights, appeared to many to mark the final humanisation of market forces. A little over 15 years later however, this vision of a rational and democratised capitalism lay in pieces as Britain, along with the rest of the advanced capitalist world, entered a new era of capitalist development defined by crisis, austerity and change.

As long as it lasted, however, this period of 'relative affluence' brought with it profound changes to the lives of the young. The gains

1

were unevenly distributed, huge inequalities remained and the lives of many stayed insulated from the considerable benefits conferred by this new prosperity. But it was during these 'golden years' that youth emerged into something approaching a coherent category, one that could with some degree of justification claim to offer young people opportunities and freedoms previously undreamt of by most of their parents. Compulsory secondary education, the raising of the minimum school leaving age and an expanded tertiary education cemented the progressive removal of children and young people from the labour market, regardless of their gender or social class, and underscored the physical separateness of children from their parents. The young too emerged as major beneficiaries of the political commitment to full employment, as employers were prepared to pay school leavers unprecedented rates of pay to meet the surge in demand for semi and unskilled labour. On top of this, new forms of state provision appeared to cement in place the very foundations of these 'good times', as young people found themselves redesignated young citizens-in-the-making through their progressive incorporation into the formal participatory structures of social democracy.

These material changes to the lives of the young provided the basis for youth studies' emergence as a distinctive field of enquiry. Against the backdrop of young people's rising affluence the work of Parsons (1942), and its subsequent elaboration by Eisenstadt (1956), loomed large (and arguably still does – see below) over social theories of youth. Beyond their theoretical complexity and sometimes impenetrable prose, their conclusion was straightforward: youth, age and relations between generations had in many respects superseded the class divisions of earlier industrial society. The expansion of secondary education, they argued, had clearly liberated children and young people from their previous economic travails and youth was now a major fault line of industrial life. Burgeoning theories of juvenile delinquency too assumed the importance of prosperity, reducing as they did already rising levels of youth crime to a pathological problem of maladjustment brought about by low intelligence, inappropriate socialisation, pockets of poverty and slum housing; or by the persistence of a conservative working class culture unable to meet the challenges posed by these more prosperous times (Mays 1972). Even those subsequent attempts to return youth to class and to the social relations of production took this relative affluence as their starting point. In the pioneering Marxist accounts of youth subcultures (Hall and Jefferson 1976), it was the post-war reconstitution of youth into a relatively autonomous and privileged site of leisure that the underlying problems of school, community, family and work could be 'resolved'; albeit in fantastic and 'imaginary' ways.

It is something of a paradox, therefore, that at the very moment when these ideas of affluence found their fullest expression in these subcultural accounts of youth, a shift of seismic proportions was already taking place. In what Hobsbawm further terms the 'crisis decades', not only did the three quick world recessions of 1973–75, 1981–83 and 1990–93 rudely interrupt what had seemed the realisation of long-standing aspirations for a planned and rational model of capitalist growth, they also provided the clearest indication that the age of welfare capitalism was all but over. 'The history of the 20 years after 1973', writes Hobsbawm, 'is that of a world which lost its bearing and slid into instability and crisis' (1994: 403). If welfare capitalism and its attendant forms of Keynesian state management had elevated youth into something positive, and if young people had emerged as a major beneficiary of the political commitment to a reformed and humane capitalism, then the crisis decades swept all this away. In education and schooling, in the labour market and at work, on the dole and on government training schemes, in relations with the welfare state and the family, and in their dealings with the law, the lives of young people were never to be the same again.

We shall explore in each of the subsequent chapters how the practical impact of the crisis decades was expressed through a series of far-reaching changes to the lives of the young. Here, however, the focus is the implications of the crisis for how we have come to understand the social category of youth. This is a necessary exercise because the crisis that engulfed young people's lives from the middle of the 1970s onwards has simultaneously been felt in terms of a crisis of theory. In the last tradition to hold sway over the study of youth, the Marxist claim that youth's defining characteristics lay in the peculiar tensions and discontinuities it posed for the reproduction of class – and later for feminists, patriarchal – relations proved progressively untenable, as the very structures upon which these cultural processes of reproduction were predicated appeared to enter a period of terminal decline. Questions of why young people were so prepared to enter 'dead-end' jobs or tolerate the prospects of stultifying personal and domestic relationships no longer appeared of relevance, when entry into 'real jobs' and the formation of 'traditional' nuclear families seemed for many to be a thing of the past. In the face of such rapid change some like Willis (1990) still hung on to their essentially functionalist

perspective on youth, while other natural heirs to the Marxist tradition sought solace in the spectacle of youth and the obscurantism of
post-modernism (Hebdige 1988). Whatever their merits, the radical
tradition that these accounts aspired to maintain nevertheless lost out
as the crisis of theorising youth was 'resolved' in terms of what Cohen
(1997: 179) describes as 'a determined returned to empiricist studies'
of the transition to adult life. In what now passes for something of an
accepted wisdom, the common starting point for the study of youth
is one that searches for its social meaning in a series of transitional
pathways – to work, family and home-making – through which
young people 'grow up' socially, as they make their journeys to the
adult social world.

It is the assumption, for often it is no more than an assumption,
that youth contains such transitional importance that occupies the
first part of this chapter. Here the intention is to take issue with the
prevailing orthodoxy within contemporary youth studies, not simply
as an end in itself but as a contribution to a process of theoretical
renewal and radical analysis already initiated elsewhere (e.g., Cohen
and Ainley 2000). The path taken here, however, is most likely an
unfamiliar one coming as it does from a position which views youth
primarily in terms of the actions of others. For as Frith (1984) reminds
us, the conventional preoccupation of youth studies is with the sub-
jective; or with those processes of learning, acceptance, refusal and
intransigence that seem so important in defining the lives of the
young. What follows is therefore in some respects a break with this
convention.

This in turn leads us on to equally unfamiliar terrain, where we
undertake to explore the importance of age to the understanding of
youth. With youth studies' return to a more orthodox interest in how
young people 'grow up' socially, somewhat curiously attention to the
role of age in determining both the form and content of youth has
been mislaid. The objective here is to rectify this through an emphasis on the politics of age. The assertion is that once we begin to ask
questions about the relationship between youth and age and the role
of state and government to this, we are forced to entertain the possibility that youth is not best understood in terms of transitions to
adult life. On the contrary, the argument developed in the later sections of this chapter, and which provides the analytical framework for
this book, stresses the significance of age in youth to the political
management of capitalist social relations and to the changing form of
the state.

The 'myth' of transition

Of course, all young people 'grow up'. We may dispute the detail, point to historical and cultural variations in timing and duration but all young people must go through a process of physiological change sometime relatively early in their life. This much is uncontroversial. Difficulties occur, however, when the marked physiological transformations of adolescence become the means to explain what is on closer examination a socially determined category. For without some ability to understand youth's existence as a social relation, the complex forces that give form and content to the lives of the young become impossible to comprehend. Public justifications of why a young person cannot legally have sexual intercourse until they are 16 years old, drive a car until they are 17, engage in armed combat until they are 18 and so on (see Table 1.1), may frequently invoke the facility, emotional or physical, to accomplish such tasks in ways that avoid damage to the individual and/or society in which they live. Are young people ready to take on such commitments, the question is often asked. But the absence of any discernible logic to the age at which rights and responsibilities are extended and the capacity of young people to exercise them, means that such questions usually miss the point. In order to be able to answer why it is that a young person's ability to procreate, control a machine or take a life occurs well before s/he is legally or morally sanctioned to do so, we must look to the social in our attempt to understand what gives shape to the category of youth. This is a realisation further underscored when we remember the 'bio-political' power of traditional theories of youth (Cohen 1997). With the emphasis on the problematic and troubled condition of youth, their enduring strength is in part explained by the ability to legitimate as innate and immutable something that has its basis in the changing and unequal political transactions of the industrial capitalist order.

For these reasons there has been a long-standing tradition of analysis that looks for youth's transitional significance in the organisation of social relations. During the late 1970s and early 1980s, for instance, the brief flirtation with radical theory and critical ethnography that left such a lasting imprint on youth studies, sought to establish youth's transitional significance from its role in the reproduction of labour power. In explaining the emergence of youth as a discernible social category from the middle of the nineteenth century onwards, critical importance was given to the changing

Table 1.1 Age in youth (England and Wales)

Age	Rights and responsibilities
10	Criminally responsible (8 in Scotland)
	Can be remanded to non-secure local authority accommodation
12	Buy a pet
	Participate in dangerous public entertainment, under licence
	Can be remanded to secure local authority accommodation
13	Minimum age for paid employment, under licence (11 on farms)
	Own air rifle
14	Ride a horse on the road wearing protective head gear
	Employed as street trader by parents, under licence
16	Age of consent
	Buy cigarettes
	Marry with parental consent (without parental consent in Scotland)
	Licence to ride a moped
	Minimum school leaving age
	Full-time employment
	Can work as a street trader
	Permitted to enter or live in a brothel
	Can be used by another to beg
17	Join the armed forces with parental consent, but not for combat
	Be interviewed by police without presence of an 'appropriate adult'
	Apply for firearms licence
	Buy or hire a crossbow
	Licenced to drive a motor car
	Can be remanded to prison
18	Engage in armed combat
	Marry without parental consent
	Vote in elections
	Participate on jury service
	Open bank account without parental signature
	Bet in a bookmakers
	Be tattooed
	Entitlement to Development Rate of the national minimum wage
	Entitlement to lower rates of welfare benefits
21	Become a Member of Parliament
22	Entitlement to 'adult' rate of the national minimum wage
25	Can adopt
	Can obtain licence to sell alcohol
	Entitlement to full rate of welfare benefits
	End of restrictions on viewing films or videos
26	Receive full rate of housing benefit

imperatives of capital accumulation and to 'the process through which potential labour power (the child) is recruited and trans-formed into actual labour power (the adult)' (Clarke and Willis 1984: 7; see also CCCS 1978). Whatever the merits of this position, and there were many, its considerable momentum nevertheless stalled and then faltered as the 'real-life' need for youth labour diminished and for a while at least seemed on the brink of collapse. As a conse-quence, these earlier connections between the social form of youth and the changing political economy of industrial capitalism were progressively diluted to the point where they pretty well ceased to exist. Today, the idea of youth as a transitional category survives and prospers, perhaps in a way as never before. But it does so by return-ing to the idea that the transitional quality to youth derives from a socially constituted process(es) of 'growing up'. Orthodox youth studies have now become, de facto, the study of young people's inte-gration into full 'adult' society (inter alia Coles 2000a; 1995; Wyn and White 1997; Furlong and Cartmel 1997; Roberts 1995; Jones and Wallace 1992; Banks *et al.* 1992).

Descriptively valuable as they are, the worth of these studies never-theless quickly comes up against an insurmountable problem: the absence of such a clearly identifiable transitional quality to the formal structures of modern youth. One of the criticisms frequently directed at modern capitalist societies is the adolescent confusion and anxiety they foster, as a consequence of their failure to allocate rights and responsibilities to young people in a logical and progressive fashion. As already noted, the relationship between the ages at which the accoutrements of full adult membership accrue to the young and their capacity to exercise these in a competent fashion is both loose and contradictory. And as Table 1.1 clearly shows, transition is far from adequate as a description of how the rights to leave compulsory edu-cation, sell labour power, wed, vote in elections, own property, enter legally binding agreements, claim welfare benefits and so on, are amassed. What governments appear to give with one hand they are prone to take away with the other, as the entitlements and obligations of full social membership are conferred at a variety of ages, with little or no sense of progress nor any apparent regard for the logic of their interconnection. For legislators and policy makers, politicians and civil servants, there is no definitive statement of the age at which youth begins or ends, and as far as current UK law is concerned, youth could begin at age 10 (the age of criminal responsibility in England and Wales, 8 in Scotland) and end at 26 (when the full range of welfare benefits are available), or any number of ages in between. If youth is a socially constituted process of 'growing up' into a fully integrated adult member of society, then the transfer of rights and responsibilities that this involves may at best be said to operate in a curiously ambiguous fashion. At worst, the absence of any clear transitional qualities to this process points to the importance of age as the product of a series of discrete historical processes that have only the most casual relevance to the notion of youth so defined.

If we approach this problem from another angle, youth's transitional quality becomes even harder to discern. Failing to establish clear transitional characteristics to the formal legal and political arrangements that shape the contours of youth, solace has more recently been sought in the idea that this transitional component can be found in a series of status changes. Couched in terms of 'trajectories' or 'careers', or those 'sequences of statuses through which young people pass as they move from childhood to adult' (Coles 1995: 20), the social quality of youth is now often explained by reference to young people's necessary movement from a state of dependence – upon parents, school and the removal of a wage – to one of independence: in living, family formation and entry into work.

As Wyn and White point out, the reality of these transitions is one of greater hesitancy, less fluidity and more imprecision than is implied in 'a perspective on youth as a steady progression through identifiable and predictable stages to a set end: adulthood' (1997: 95). There is also a more fundamental problem of isolating those precise statuses that characterise this transitional category. It cannot be the status of being in education, for instance, because large numbers of young children are obviously in education and, less obviously, mature students now numerically dominate higher education. It cannot be the absence of work because children do not work, unemployment is again more numerically significant among adults and economic inactivity is endemic to the adult population (Pullinger and Summerfield 1998). Neither too is dependence upon the family the exclusive preserve of the young, as both trends towards what is euphemistically termed 'care in the community' and the one in four males aged 25 to 30 still resident in the parental home, can readily testify.

Paradoxically, difficulties in identifying youth's transitional qualities take us back to the question of age. Without some reference to age, accounts of youth-as-transition risk a descent into the absurd, for when status is the defining condition we must take seriously as youth, as Irwin (1995) asks us to do, any individual between the ages of 16 and 35; provided that they are either unemployed, living at home, outside of a long-term relationship or have no dependent children. This may be appropriate for purposes of market research, where the youthful consumer is judged no more when s/he 'settles down' to a job or a family, but it is certainly not the stuff of robust or critical analysis. When judged in terms of status alone, how else can we differentiate between the secondary school student and the mature student, the working school student and the part-time adult worker or the unemployed school leaver and the factory worker made redundant after 30 years, without reference to their age?

This is because beyond its undoubted cultural resonance, age also possesses considerable material significance. Why this is so we will come to later. It may not be possible, nor is it probably desirable, to establish a definition of youth couched in precise chronological terms so that we can say that youth begins at age X and ends at age Y. It does not even matter that the permissive character of formal age entitlements often fail to correspond with the detail of young people's actions. Even accepting that young people get up to all sorts of things that the letter of the law is supposed to prevent them from doing, age criteria still provide the principle means through which their lives are organised into something approaching a coherent and meaningful category. It is on the basis of their age, for example, that young people are assigned to those institutions that we have come to recognise as characteristic of youth. The simple fact of possessing a certain biological age brings with it differential access to social power, while age also provides the means through which young people are brought into a more or less common relationship with many of the central institutions of modern life. From the sublime – schooling, paid employment, the criminal justice system, taxation, the armed forces, sexual conduct, enfranchisement, property rights, relationships with parents and so on – to (what may often now seem) the ridiculous – purchasing a pet, participating in dangerous public entertainment, entering or living in a brothel, being tattooed, begging for another, or participating in a performance of hypnotism – youth is most fundamentally a question of age (Table 1.1).

Age, difference and relations of generation

Age is also distinctive in another way: it gives substance to youth's existence as a universal social category. For the study of youth transitions this raises a further intractable problem again clearly identified, if in somewhat understated terms, by Wyn and White when they comment: 'the concept of youth involves a tension between the social significance of age, which gives young people a *common* social status which is different from adulthood, and the social significance of other social divisions which *differentiate* young people from each other' (1997: 15, original emphasis). For in the concern with youth-as-transition, it is necessary to retain some idea of what makes youth a common condition since, after all, if youth is about 'growing up' socially then by definition all young people must eventually become adult. In practice, however, the acknowledgement of what it is that exactly ties young people together in ways that can permit us to talk about 'youth', is usually submerged under a concern with those sources of division between the young; for instance, 'where it is misleading to emphasise the qualities of youth *per se*, since the young are neither a homogeneous category nor a static one' (Jones 1988: 707). One of the lasting contributions made by orthodox youth studies over the past decade or so has been the detail with which it has mapped out how young people's lives are shaped by differing levels of economic (dis)advantage and by divisions of gender, ethnicity and location (Roberts 1995; Bates and Riseborough 1993; Banks *et al.* 1992). But without some logical idea of where this process of dis-aggregation should begin or end, or how these divisions relate to the source of youth's social coherence, the risk is that youth studies are set in motion upon an ultimately nihilistic trajectory. Why stop with only four variables, why not 14, 40 or 400? To adopt this course of action would, of course, reduce the study of youth to little more than the collection of 'coming of age' stories and for this reason holds little attraction. It is also instructive to note that even the radical pluralism of the 'post-modern turn' in youth studies has been forced to return to the realisation that, 'there are none the less a sufficient number of age-related experiences among young people which still allow us to talk meaningfully about youth' (McRobbie 1995: 178).

For this reason it is similarly insufficient to dismiss the universalism of youth as simply an illusion. As already noted, appeals to the universalism of traditional theories of youth and adolescence undoubtedly serve an ulterior 'bio-political' purpose (Cohen 1997). Like all the most potent forms of ideological mobilisation, however, claims upon youth's universalism have their roots in concrete social practices. Whatever the other sources of division between the young – and there are certainly many of them – it is primarily on the basis of their age that young people's every day relations are constituted.

Rather than by reason of their class, gender, ethnicity or sexuality, it is because they are under 16 years old that all young people must endure some type of schooling; under the age of 17 that all are subject to the practice of 'youth justice'; under the age of 18 that all are excluded from the democratic process; under the age of 22 that all are excluded from the full rate of the national minimum wage; and so on. What is more, as we shall see below, it is the real universalism that age ascribes to the lives of the young which provides the means through which social divisions are reproduced.

Coyness surrounding the importance of age to youth is, however, a relatively recent state of affairs. In the work of the direct theoretical forbearers of the current orthodoxy in youth studies, the classic structural functionalist accounts developed in the sociology of Eisenstadt (1956) and less systematically by Parsons (1942), centre stage was given to the role of age. Contemporary youth studies owes a considerable if unacknowledged debt to structural functionalist theoretical elaborations of youth, but whereas the former has shied away from making clear the importance of age to the social construction of youth the latter made age and age relations a priority. For Eisenstadt in particular, the very ubiquity of age and age hierarchies to all societies was proof of their functional significance as a means of transmitting normative patterns of behaviour *from generation to generation*. As he wrote, 'the function of differential age definitions is to enable the individual to learn and acquire new roles, to become adult etc., and in this way to maintain social continuity' (1956: 29). Along with Parsons, Eisenstadt saw this process of social reproduction as taking a specific form to industrial society, as the separation of home and work, family and education – or in Parsonian terms the division between the collectivist and particularistic orientations of the family and the competitive, individualistic, universalistic and diffuse ones of the industrial order (see Smith 1983) – required the development of new modes of socialisation. It was from the structural hiatus between the 'worlds' of the family and wider public life brought about by industrialisation, that age relations were embedded into a more formal, complex and protracted set of arrangements as a means of preparing the young for, and integrating them into, full adult life. Finding expression in a series of institutions – schools, youth clubs, apprenticeships, peer groups, a self-conscious youth culture – age may have been the means of organisation but Eisenstadt saw it as the unequivocal expression of adult authority.

The structural functionalists were not wrong to stress the importance of age as a principle of social organisation, nor were they incorrect to stress its pivotal role to youth. Their mistake came in assuming that its importance lay in the power of adults over children. Ascribing youth's importance to the activities of adults vis-à-vis the functional utility of age, misrepresents both the significance and origins of inter-generational divisions and the power relations that they express. In the same way that 'there is no necessary internal connection between men and women as gendered subjects which defines a self-perpetuating material dynamic or economic/social system' (Pollert 1996: 643), so too is there nothing inherent in the relations between adults and younger people that can *explain* the existence and reproduction of those age relations that divide the young from the old. Age may bring individuals together into distinctive social groupings and place them into certain institutional settings. In the process, it may also establish a distinctive hierarchical distribution of power. But as the recent debate over the changing terms of the 'generational contract' show, there is little substance to the view that adults as a social group pos-sess a shared set of interests vis-à-vis the young, and that neither per-ceive their interests to be significantly different to, or in conflict with, those of other 'generations'.[1] Indeed, the existence of a 'genera-tion gap' is probably no more than a popular misnomer (Coleman and Hendry 1991).

This is the case because those sources of social power that give age its practical authority over the lives of the young, lie primarily outside of the relations between generations. In complex and dynamic societies governed by the imperatives of capital accumulation and production for profit, the undoubted significance invested in these 'generational' divisions – whether manifest in the relationships between parents and children, teachers and students, young workers and their employers, youth workers and clients, young offenders and the police – is to be found elsewhere, primarily in the political configuration of capitalist social relations and the changing form of the state. Thus it is not the relations between the generations that are responsible for the endur-ing importance of age. On the contrary, as Sheila Allen argued over 30 years ago:

> Age relations (including youth) are part of the economic relations and the political and ideological structures in which they take place. It is not the relations between ages which explain the changes or stability in society, but changes in societies which explains the relations between ages. (Allen 1968: 321)

Bringing the state back in?

How then may age in youth be politically significant? One possible means to establish this could be via the recent interest in youth and cit-izenship (e.g. Hall *et al.* 1998; France 1996; Coles 1995; Jones and Wallace 1992). Citizenship as a way of comprehending the importance of politics in determining access to full social membership and the role of the state in managing the historical development of struggles over the distribution of rights in capitalist societies, has undergone some-thing of a renaissance in recent years. Yet when applied to youth, the notion of citizenship intriguingly loses much of its potential as a means to comprehend those historical and political processes responsible for this construction, and instead citizenship becomes another benchmark against which we can judge the process of 'growing up': 'youth can be seen as that period during which the transition to citizenship, that is, to full participation in society occurs' (Jones and Wallace 1992: 18). Rather than exploring the potential of citizenship to illuminate why it is that youth has come to assume a particular form – or why it is that age has historically assumed such political importance as a means of distribut-ing rights and resources – we are left with a one-dimensional approach, in which the rights and responsibilities of citizenship become another marker of 'growing up'. Not only are we back to the thorny problem dis-cussed above: whether or not the acquisition of these rights can be held to take a genuinely transitional character. But even if we are prepared to take a considerable leap of faith and conceded that they do, we are also required to opt in to a rather tenuous analogy between the development of models of citizenship as the means to grasp historical causality and political efficacy, and young people's integration as full social members: 'what [citizenship] describes as happening at the level of society over historical time, appears to apply at the level of the individual during the life course' (*ibid.*: 21).

Whereas the political significance of age and youth is rendered neutral by appeals to citizenship, the state and age are central to Wallace and Kovatcheva's account of youth and late modernity. In their impres-sive if sometimes jumbled survey of youth in contemporary industrial society, they argue unequivocally for a view of youth as the 'product of state systems through which age became bureaucratically calibrated. Without such a definition of age youth would not have been possible' (1998: 83). It is through the development of the modern state, they argue, that pre-industrial patterns of age relations were reconfigured into the more familiar age hierarchies characteristic of modern times. The reasons for this, the argument goes, is that age provides a precise method for the calibration of state administrative practices, ostensibly in the name of young people's welfare but more pressingly to define subordinate populations in order to effect their control. Culminating after the Second World War, the high point of youth is seen to be the institutional configuration of age into a clearly defined stage of the life course through the development of welfare states – replete with their attendant institutions, pathways and cultural forms; and the emergence of a pervasive ideology of adolescence, as a way of legitimating the pattern of subordinate relations that this political construction of youth involved.

There is clearly potential to this thesis: the importance it gives to state practice and to the role of government in the organisation of youth, a clear sense of the importance of age as a method of political and bureaucratic administration, the linkages between state practice and the emergence of youth institutions and at least some measure of youth as historical process. However, when all is said and done, they too ultimately exclude a sense of those social forces that give age its political clout. Not only does the absence of a clear elaboration of the relationship between the state, age and youth stand in stark contrast to the breadth of their historical and comparative detail. In the last resort, the political and administrative significance that age so clearly possesses is reduced to the technical requirements of industrial society. This is evident in their rather Panglossian reading of the historical development of youth as unfolding through a progressively more benign relationship between the 'modern' state, a new class of welfare professionals and the emerging category of youth; the apotheosis of which was expressed in the importance of age and youth to the construction of post-war citizenship. More tellingly, however, is their reduction of state formation in education and training – a formative site of intervention as far as the social organisation of youth is concerned – to the changing technical requirements of modern productive systems. As they note, 'the increasingly complex division of labour in modern societies and the needs of ever-changing skills have necessitated longer period of preparation of work and retraining or re-education for life' (Wallace and Kovatcheva 1998: 85). Youth, it would appear, is ultimately a technical relation.

A political economy of youth and age

To put the politics back into age and youth we must therefore avoid such a technicist standpoint. In this respect, there is much to be gained from exploring 'the lost threads of a Marxist tradition' (Meiksins Wood 1995: 53) which has recently resurfaced inter alia in the guise of an 'Open Marxism' (Bonefeld *et al.* 1992) or 'political Marxism' (Meiksins Woods 1995), and to which is allied an understanding of the state as a *form* of the *social relations of production*[2] (Clarke 1991). This involves a rejection of both the reductionist view of the state advocated by 'classical Marxism'; where the existence of the state is reduced to crude economic or technical imperatives; and the base/superstructure metaphor of more recent times, in which the state is accounted for by reference to some deep and hidden essence. On the contrary, such a position understands the state as an actually existing social relation that derives its existence from the historically unique separation of capitalist social relations into real and distinctive 'economic' and 'political' forms. To the former is confined the immediate process of production and the direct extraction of surplus value (i.e. the direct exploitation of workers), while to the latter the means to constitute, manage and enforce the exchange between the 'free and equal' partners that this is held to involve (Holloway 1992; Holloway and Picciotto 1978).

So what has this to do with youth and age? When it is accepted that the state is a form taken by capitalist social relations of production – the exercise of political power in ways that seek to uphold, protect and consolidate the integrity of the direct process of exploitation – it becomes necessary to think about the state in a different way. Not only do we have to think about the state in terms of *what* it does, but we must also look at the state in terms of *how* it does things. In the case of youth, age then becomes politically important not simply because of its administrative convenience, technical utility or because of its functional value in the reproduction of labour power. Nor can age be treated simply as a matter of state and government because of the imperative of regulating a surplus youthful population through make-work schemes or a more overtly repressive system of youth justice. Rather age becomes equally important as a politically constituted method of division, one means through which the state can go about its everyday business of managing social relations by organising them into real distinctions and categories that work to obscure the exploitative content of social life. 'More precisely, it [i.e. the state is] a process which projects certain forms of organisation upon our everyday activity, forms of organisation which do not pose any threat to the reproduction of capitalist social relations' (LEWRG 1980: 57). It is thus from the form of the state that those categories now characteristic of capitalist society arise: citizen, parent, resident, patient, taxpayer, claimant, consumer and such other. And of course through age we find the political construction of youth.

Keynesianism, monetarism and the changing state of youth

As an instrument of division, age also has further value as a means of effecting young people's (re)integration into society on the terms set down by the broader political configuration of society. For our purposes, this process of integration can be divided into two distinctive phases. The first, stretching from the Second World War until it entered a period of terminal crisis during the middle of the 1970s, can be termed Keynesianism and the second, emerging out of the crisis of Keynesianism and continuing on to the present day, monetarism. To many these are familiar terms from economics but they also have value as a way of expressing a much broader relationship between state and civil society characteristic of each specific period of post-war development (Clarke 1987). State practices associated with each were not confined to a narrow set of economic doctrines aimed at managing demand or controlling the money supply, but involved the state in the systematic (re)construction of the whole edifice of social relations.

In relation to the Keynesian mode, two elements need to be highlighted here. First, at its core was a strategy of inclusion. Under the Keynesian state form, the emphasis was on the direct political management of social relations according to principles of conciliation and incorporation. Strong economic growth coupled with full employment saw attempts to reconcile the demands of a well-organised working class and increasingly militant labour movement with continuing capitalist profitability, through an enormous programme of concession. The product of this included the creation of a welfare state, a complex and sophisticated machinery of social administration, a generalised system of industrial relations and the expansion of the means for formal democratic participation, all of which were underwritten by the political commitment to the maintenance of full employment. Second, this strategy of inclusion therefore necessitated a highly interventionist state. In the development of these more inclusive ways of managing social relations, the form of the state underwent profound change as, on the one hand, its influence was taken deep into the fabric of society. From the workings of the family and some of the most intimate aspects of personal life, through to the public worlds of schooling and employment, the influence of the state stretched further than ever before. On the other hand, as well as bringing about a new found closeness between state and civil society, this process of interventionism was accompanied by qualitative changes in which old social categories were destroyed, new ones created and others reconstructed according to the political commitment to concession.

As we shall see in the following chapters, youth was elevated into one of the biggest beneficiaries of the Keynesian strategy. Expressed most clearly in the social democratic ideal of youth as a key site through which the commitment to greater equality of outcome could be reconciled with the more exclusive imperatives of capitalist development (Davies 1986), Table 1.2 shows how youth was subject to an extensive process of reorganisation. Through criteria of age, more young people were brought within new and extended opportunities for schooling and an expanded tertiary education free at the point of demand. The political commitment to full employment underwrote jobs for all school leavers and rising youth wages. The conditions under which youth crime and delinquency were regarded underwent a redefinition in terms of the needs of young offenders. And the young also

Table 1.2 Examples of youth under Keynesian and monetarist forms of political management

Keynesian youth (the politicisation of youth through age)	Monetarist youth (the de-politicisation of youth through age)
• Direct state support for parents e.g. family allowances	• Move cost of child support back onto the family – erode value and scope of welfare benefits for children and young people
• Consolidate and reorganise secondary schooling: 　• Raise school leaving age 　• Comprehensive reform, end selection 　• A 'child-centred' curriculum	• Reorganise secondary schooling through: 　• Age-standardised testing 　• Promote market forces, selection and competition 　• Make schooling more relevant to the 'needs' of industry
• Expand further and higher education free at the point of demand; mandatory maintenance awards	• Expand further and higher education by shifting the cost onto young people and their parents – fees and loans
• Guarantee full employment	• Guarantee place on a work experience or training scheme
• Raise youth wages	• Actively depress youth wages
• Extend welfare benefits to young people in their own right e.g. supplementary benefit, unemployment benefit and housing benefit	• Relate welfare entitlements more closely to age as a means of limiting provision and introduce harsher eligibility criteria as a deterrent
• Decriminalise and divert young offenders	• Confine young people within the rule of law, criminalise, incarcerate and surveillance

found themselves progressively incorporated into mainstream civil life through an expanded framework of civil, legal and political rights.

As a way of managing social relations, Keynesianism proved both costly and unstable. Not only did it in involve increased levels of public expenditure to finance these new schools, universities and welfare benefits, and higher rates of borrowing and taxation to pay for them, but in assuming direct responsibility for managing capitalist development it also risked attributing to government responsibility for any failures. While the 'good times' continued to provide strong growth and full employment, Keynesianism permitted governments to take much of the credit, even though little of this was directly of their making. But when boom turned to bust, governments were also faced with responsibility for these failures and it was in response to this political crisis of the interventionist state that a successor in the form of monetarism emerged. Gaining strength from the practical failures of Keynesianism, monetarism asserted that the roots of the crisis were not to be found in the instability of market relations, but with the interventionist state itself. Through the arbitrary judgement of politicians and the self-motivated decisions of the growing cadres of welfare bureaucrats and state functionaries, state intervention had undermined incentives and corrupted the work ethic. To overcome this, the state needed to withdraw from its intervention into markets and the link between effort and reward so crucial to capitalist profitability re-established.

Thus monetarism did not emerge as a 'solution' to the deepening economic crises of the late twentieth century. As Clarke makes clear,

> the driving force behind this restructuring was not so much the attempt to provide a solution to the economic crisis, as the attempt to resolve the political crisis of the state by trying to disengage the state from the economy so as to depoliticise economic policy formation. (1990: 27; see also Burnham 1999)

Monetarism was therefore no more a simple matter of economics than Keynesianism was. What hold it had over the Treasury at the beginning of the 1980s, for instance, was as brief as it was disastrous. Rather, the continuing importance of monetarism lay in the 'solutions' it offered to the political crisis of the interventionist state. By replacing the direct political management of social relations with new forms that looked to money and the market, governments could thus attempt to bring about their own political disengagement from the crisis of the interventionist state and the previous direct responsibilities they had assumed.

For the monetarists, such a strategy was justified in terms of, 'getting the state off the backs of the people' (Bosanquet 1983). Never more than of rhetorical significance, in the process of restructuring the role of the state was not diminished but underwent a change in form. As Burnham makes clear, 'the act of depoliticisation is itself highly political' (1999: 28) and one that requires the active use of state power in the restructuring of social relations; or to paraphrase von Hayek, doyen of the monetarists, 'the road to freedom requires a little coercion' (Standing 1997: 14). In this respect, the process of 'deregulation' advocated by monetarism is more accurately a process of 're-regulation', where, for example, 'the state is forced to bring ever greater coercion to bear upon the low-paid and the unemployed, in an attempt to make them subject to the "disciplines" of the labour market which the welfare state is said to have mitigated' (Deakin and Wilkinson 1991: 143). In looking to money and the market as key agents of restructuring, practical changes to the organisation of the state were therefore simultaneously expressed in terms of the restructuring of the entire framework of post-war social relations.

Practically speaking, therefore, the implications of this were immense. Where previously government had sought to address popular aspirations through conciliation and concession – delivered in the form of a commitment to comprehensive schooling, jobs for all, security of health and welfare from 'the cradle to the grave' – monetarism articulated a new and more austere approach. By removing from government direct responsibility for meeting popular aspirations, monetarism involved the development of new state practices in which aspirations for schooling, jobs and welfare were increasingly confined within the limits imposed by money and the market. Thus, as governments of first the left and then the right looked to money and the market as a 'solution' to the deepening political problems that they faced, so too was the previous inclusive strategy reconstructed through new state forms whose hallmark was their greater exclusivity (see Young 1999).

It is within these terms that the recent political reconstruction of youth has been pursued (see Table 1.2). Given its centrality to the Keynesian strategy, the crisis of the interventionist state was simultaneously expressed in terms of the crisis of youth. If being a certain age was elevated into a relatively good 'thing' to be and if being young meant access to an expanded education, financial support for parenting,

state support for independent living, greater inclusion in social
security, jobs paying relatively high wages and the rehabilitation of
offenders, then all this needed sweeping away. Age, indeed, became
deeply implicated in this process of monetarist restructuring. New age
divisions were introduced to bring young people's aspirations within
both the limits imposed by money and the market, and their complement the rule of law. At the same time, the maintenance of pre-existing
age divisions were also reshaped within these new parameters.
Possibilities for even the most cursory form of independence were curtailed, as public support for the costs of young people's reproduction
were transferred back onto the family. Education was both intensified
and bound more closely to the 'needs' of employers and the market.
Opportunities for work and the levels of income that flowed from
them were tied more closely to what the market was prepared to offer.
Welfare too was subject to the discipline of market forces and brought
within rigid financial constraints. And age became the basis of ever-
more finely graded attempts to confine the behaviour of the young
within the rule of law.

Conclusion

Before moving on to consider in greater detail the particular ways in
which this political restructuring of youth has been effected, it is worth
reiterating a number of themes. In considering the changing state of
youth, this book emphasises the centrality of age to the organisation of
young people's lives; to the activities of the state in its day to day
endeavours to manage social relations expressed through policy and
the structures of the law and social administration; and to the recent
history of the political restructuring of social relations. As this chapter
has stressed, it is the political importance attributed to age that in
many respects determines the shape of young people's lives. This is the
case because criteria of age provide government and the state with one
method of partition, a way to both create and impose particular sets of
divisions on young people's lives that result in their separation from
their families and communities. And in separating them off in this way,
age also provides the basis through which young people can be (re)inte-
grated into the broader political strategies that states adopt in their
attempts to manage the contradictions of capitalist development.

In concluding this chapter, it also needs affirming that there has
been nothing inevitable about the developments explored in what

follows. This is because there is no functional, administrative or technological requirement that means states continue to relate to young people primarily upon the basis of their age. Youth in this sense is fundamentally a social relation and the product of self-conscious political decisions. To answer questions seeking clarification as to why age came to assume such a significance, we would need to undertake a historical study of much broader ambition and scale than that attempted here, and one that would most likely concentrate upon the reconstruction of the relations of family authority produced by the capitalist separation of home and work (Meiksins Wood 1995). Such a diversion cannot detain us but it is worth pointing out that the contingency of age is clearly illustrated by the fact that while many of the issues played out in the political restructuring of youth in Britain are common across the entire industrial capitalist world (OECD 2000), the terms upon which they have been dealt with are ones set down by distinctive national conditions. At the same time, we must also avoid resorting to functional explanations of why Keynesianism gave way to monetarism, in the way that is often inferred by theories of post-Fordism and post-structuralism. There was no technological necessity that the Keynesian welfare state and its commitment to a more inclusive youth would be reorganised more closely in line with the dictates of money and the market. Such a 'resolution' was ultimately decided by the shifting balance of social and political forces in play at the time; and for all their considerable agency one in which the young remained at best a relatively minor player.

It is also worth noting from the outset that while some young people benefited enormously from these changes, the resulting condition of exclusion and division has found little enthusiasm among the majority of young people. Furthermore, that this process of restructuring has also had an uneven impact *between* different groups of young people returns us firmly to the fact that youth is far from being a homogeneous category. Indeed, in most walks of life the turn to money and the market has reanimated and exacerbated long-standing sources of social division between the young: middle and working class, black and white and male and female. Therefore, in stressing that state, class and the social relations of production are central to our understanding of youth and age, the intention is not to collapse youth back into class; if this is understood to mean that all young people are working class or that age and youth are simple effects of some more fundamental economic process. Even the most cursory examination reveals that the Bengali girl struggling through on an inner city housing estate is in a qualitatively different position from the son of the new class of millionaires that gets bigger every week. On the contrary, to stress the political significance of youth and age in this way is to emphasise that the very universalism that states attribute to age provides the means through which traditional sources of inequality between the young can be reproduced, in the same way that, for instance, 'the universal citizenship *form* may have been the medium for promoting interests within a much more traditional class based political and economic content' (Pierson 1991: 37, original emphasis). It is to the detail of these divisions and the processes of restructuring from which they arise, that we shall now turn.

CHAPTER 2

The Changing State of Education

In examining in more detail the changing state of youth we begin with education; or more accurately the schooling of children and young people from age 11 onwards. Why start here? Well because the imposition of a period of compulsory schooling provides one of the starkest examples of youth's political construction. Schooling marks in perhaps its most distinctive form the way in which the state uses age criteria as a means of shaping the lives of the young through inserting them into particular institutional contexts, which are themselves subject to specific modes of organisation. Through the removal of young people from their parents and families, communities and culture, and their insertion into full-time education, schooling provides us with one of the clearest expressions of the political construction of youth (Clarke and Willis 1984).

Therefore, to explore the politics of youth is simultaneously to investigate the politics of education and when we consider the changing state of education over the past three decades, we find one of the clearest examples of the changing state of youth. This is because education was central to the Keynesian strategy of inclusion, as the transformation of schooling was given responsibility for reconciling working class aspirations with the imperatives of post-war development. Characterised by concession and underpinned by the commitment to education as the source of an inclusive youth, schooling held out the prospect of unifying aspirations for social progress with those of greater national efficiency. By 1976, however, this strategy openly lay in ruins. The deterioration of 'school leavers' employment prospects combined with rapidly escalating levels of youth unemployment, provided one of the clearest indications that the social democratic commitment to education as the basis of a more inclusive youth had ended in practical failure.

In the 'resolution' of this crisis the state of education was literally turned upside down. Most clearly evident in what became known as the 'new vocationalism', and then when this ran into the sand the embrace of market forces, education's ostensible purpose of fostering greater inclusiveness was progressively questioned. In supposedly concentrating on the personal 'needs' of students and by answering to a liberal curriculum, the construction of a more inclusive form of schooling was now held responsible for young people's apparent lack of preparedness for work, for escalating levels of youth unemployment, for the growing 'gap' between school and work and, ultimately, for national economic decline. As we shall see, this critique of education and schooling was (and is) a deeply ideological one. The claim to be able to school young people in anticipation of the future needs of industry and technology, let alone the belief that cohorts of well-educated and skilled school leavers can solve the problem of insufficient demand for youth labour, is even more of a mirage than the previous belief in education as a means to humanise market forces.

Nevertheless, these claims derived their strength from a number of practical developments. By the middle of the 1970s, governments were already actively distancing themselves from their previous substantive commitments in a clear signal that education's 'party' was well and truly over. For Labour the retreat from education as the basis for an inclusive youth was always more an issue of pragmatism than one of conviction, but with the election of the Conservatives the requirement that education should be subordinated to the 'needs' of employers and the market was more enthusiastically embraced. Hesitantly at first, the reconstruction of education subsequently took on added momentum, initially through the consolidation of vocationalism and then later through the resort to market forces. By the time the Conservatives lost power in 1997, the state of education had been transformed.

It is commonplace to explain these developments by pointing to the changing 'correspondence' between education and the post-war economy (Bowles and Gintis 1976). Proponents of the post-Fordism thesis, for instance, point to the development of qualitative changes in the nature of British capitalism which by the 1970s, were progressively displacing mass production techniques with new methods of 'flexible specialisation'. The impact of the new technology used to drive such production processes is then seen as rendering obsolete post-war education's function of providing the hierarchies of skill and class that defined much of the post-war boom (Ainley 1999a; Brown and Lauder 1996).

With fewer jobs, redundant skills and the reorganisation of the workforce into categories of supposedly 'core' and 'peripheral' workers – the former enjoying secure and well remunerated work, the latter destined to unskilled and semi-skilled work interspersed with periods of unemployment – the restructuring of schooling became necessary to service both the new division of labour and the problems of control and containment that it posed. Not only did a generation of school leavers need socialising into accepting the often cruel consequences of this new and austere regime, but education was also imbued with a responsibility for servicing the radically altered skills requirements of the emerging post-Fordist phase of capitalist development.

There is much of merit in this position,[1] particularly the emphasis it gives to the relationship between schooling, education and youth, and the changing imperatives of capital accumulation. The linkages between vocationalism, the turn to markets in education and the restoration of capitalist profitability are clear. The approach developed in this chapter is somewhat different, however. In pursuing the restructuring of education, this chapter argues that the primary objective was not so much rooted in the need to 'resolve' the deepening economic crisis, nor respond to changing technological imperatives. As Dale explains, 'it is much more difficult to explain the content and form of schooling as positively designated to support capitalism than it is to see it as excluding elements considered potentially or actually threatening to capitalism' (1989: 46). Thus, it is argued here that the restructuring of education played out from the middle of the 1970s is equally significant in terms of its political importance. Through the resort to vocationalism, the requirements of employers and market forces, the driving force has been the desire of governments to politically disengage themselves from the previous direct responsibilities they had assumed for education as the basis for a more inclusive youth.

Education for all

Education's importance as a source of inclusion culminated with Labour's return to governing power in 1964 (and again in 1966). Growing unease over the institutionalised elitism of the tripartite system laid down by the 1944 Education Act, combined with deepening concerns over stagnating economic performance, ensured education a prominent role in Labour's pledge to bring about national renewal. Indeed, under Labour education was positioned as uniquely capable of solving the problem of how to reinvigorate Britain's waning international competitiveness, while simultaneously addressing the frustrated aspirations of a well-organised working class. On the one hand, a programme of progressive reform could rationalise a clearly inefficient and manifestly unfair system of selection at 11 plus, which condemned large numbers of working class young people to a lower quality education and a life of manual labour. On the other hand, these newly liberated sons and (only later) daughters of the manual working class would be free to embrace the new employment opportunities created by the force of technological innovation. In what appeared to square the circle, 'new schools and universities open to all would produce the white-coated technicians capable of fusing the white heat of scientific revolution with rapid social advance' (Ainley 1988: 66).

The centrepiece of this was the push towards comprehensive secondary education and its corollary, the ending of selection at 11 plus. Comprehensive secondary education was nothing new, with 10 per cent of schools in England and 28 per cent in Wales already comprehensive by 1965 (Smith 2000), but shortly after gaining office plans for a national programme were rolled out. By requesting that all local education authorities (LEAs) submit plans for comprehensive reorganisation, the intention was to bring all secondary school age children within a comprehensive system that would confront head-on the role of schooling in reproducing inequality. A comprehensive regime, it was argued, would liberate the vast numbers of working class children the current system condemned to educational (and, in turn, social) failure at 11 plus, and the 'national interest' would be served by tapping into the vast pool of working class 'hidden talent' that had previously gone to waste.

Evidence of education's new-found importance was also apparent elsewhere. In spite of the absence of new monies for early comprehensive reorganisation, public expenditure on education did enjoy real increases of about 4 per cent per annum throughout this period. Total public expenditure on education rose from 3.2 per cent of Gross Domestic Product (GDP) in 1951, to a high point of 6.5 per cent in 1975 (Davies 1986). Some of this new money was directed towards the modernisation of the curriculum in ways that would qualify its role as a means of differentiating between the young (Tomlinson 2001). For those older working class students alienated by the prospect of a more protracted schooling, the curriculum could be tailored more closely to their personal needs, while all secondary school students would benefit from the introduction of new and progressive pedagogical techniques, like 'child-centred' teaching practices and independent learning and inquiry. New money would also be spent on those school students deemed 'most severely handicapped by home conditions' (Simon 1991: 368). Through designated Educational Priority Areas (EPAs) created in 1967, an alluring mix of extra resources, smaller class sizes, additional teaching support, new buildings, equipment and books, and the promise of highly motivated teachers could be directed at tackling the persistent and deep-seated forces still working to marginalise significant groups of the young.

Higher education was also reconstituted within these more inclusive terms. At one level, the reform of higher education was a necessary condition for the success of the general programme of educational reform. Only through a modernised and technically efficient system of teacher training delivered in universities and polytechnics, could young people benefit from cutting-edge pedagogical techniques. At another level, young people beyond the age of compulsory education would also enjoy expanded opportunities. Set in motion by the Conservatives, Labour readily committed itself to implementing the recommendations of the 1963 Robbins Report. Echoing the broader themes of 'wasted talent' and gross inequity, the Report underwrote a period of major expansion and from a small (and socially exclusive) base, the total higher education student population doubled between 1963 and 1970, and seven new universities were founded in England and one more in Scotland (Halsey 2000). To give this substance, provision remained free at the point of demand and all students enjoyed an entitlement to financial support through a mandatory grant for living expenses, paid through LEAs, subject to a parental test of means.

With the social democratic reform of education, thus came the practical transformation of youth. In a highly interventionist programme, selection by ability at age 11 plus would cease, all secondary school students would enjoy a common learning experience and greater equality of outcome could be achieved. The intrinsic benefits of an education would therefore be substantially widened and the rewards that followed on from the possession of certain qualifications – whether measured in terms of employment, status, career or earnings – tied more closely to merit and individual ability. For this reason, comprehensive reform in particular contained the basis of an important and rational attempt to confront schooling's historical role in the reproduction of social inequalities, by raising the possibility that schools and universities could be made responsive to the needs of all.

The progressive impulses clearly embodied in this reform agenda ultimately came up against a familiar set of concerns. It was not just that 'the starting point [of education reform] was – even during the boom years – the underlying economic weaknesses which had plagued Britain for decades' (Davies 1986: 24). Belief in education's value as an economic asset certainly remained of paramount importance, although the precise connections were (and are) poorly understood. Even at the height of the social democratic commitment to reform, familiar concerns that linked educational development to productivity, technical innovation and the decline of Britain's international competitiveness were never far away. Rather, beyond the more grandiose claims to be loosening the social ties that education continued to bind, in the formal democratisation of education the needs of large numbers of young people continued to be subordinated to a more traditional set of interests.

At its most glaring, the opening up of universities simply moved higher education from the preserve of a narrow ruling elite, into a more general middle class experience. The proportion of higher education students with working class parents changed very little as a consequence of 1960s expansion (Halsey 2000). Of greater numerical significance was the failure of comprehensive reform to pose a fundamental challenge to the patterning of educational inequalities. Part of this can be explained by the timidity of Labour's reform programme, despite the obvious and extensive popular support that comprehensive reform often enjoyed (Simon 1991). Around 30 per cent of all secondary school pupils in the maintained sector were in comprehensive schools by 1970, but the permissive status of early legislation both hindered the pace of reform and gave succour to opposing forces. The absence of any clear guidelines also opened up divisions over the direction that reform should take. One obvious consequence was that within the same LEA, newly founded comprehensive schools could find themselves alongside retained grammar schools and the continuation of the 11 plus.

More fundamentally, the comprehensive movement also belied its eponymous commitment to universalism by continuing to divide the young (Finn 1987). The failure to confront the dominance of 'official knowledge' in determining the content and form of education – 'the mental work of organising the efforts of others' or, more simply, 'the knowledge necessary to rule' as Ainley (1999b: 5) terms it – ensured that comprehensives continued to serve a narrower set of dominant interests. 'Streaming' on the basis of academic ability, the maintenance of separate curricula for 'non-academic' students and girls, and the continuation of selection and differentiation through examination, all ensured that divisions were replicated and reproduced within the form of comprehensive schooling.

Unravelling universalism

Labour's surprising defeat to the Conservatives at the 1970 General Election marks the beginning of the end of the inclusive strategy. Labour's reform of education had from the beginning come up against bitter opposition, with comprehensive change often provoking vehement hostility. A number of Conservative controlled LEAs were noteworthy for their obstructionist stance, although party political allegiance proved no necessary indication of a LEA's likely stance; most Conservative controlled LEAs supported and a number of Labour controlled LEAs opposed comprehensive reorganisation. Opposition also came from modest but vocal groups of parents and local campaigners determined to defend selection, and from a small but vociferous group of academics and educationalists bemoaning the malign influence of what they saw as permissive reform (Simon 1991). Yet despite the increasing level of noise made by the 'traditionalists' and those determined to defend their children's educational privileges, it was not until the Conservative's return to power in 1970 that these points of opposition found a more coherent focus.

From the outset, the Conservative government made clear its desire to apply the brakes to the reform agenda. Already signs of rising unemployment coupled with faltering economic growth, posed awkward questions to the claim that education could marry social progress with the requirements of capitalist profitability. Indeed, during the early years of the Heath government of 1970–74, the Conservatives began to distance themselves from their earlier support for educational reform. Shortly after the 1970 election, Margaret Thatcher, in her capacity as Minster for Education and Science, removed the earlier requirement on LEAs to plan for comprehensives. The practical impact of this was limited, since the considerable local momentum often built up around reorganisation ensured that by the time of their election defeat in 1974, the number of students in comprehensive schools had actually doubled. Nevertheless, the Conservative's early attempts to distance themselves from their previous support for comprehensives provided both a statement of intent and a sign of things to come.

Plummeting popularity did goad Heath's government into outlining a ten-year expansion plan for education in 1973, in what amounted to something of a restatement of the reform agenda. But the effect of this was short-lived and following the first short recession of 1973, education was identified as ripe for significant expenditure cuts.

When it came, however, the end of the political commitment to education as a source of inclusion was brought about by Labour. In his now notorious 1976 speech supposedly initiating a 'Great Debate' on education, the Labour Prime Minister James Callaghan articulated a set of themes explicitly critiquing Labour's previous approach. In his speech, Callaghan stressed the mistakes of the past and claimed that reform had not so much provided the 'solution' to Britain's deepening social and economic difficulties, but that comprehensives were a source of the problem. Egalitarianism, claimed Callaghan, had supposedly been at the expense of nurturing individual initiative and ability, and 'progressive' teaching techniques, a curriculum infused with permissiveness and an anti-industrial bias among teachers were all held to account for producing ill-disciplined and poorly qualified school leavers. In what amounted to another version of the 'British labour problem' (Cutler 1992), questions of failure of long-term investment, low productivity, inadequate training and poor management were thus effectively sidestepped. In their place, the political crisis that progressively engulfed Labour in power was redefined as an educational one, most clearly evidenced by the growing numbers of young people unable to find work.

Callaghan's 'Great Debate' was therefore significant in two ways. First, it marked an inversion of the previous commitment to education as social progress by redefining schooling as the problem and re-articulating its purpose in terms of the 'needs' of industry and employers, rather than the needs of young people, their parents and communities. The fact that most employers had little specific idea what they needed from their new recruits, beyond basic literacy and numeracy and a suitable degree of deference (Finn 1982), did not seem to matter. By articulating these sentiments as a pragmatic response to changed conditions, Callaghan also took his cue from the Right, particularly the dissenting views of a group of disillusioned right wing academics and educationalists that had coalesced around the notorious 'Black Papers' (Education Group 1991).

Second, Callaghan's speech not so much initiated a debate on the future of education as confirmed the direction that policy was already taking. Labour's early promise of radical reform in the immediate aftermath of the 1974 election proved both brief and illusory. By 1975, the commitment to reform had already been exhausted and Labour too was looking towards retrenchment, most notable in the decision to carry through the cuts to education announced by the Conservatives in 1973. Further plans for reform of the curriculum and examination system were also quietly abandoned and expectations for further change dampened down. While the considerable momentum behind reform continued – by 1977, 80 per cent of students in the maintained sector were in comprehensive schools (Simon 1991) – it was nevertheless the case that by the time of the Great Debate, the political commitment to education as the basis of a more inclusive youth had, for all intents and purposes, been abandoned.

The reasons for Labour's repudiation of its own earlier position are to be found in the deepening crisis of education. One of the reasons that the previous Conservative government had been unable to bring about any significant shift in education policy was that popular support for reform, particularly comprehensive reform, remained strong. Any frontal attack therefore risked uniting parents, educationalists and trades unionists in opposition, many of whose own children had experienced tangible benefits as a consequence of educational reform. However, these tangible benefits were, for increasing numbers of school leavers, swiftly diminishing as young people's sensitivity to rapidly worsening labour market conditions, ruthlessly exposed the limits of the social democratic 'education exchange' (Stafford 1981; Willis 1977). For Labour this presented a fundamental political problem. In taking responsibility for creating an education system directly answerable to the needs of all young people, rising youth unemployment in particular meant that it now faced blame for failure. By looking to vocationalism and employers as the agents of change, Labour thus sought to politically disengage itself from the direct responsibilities for meeting the educational aspirations of all young people that it had previously assumed. Importantly, in doing so, Labour was also much better positioned than the Conservatives to disarm potential sources of opposition. As the 'natural' party of a system of inclusive education, Labour could, for a while at least, claim with some credibility that its actions were being taken in the name of pragmatism rather than any desire to effect a more fundamental retreat from the principles of comprehensive education.

Reaction and reform

Reviewing Labour's time in power between 1974 and 1979, the historian of education Brian Simon concludes, '[t]here is no doubt ... that it paved the way, or provided the soil, for the surge of the radical right – for the Thatcherite domination of the 1980s' (Simon 1991: 431). In retreating from its previous commitments, Labour set the broad terms within which the restructuring of education would be pursued over the next two decades or so. Against the social democratic promise of universalism and greater equality of outcome, this new direction was expressed in much narrower terms of the 'needs' of employers and the market. As such, the subsequent development of new forms of education provision provided the basis for a new and more painful relationship between the state, the education system and the young. Whereas comprehensive reform at least offered some rational basis from which to address the needs of all young people, the turn to vocationalism and the market ushered in a new and more exclusive approach to the educational needs of the young.

This more exclusive approach developed only hesitantly over the following decade. Throughout much of the first two terms of Margaret Thatcher's time as Prime Minister, the tentativeness of education policy belied the belligerence of government rhetoric. Education reform may have been central to the Conservative's 1979 General Election campaign, but it was not until several years later that something approaching a coherent and more forceful restructuring programme emerged. In between, the Conservatives continued to occupy a similar terrain to the one already mapped out by Labour, only this time fuelled by firm ideological belief. It was only towards the end of the 1980s that a more methodical restructuring programme emerged, this time around the imposition of market forces.

Immediate reform after 1979 thus sought to extend the retrenchment process already begun. Once again, early Conservative legislation sought to obstruct the considerable momentum behind comprehensive reform by removing the statutory obligations on LEAs to plan for reorganisation, a requirement somewhat posthumously introduced by Labour at the end of its time in power. Education was also identified as ripe for further expenditure cuts, as the obligations on LEAs to provide students with lunch and subsidised transport to and from school were relaxed. Moves were also made to promote 'parental choice' although, to begin with, the value of this was largely rhetorical. Of more substance was provision in the 1981 Education Act for an Assisted Places

Scheme (APS), in which monies for the hard-pressed public sector were siphoned off in order to allow between 12000 and 15000 students each year to transfer from state maintained to independent schools. Under the guise of extending 'choice' and opportunities for a 'first-class' education to students not in a position to receive a private education, for almost two decades the practice of APS was to socialise some of the costs of private education for hard-pressed sections of the middle class, while simultaneously throwing a lifeline to independent schools that may otherwise have gone to the wall.

The shape of things to come did appear, however, in the form of the Technical and Vocational Education Initiative (TVEI), announced in 1982. TVEI drew upon the experiments in vocationalism introduced by Labour's Youth Opportunities Programme (YOP) and was later extended by the Conservatives through the Youth Training Scheme (see Chapter 3). It also looked ahead by anticipating wider moves towards greater central control over the curriculum (Ainley 1999b). Through TVEI schools were encouraged to bid directly to the Manpower Services Commission (MSC) for much needed funds, for projects that introduced a stream of technical education into the curriculum for 14 to 18 year olds. In doing so, the redefinition of education in terms of a closely defined period of vocational preparation for students not deemed 'academic', signalled a decisive shift away from the comprehensive ideal (Gleeson and McLean 1994). This move was somewhat less successfully reinforced by the provision of a more practically 'relevant' education to the least 'academically able' 40 per cent of students, through the Low Achieving Pupil Project introduced the same year. Although the new monies that flowed from TVEI were often used to subvert its original intent (Ainley 1999b), it nevertheless constituted both a significant challenge to the principle of a universal education and a marked concentration of state power over the content of schooling.

Using vocationalism as a means to formally differentiate students within the comprehensive system subsequently became a major objective. Popular support for comprehensives may have been on the wane, particularly as youth unemployment steadily worsened, but a head-on confrontation remained extremely risky, with sources of national and local support still well organised. Momentum behind comprehensive reform in fact remained strong enough to ensure that reorganisation continued well into the 1980s, since the return to explicit selection and the 11 plus held little popular appeal. In England, nearly 90 per cent of all maintained schools were comprehensive by 1988 and 92 per cent of all secondary school students were in maintained schools; the respective figures for Wales were 97 and 99 per cent (Simon 1991). Such figures did disguise the fact that only half of these schools were genuinely comprehensive. Existing divisions were nevertheless further exacerbated by the further institutionalisation of different curricula and examination systems for those deemed either vocationally or academically oriented. More indirectly, the influence of parental background also began to reassert itself in a much more brazen fashion, as hard-pressed schools looked to parents for cash for books, extra-curricular activities and for much needed basic classroom equipment.

Education, exclusion and class strategy

The restructuring of education took on a greater urgency from the middle of the 1980s. Up to this point, practical reform had been limited to experiments in vocationalism, the abandonment of any pretence to a common curriculum, tentative attempts to widen divisions between students on the basis of judgements of academic aptitude, and populist appeals to parental choice. After 1988, however, education assumed a new urgency and with the election of the third consecutive Thatcher government, plans were laid out for a root and branch reorganisation around market forces. Of course, resort to market forces in education was itself a political act and one, moreover, that said more about the needs of government than it did about the needs of the young. Not only did government undertake to reorganise schools, colleges and universities in a systematic fashion, it was also hoped that by doing so the process of political disengagement began a decade earlier could be further accomplished.

One of the prime reasons for this was the by now clear failure of vocationalism. Giving over greater parts of young people's education to the requirements of employers had been even more of a dismal failure than the comprehensive approach it had displaced. By the middle of the 1980s, young people were experiencing a slump in the demand for their labour, youth unemployment was approaching historical highs (see Chapter 3) and for this government continued to take much of the blame. Thus the turn to market forces was not so much a consequence of the changing economic or technical imperatives to which education was now supposed to answer. On the contrary, the nature of the flows that take place between investment in education, skills, human capital formation, economic performance and technological innovation are still poorly understood. The belief that a more intensive and efficient education system can on its own create the 'supply-side' conditions necessary to stimulate economic activity, bring about technological innovation and thus increase the demand for youth labour has at best uncertain empirical foundations (O'Higgins 2001). 'In fact, the adoption of educational solutions to economic problems... in the [1980s and] 1990s tells us less about economic realities than it does about political ones' (Coates 2000: 120). By containing aspirations for education more closely within rigid financial constraints and by reorganising schools and colleges more fully around market forces, Conservative governments hoped to be able to shield themselves from the political fallout arising from the consequences of their own policies, while offering some relief to young people and their parents who were increasingly anxious about what the future held.

A necessary aspect of this was an unprecedented increase in state control over education. As we saw in Chapter 1, markets are inherently 'political' in that the 'economic' rests firmly upon the prevailing disposition of 'political' power, as 'the market needs the State to bring into being the conditions under which it can flourish' (Dale 1989: 116; see also Whitty 1989). The first step towards greater centralised control came in 1985 with the announcement of a new qualification for 16 year olds: the General Certificate of Secondary Education (GCSE). What appeared initially to consolidate a unified system of examinations so central to aspirations for comprehensive reorganisation, in reality brought all school students within a more finely calibrated system of differentiation. At the same time, the greater degree of prescription involved in the GCSE, also marked a significant erosion of the professional integrity of teachers and their ability to tailor an education to the needs of individual students.

Of more significance was legislation announced the following year proposing a national curriculum. In what emerged as one of the key pieces of legislation for the third Thatcher government, the passing into law of the 1988 Education Reform Act (ERA) brought about an unprecedented extension of state control of education for the young, by empowering Ministers to lay down the framework for a common primary and secondary school curriculum, order its content and appoint members to those bodies created to advise on the issue (Whitty 1989; Simon 1988). The Act specified a number of 'core' and 'foundation' subjects that schools were now required to teach, the content of which was determined by working groups established specifically for the purpose. The Act also paved the way for market forces by dividing the curriculum into four 'key stages' spanning the entire years of compulsory education and testing through national standard assessment tasks (SATs) at ages 7, 11 and 14. Later, this was enforced by a privatised and increasingly prescriptive system of school inspections in the form of the Office for Standards in Education (OFSTED), which was also used to identify failing schools and weed out incompetent teachers. In 1993 the government did relax ERA's framework for learning and assessment, in some acknowledgement of the burden schools and students were facing. But the imposition of the SATs regime remained inviolate, since it underpinned a role for the market through the use of raw examination performance data to create school 'league tables' that would foster greater inter-school competition.

ERA also reconstructed the education functions of local government. Strengthening local government's role in education had been an important component of the inclusive strategy, since it could ensure that schools and colleges were to some degree responsive to the needs of all students (Troyna 1993). Throughout the 1980s, LEA influence over the curriculum and education expenditure had been progressively weakened and this trend was further intensified by ERA, relaxing as it did local government responsibilities for the planning and implementation of local provision (Taylor Goodby 1992). Under the Local Management of Schools (LMS) budgets – that is money for teacher salaries, equipment and books, heating, lighting, maintenance and so on – were devolved to head teachers and boards of governors dominated by parents and representatives of local business, and the method of calculation further linked to student numbers. Funding for schools according to socially determined notions of need was therefore significantly compromised, with school budgets more closely related to individual success in attracting students. As is the way with markets, the devolution of budgets certainly gave academically successful schools a degree of greater financial independence, but LMS also underscored widening divisions by financially punishing schools already struggling to serve hard-pressed youth in rapidly deteriorating communities.

LMS also divided school students in other ways. On the one hand, individual schools could choose to remain under local authority control in exchange for which LEAs would 'top-slice' their budgets to provide services like 'special needs' education. On the other hand, if a ballot of parents decided to opt for grant maintained (GM) status, individual schools could receive their budgets directly from the state and so formally sever ties with their LEA. To encourage this, schools choosing GM status were provided with additional resources for items like capital expenditure or technology grants, and were given greater latitude over student selection. The intention behind the creation of GM schools was clear. LEA control over education could be further limited and individual schools more fully exposed to competitive pressures. Despite this, however, the impact of GM status on schools was only slight; at least to begin with. By 1993 only 315 of 25 000 secondary schools had opted out and by the time the Conservatives lost power four years later, only 3 per cent of primary schools and 20 per cent of secondary schools had opted out (Smith 2000).

The 'awful example' of sixteen plus

If ERA 1988 marked a defining moment in young people's secondary education, for those aged 16 plus a counterpart can be found in the Further and Higher Education Act 1992. In what Ainley (1999b: 149) describes as 'the awful example of further education', the 1992 Act vigorously sought to impose market discipline upon further education, through the reconstitution of colleges into freestanding 'corporations'. Freed from the constraints of local accountability and managed by new boards heavily populated by business interests, these corporations were required to enter into contracts to deliver a set number of services agreed with the Further Education Funding Council (FEFC), which had been newly established for the purpose. The principal goal of the FEFC was to bring the further education sector under more rigid financial discipline, by rationalising an erratic and impenetrable system of college funding through common levels of funding linked to student recruitment, retention and course outcomes. In a hugely bureaucratic and often labyrinthine system of administration, colleges would now be funded according to student numbers rather than the needs of the communities they had previously served, and their ability to generate additional government funds made contingent upon competitive success in expanding their student base.

The implications for young students in the sector were profound. Student numbers in further education certainly increased significantly throughout the 1990s although, as we shall see, the extent to which this was a direct consequence of government policy is debatable. This expansion was undertaken on the basis of a significant contraction in real levels of funding for the sector and especially pernicious was the requirement that on each annual renegotiation of their contract, colleges were only entitled to a maximum of 90 per cent of the previous year's funding allocation. To retain a consistent level of funding, let alone secure an increase, colleges were required to bid for additional student numbers year-on-year. Failure to realise these contractual obligations would risk exposure to considerable financial penalties in the form of a 'claw back' of resources. As Ainley (1999b) points out, for students in further education this new funding regime amounted to a real year-on-year reduction in resources of around 3.5 per cent per annum. To make matters worse, further education was subjected to further expenditure cuts in the 1995 budget, in which capital expenditure on buildings and maintenance alone was reduced by two thirds. By the time the Conservatives lost power in 1997, two thirds of further education colleges were in debt, around 70 per cent were technically insolvent and four out of 10 colleges were unable to guarantee the FEFC that they had their finances under control.

If young people in further education were exposed to concerted attempts to recompose their education within the discipline of market forces, those in higher education were not immune. Higher education continued its historical expansion throughout the 1970s and 1980s, although there was nothing linear or inevitable about this as the cuts in student places during the early 1980s testified (Halsey 2000). With ERA 1988, however, higher education too was brought within a more coherent strategy of market reform, as polytechnics and some colleges of higher education were removed from LEA control and, like the colleges of further education, reconstituted into competing corporations resourced through another newly created funding body. In swapping dependence upon local government for the largesse of the central state, the new found 'independence' of these institutions provided the foundation for a huge expansion of higher education places. Between 1989 and 1992, polytechnics alone accounted for 50 per cent of the growth in student numbers from 250 000 to 382 000 (Ainley 1999b); a feat made all the more impressive by a reduction in unit costs of 25 per cent across the same period.

The much more aggressive marketisation of higher education took place through the Further and Higher Education Act 1992. As with the further education sector, the Act introduced a new funding regime that linked payment to student numbers. On top of this, competition was strengthened by the formal removal of the so-called binary divide in higher education – a division between polytechnics as centres of vocational education and universities as institutions of academic research and scholarship – as polytechnics were permitted to redesignate themselves universities (now commonly referred to as the 'new' universities) able to award their own degrees. The student experience too was reconstituted within the discipline of market forces. Throughout the 1980s, state support for students in the form of travel allowances, housing costs and vacation benefit payments were steadily removed. In 1990, the level of maintenance awards for students was frozen and provision for cost-of-living increases was financed through the introduction of student loans, repayable at a certain threshold of graduate earnings (Winn 1997).

Counting the cost

The growing importance of money in determining what type of education and schooling the young received represented not only a method of financial control but also a means of restructuring their lives. By containing education expenditure within strictly enforced financial limits, the political and administrative discretion so central to the inclusive strategy could be progressively eroded and the provision of education according to socially determined notions of need, ruthlessly subordinated to the anonymous discipline of money. Education had certainly always struggled for sufficient resources but the concessions contained in the inclusive strategy did ensure that the funding of education steadily improved. Paradoxically, however, it was also this relative success that marked education out as a prime target for subsequent cuts. As we have already noted, the writing was already on the wall from the early 1970s when real cuts to the education budget were carried through for the first time in the post-war period (see Table 2.1). Following the Conservative's election victory in 1979, education was the target of further cuts and these were followed two years later by a long-term planned contraction to education spending (Dale 1989). The axe fell particularly hard upon capital expenditure and over the next decade the physical fabric of British education was put under intense strain, as monies for routine repair and maintenance of school buildings, let alone the construction of desperately needed new ones, underwent a marked contraction. Similar pressures were felt upon basic equipment like text books, writing materials and classroom furniture, while individual schools and LEAs were given the powers to

Table 2.1 Expenditure on education as a percentage of GDP

Year	Public expenditure on education	Private expenditure on education
1973–74	5.8	1.6
1974–75	6.4	1.5
1975–76	6.5	1.6
1976–77	6.2	2.0
1977–78	5.6	2.2
1978–79	5.4	2.3
1979–80	5.2	2.3
1980–81	5.6	2.4
1981–82	5.5	2.6
1982–83	5.4	2.7
1983–84	5.3	2.5
1984–85	5.1	2.6
1985–86	4.9	2.6
1986–87	4.9	2.8
1987–88	4.8	2.9
1988–89	4.7	3.0
1989–90	4.8	3.4
1990–91	4.8	3.8
1991–92	5.1	4.5
1992–93	5.2	5.1
1993–94	5.2	5.4
1994–95	5.2	5.8
1995–96	5.1	6.4

Source: Glennerster 1998.

ride the wave of property speculation by selling off school playing fields in a desperate attempt to raise revenue.

The scale of these cuts is well captured by Glennerster, when he remarks:

> The result of the spending strategies of successive Governments was to reduce the share of the GDP allocated to publicly funded education from 6.5 per cent in 1975/76 to 4.7 per cent in 1988/89. No such previous reduction in education's share of the nation's resources had occurred this century ... It is not to be found in the experience of any other leading nation. (Glennerster 1998: 36)

As Table 2.1 shows, the proportion of GDP going into education increased a little following the nadir of 1988–89 but by the middle of the 1990s the modest increases of the previous years had once again been reversed. The real value of funding per pupil also deteriorated across the 1990s (Smith 2000) while, as we have already seen, unit costs in further and higher education were subject to a sharp and relentless decline (MacKinnon *et al.* 1996). Throughout the 1990s the student: teacher ratio was also steadily eroded.

'Is educashun wurking?'

Ball well recognises the significance of the turn to markets when he comments that, 'the implementation of market reforms in education is essentially *a class strategy which has as one of its major effects the repro-duction of relative social class (and ethnic) advantages'* (1993: 4, original emphasis). In turning to the market, existing sources of inequality are further valorised to the point where, 'in effect, we have to understand the market [in education] as a system of exclusion' (*ibid.*: 17). In aban-doning the political commitment to an education system geared towards the need all young people and by returning education to employers and the market, young people were promised the develop-ment of a new structure of provision that would provide them with the practical and intellectual skills necessary for a prosperous working life. The reality has actually been somewhat different and the restruc-turing of education played out since the middle of the 1970s has, in many respects, exacted a high price.

One notable example of this has been a huge expansion in educa-tion's influence over the lives of the young. Education provision has grown steadily throughout the twentieth century and over the course of the last 100 years or so, we have moved from a position where education beyond the age of 11 was still the preserve of a minority, through compulsory secondary education and on to the emergence of something approaching a system of mass higher education. We have already seen how the expansion of secondary education was regarded as a key part of the inclusive strategy pursued during the 1960s and early 1970s. Yet while the raising of the school leaving age to 16 in 1972 was the last formal extension of compulsory schooling, the restructuring of education during the 1980s and 1990s has de facto produced an equally significant expansion. Take participation beyond the minimum school leaving age. Rates of participation in full-time education for 16 year olds increased from around one in three in 1974, to around one in two in the early 1980s (Furlong and Cartmel 1997). Ten years later the number of 16 year olds staying in full-time educa-tion had reached around seven in ten; a figure around which it was to hover for the rest of the decade. Equally remarkable were the increases in the numbers of 17 and 18 year olds in full-time education. At the beginning of the 1990s, four in ten 16 to 18 year olds were still in full-time education and by the end of the decade the figure had risen to 55 per cent. When figures for young people on government supported work experience and training provision are included, by the time the Conservatives lost power the majority of young people aged 16–18 were in some form of full-time education or training.[2]

Young people's participation in higher education expanded in similarly dramatic ways. Again we have seen how the social democratic reconstruction of higher education saw the number of young people experiencing a university or polytechnic education more than double during the 1960s alone. Although the proportion of 18 and 19 year olds entering full-time higher education after 1971 (14 per cent) subsequently dropped, and did not recover to this earlier level until the mid 1980s, between 1991 and 1998 those entering full-time higher education courses increased from just under one in five to one in three of the age group (Halsey 2000). The significance of this expansion nevertheless requires qualification. While we have also seen that the supply of new places in higher education was driven by the re-regulation of universities and changes to the method of their funding, the increased demand for these places is more difficult to explain. Certainly this process of expansion compounded higher education's exclusionary role, since the vast majority of these new entrants were drawn from the middle class. The proportion of working class young people entering higher education changed little throughout the 1990s. But the fact that employers responded to the recession of 1990–93 in particular by rationalising many of the middle management segments of the labour market, which had until then emerged largely unscathed from the previous two quick recessions, undoubtedly accelerated the trend. In response to the intensification of competitive pressures, entry to most professions and large swathes of middle management have been progressively reconstituted as graduate level occupations.

Increased rates of staying on in full-time further education are therefore not so much a reflection of the success of educational restructuring, as testament to the broader failure of the monetarist strategy. As we shall see in the next chapter, the initial surge in school leaver participation in government work experience and training programmes was primarily a response to the collapse in those semi and unskilled employment opportunities traditionally the preserve of working class school leavers. Their replacement by schemes and programmes patently unable to meet their aspirations for *real jobs* paying decent wages ensured that any initial goodwill was quickly exhausted and by the early 1990s these schemes were haemorrhaging their recruits. It was the lack of credible training opportunities together with the absence of meaningful job opportunities that, to a large degree, account for the growth in increased rates of participation in education post 16. As Ainley (1999b) notes, during the 1990s further education took over much of the warehousing role of unemployed youth assumed by training programmes during the 1980s. The development of a new range of courses and qualifications for this army of reluctant participants may have provided a *post hoc* source of legitimation, but for large numbers of young people their participation in further education was more a reflection of the absence of credible alternatives than a ringing endorsement of educational change.[3]

As well as quantitative changes, the qualitative impact of restructuring has further underwritten education as a source of differentiation between young people. As we have seen, the maintenance of selection and streaming maintained historical sources of division within the comprehensive movement. As Willis (1977) so memorably demonstrated, working class kids still got working class jobs. But as the reform agenda was halted and then abandoned, education's importance as a site of division has become even greater. It is true that the national curriculum, regular testing and the reorganisation of the examination system have produced a large increase in general levels of qualification. In 1970, four in 10 young people left school with no qualifications but by 1992 only 7 per cent of school leavers remained unqualified (MacKinnon *et al.* 1996). But it is also the case that with the growth in qualifications, middle class young people have continued their domination of higher grade GCSEs and 'A' levels. As Smith points out, '... while the overall level of qualifications has increased dramatically, particularly in the final 20 years of the [twentieth] century, the relative chances of people from different social backgrounds of acquiring these qualifications has remained remarkably constant' (2000: 218).

For young black people too, the turn to markets compounded previous sources of exclusion. As Cregan (2002: 30) argues, the general increase in rates of qualification among school leavers has done little to overcome the relative educational disadvantages of young people of African-Caribbean or Asian descent: 'blacks were still less qualified than whites when they left school'. Higher rates of participation in full-time education post 16 among young blacks are also more a reflection of continuing disadvantage than sign of relative progress. By the early

1990s, 78 per cent of young people of African or Caribbean descent and 77 per cent of Asian descent were staying in full-time education, compared to 63 per cent of whites. However, the primary reason for this was often acute experience of unemployment, as black school leavers faced additional barriers to securing those jobs still going in the form of employer-discrimination and a lack of credible qualifications. As Cregan makes clear, for all the changes, 'the policies of successive governments in the last thirty years of the twentieth century had no overall advantageous effect on the relative experiences of the majority of young blacks' (*ibid.*: 25).

Perhaps the most visible source of division has come from the large numbers of students who have chosen to physically absent themselves from this structure of education. With the de facto extension of compulsory education and the sharp intensification of the 'learning' experience, many young people have responded to the prospect of a protracted education, a rigid and often irrelevant curriculum, and an intense regime of testing and examination, by excluding themselves from school in ways similar to those detailed by Corrigan (1977) some years earlier. Official records of school truancy suggest that a little under 1 per cent of secondary school students are absent from school without good reason, with rates among 13 to 15 year olds the highest (DfEE 2000). Few regard these figures as credible and alternative estimates point to around 30 per cent of secondary school age students playing truant, most of which occurs post-registration (O'Keefe 1993). Anywhere between 500 000 young people are unauthorised absentees from school each week and up to one million play truant each year (Milner and Blyth 1999). A significant minority of this is regular or persistent absenteeism, with one in 10 students playing truant on particular days, one in 20 for days at a time and 2.5 per cent of students truanting for weeks at a time. Interestingly, while boys are over-represented in the official figures on truancy the findings from self-report studies point to only minimal differences between the genders (Casey and Smith 1995). In some areas, particularly inner city and estates dominated by social housing, truanting has become a long-standing and routine feature of young people's lives. As Reid comments, 'present reported average rates of attendance in some parts of London of 80 per cent for secondary age pupils are no higher than they were in 1918. Similar findings have been reported in Scotland and urban and rural areas of England' (1999: 21).

Truancy may be one sign that young people have not accepted the changing state of education lightly. Another is the growth in school exclusions. In constructing a more protracted and intensive education, long-standing problems of managing the student body have been exacerbated. Historically, the rejection of teacher authority, disaffection, disillusionment, boredom and cynicism, and their manifestation in terms of bullying, disruption, vandalism and the physical and verbal abuse of teachers (Carlen *et al.* 1992; Humphries 1990), have been an endemic feature of compulsory schooling. Yet with the introduction of school 'league tables' and greater competition for students, the ready use of temporary or permanent physical exclusions has become a more important tool in managing the consequences of this new regime. As pressures on schools and their students have intensified, so too has their willingness and ability to resort to exclusion grown. Figures point out that permanent exclusions increased from 3000 to over 13 000 per year between 1990 and 1997 (an increase of 450 per cent). Across the same time the number of fixed term exclusions rose to over 100 000, after which a slight reduction occurred (Parsons 1998). The vast majority of these exclusions were boys, but rates of exclusion among young people of African-Caribbean origin have been around five to eight times higher than rates for whites (DfEE 2000; Osler and Hill 1999).

If market forces in education have worked to deepen the educational exclusion experienced by working class and some young ethnic minority people, then there were some benefits for a small number of girls and young women. Reflecting broader changes to the occupational structure and the gradual opening up of the professions to middle class young women, rather than any progressive shift in the form of schooling, the reorganisation of education has both expressed and consolidated broader shifts in gender relations. Throughout most of the post-war period, education remained a key site for the subordination of girls, as post-war policy was directed primarily at educating boys for the task of reconstruction (David 1993). Gender stereotypes continued to inform schooling and a differentiated curriculum underpinned girls' gendered 'choices', so that as late as the 1970s girls continued to suffer lower rates of participation in public examinations, particularly from age 16 onwards, and tended to under perform in comparison to boys.

The introduction of 'core' subjects under the national curriculum did go some way towards formalising a general curriculum, with the consequence that girls' examination performance underwent a significant improvement (Tomlinson 2001; Weiner *et al.* 1997). By the early 1990s, girls' performance at GCSE level surpassed that of boys and girls were beginning to record greater success at A level too. At both GCSE and A level, subject 'choice' has remained heavily gendered, most evident in a feminised arts and humanities and the continuing masculine domination of the physical sciences. Higher education did remain more resilient to these changes, particularly at postgraduate level, but even here the gender composition has changed notably. By the mid-1990s, girls 'were maintaining their primary school lead over boys throughout secondary and into higher education. Girls today out-perform boys in GCSEs, do better at A levels, and are more likely to enter higher education' (Furlong and Cartmel 1997: 47). Yet the bene-fits for girls were thinly spread. While some previously excluded areas of education were opened up to girls and young women, for many the reorganisation of education confirmed more recognisable patterns of inequality. For working class girls, greater competition from adult women and those women returning to work after child care responsi-bilities, particularly for those semi, unskilled and 'dead-end' jobs traditionally the preserve of low qualified female school leavers, meant that employers were demanding increased levels of qualifications from their recruits. Many more girls also sought shelter in education in the absence of any wider opportunities for work. Running even faster just to stand still, 'in relation to young men, most young women face an equally disadvantaged labour market position than in the [earlier] post-war years despite taking advantage of increased schooling by perform-ing better than young males in examinations' (Cregan 2002: 40–1).

Conclusion

By the middle of the 1990s, therefore, what it meant to be a young student either in school, college or university, had changed; possibly beyond what would have been recognisable as recently as a generation earlier. Up to the middle of the 1970s, being young had been a rela-tively advantageous thing to be as education became a central point in the political commitment to a more inclusive youth. The extension of compulsory and post-compulsory opportunities for education, new resources, curriculum and examination reform and an enhanced teaching profession offered the basis for a rational reorganisation of a system of education deeply imbued with relations of inequality. The expansion of higher education followed. However, within this political commitment to greater equality and inclusion, deeply entrenched and fundamental inequalities remained. The failure of reform to confront education's importance as a source of social division between the young was clearly evident in the survival and then prospering of the private sector, where ability to pay and ruthless selection continued as the only significant criteria of entry. In the maintained sector, the secondary schools remained 'the prime site of the process of selection through examination for manual or mental labour' (Ainley 1988: 63), as the reforming promise of a non-selective admissions procedure, a common curriculum and examinations system, and more responsive teaching and learning methods failed to alter the balance of forces dividing the young. Social democratic reform had brought about significant and important changes to the form of education and raised the possibility of its rational reform. But within the political commitment to universalism, the content and outcome of education remained depressingly familiar.

The instability of the social democratic form of education proved its eventual undoing and by the middle of the 1970s, to all intents and purposes it had been repudiated. There was nothing inevitable about the direction that the restructuring process took, particularly as popular support for the comprehensive reorganisation remained strong for well over a decade after the programme had been abandoned. But in taking responsibility for education as the basis of youth's inclusion, the deterioration in young people's employment prospects meant that governments were also faced with the cost of these failures. Swamped by a stagnating economy, rising unemployment and a sharp change in the demand for youth labour, Labour's turn towards vocationalism as the 'solution' to this deepening crisis – always more a mark of pragmatism than of any fundamental change in conviction – set the terms within which education restructuring would be played out over the next 25 years. Embraced by Thatcher's Conservatives and then John Major, the subsequent reconstruction of young people's education, first in the name of vocational reform and then in-line with market forces, expressed a series of deep political forces. Through resort to employers, money and the market, governments sought more fully to politically disengage themselves from the previous responsibilities they had assumed, provide a degree of cover for the consequences of the policies they had chosen to pursue and, along the way, hold out some comfort for growing numbers of alarmed young people and their parents.

The subsequent destruction of the institutional forms of the inclusive political strategy and their reconstruction in new ways therefore simultaneously involved the practical transformation of youth. The influence of education over young people's lives has become more dramatic during the last quarter of the twentieth century, as more young people spent more time in formal education than ever before. At the same time, the experience of education has been intensified to an unprecedented degree. The consequences of this for all young people have been dramatic, but the latter reconstruction of education has heightened divisions between the young. For some, a protracted and marketised system of education continues to underscore their dominance over the examinations system and thus those segments of the labour market that offer unparalleled opportunities for wealth and material acquisition. But for many more – the unskilled and semi-skilled working class, young black people and large numbers of young women – education has become a means to effect their continuing exclusion: from knowledge, from skills, from meaningful qualifications and ultimately, as we shall now explore, from decent jobs.

CHAPTER 3

The Changing State of Work

In continuing our examination of the changing state of youth, the changing state of work may at first glance seem an inappropriate topic to include. After all, at one level issues of youth employment and unemployment have little to do with politics and the state. Beyond exhortation, the state holds little direct sway over employers' recruitment practices or the roles assigned to young people at work. Still more significant is the 'mythical' status of the commitment to full employment. An unforeseen and largely fortuitous product of the post-war global boom (Glynn 1991), for 30 years after the end of the Second World War governing orthodoxy nevertheless laid claim to full employment levels of growth as a direct consequence of the willingness of governments to intervene to manage economic activity. Far from rationalising post-war economic development into a planned pattern of growth, the limits of government in this respect were rudely underlined by the return to mass unemployment from around 1975. Indeed the failure of the social democratic state to substantiate its commitment to full employment had, as we shall see in the first sections of this chapter, historic implications for the young. As the political strategy of inclusion through jobs for all crumbled in the face of global recession, young people's purchase on the labour market was exposed as far more tenuous than many had supposed. As government scrambled to distance themselves from their earlier promises of work, the continuing long-term decline of manufacturing, the acceleration of the displacement of semi- and unskilled jobs by technology, changing patterns of employment in the service sector and new modes of employer control all contributed to a far-reaching change in young people's relationship to the labour market.

Yet it is precisely because youth unemployment broke into pieces the social democratic vision of a managed and inclusive capitalism, that the changing state of work is also political. Most immediately, the crisis of unemployment that unfolded over the last three decades of

49

the twentieth century was simultaneously articulated in terms of a crisis of the Keynesian state. In giving a commitment to the maintenance of full employment, governments had been keen to take credit for relatively buoyant job prospects and steadily rising wages. But just as governments were eager to bask in the glory conferred by full employment, they also found themselves faced with the threat to their political authority posed by a return to pre-war levels of unemployment. Young people had been major beneficiaries of the long post-war boom. A buoyant labour market, full employment, nominal levels of unemployment and rising wages all suggested that youth had finally 'come of age'. But as boom turned to bust and recession was followed by recession, the rapidly deteriorating prospects of young workers and a marked change in the demand for youth labour provided one of the starkest examples of the practical failures of the Keynesian dream.

Youth unemployment is political in a further way. In abandoning the commitment to full employment, the rejection of the state strategy of inclusion was signalled in perhaps its starkest terms. In seeking to politically disengage itself from its previous responsibility for ensuring all who wanted it had work, the interventionist state and the politics of security through 'jobs for all' was progressively abandoned in favour of the monetarist commitment to prioritising inflation. As Bonefeld *et al.* point out, in identifying inflation as their priority, governments signalled more than a change in economic policy. The 'prioritisation of inflation amounts to an underwriting of market forces as the key determinant of inequality...the major, but not the only, illustration being an increase in unemployment, to an unknown level for an indeterminate period' (1995: 78). Monetarism understood in the narrow sense of strict control of the money supply in order to squeeze out price inflation, was briefly (and disastrously) applied at the beginning of the 1980s. But, in adopting an anti-inflationary stance, governments clearly signalled a broader change in strategy, which underscored the centrality of markets as the key determinant in the allocation of jobs and income.

In this way, the political retreat from full employment in favour of the pursuit of monetary stability and low inflation, also expressed a marked change in governing practice. The monetarist conviction that unemployment in general and youth unemployment in particular could be 'solved' through deregulating youth labour was never more than a chimera. The belief that jobs for young people can come alone from changes to the characteristics of youth labour coming onto the labour market, as we shall see, has little substance. Yet the considerable force with which this monetarist ideology came to define the limits of political activity, had as its basis practical changes to the activities of the state. Where governments had once proclaimed the sanctity of full employment through tax and spend, there was the withdrawal of state support in favour of the 'guarantee' of a place on a work experience or training scheme. And where there had once been the commitment to exercise some degree of direct and benign regulation over young people's entry into work, the terms of young people's relationship to the labour market was subject to systematic re-regulation.

The crisis of youth employment

That the collapse in youth unemployment dealt such a blow to the political strategy of incorporation, derived in large part from the position of young workers as one of the principle beneficiaries of the 'golden age' of post-war capitalist development. The buoyant demand for youth labour during this period is well illustrated by Finn's (1987; see also Maguire 1991) reference to the early 1960s. Of approximately 600 000 young people leaving school each year, few would suffer the ignominies of unemployment. High demand for semi-and unskilled labour in the manufacturing sector drew in around one third of school leavers. Another fifth of boys entered the distribution trades and around one third of girls were employed as shop assistants. Few of these jobs offered opportunities for formal training, even if demarcations of age ensured that young males enjoyed an effective monopoly over a relatively healthy, if declining, apprenticeship system. By the middle of the 1960s, a quarter of a million young people were finding manufacturing apprenticeships, although only 6 per cent of young women were apprenticed and most of these were in hairdressing. Unemployment rates for young people during this period were actually lower than those for the working population as a whole, which itself averaged 1.8 per cent from the end of the war through to the middle of the 1960s (Glynn and Booth 1996). In 1961 for instance, of a recorded unemployment rate of 330 000 only 10 000 were under 19 years of age.

Looking back to this period from the vantage point of today, it would be tempting to view these years with sanguinity. That most of these jobs were low quality, mundane and valued for their ability to offer some degree of immediate financial gratification, should nevertheless be underlined (Carter 1966). Even at the height of the post-war boom, it is sobering to remember that the idea of straightforward transitions to work combined with security of employment, so often associated with the Keynesian period, were ones still alien to the vast majority of working class people (Titmus 1958). In any case, such relative fortunes proved brief and unsustainable. Concerns about the ability of the British economy to sustain levels of growth necessary to maintain full employment were openly aired throughout the 1950s, as the unemployment rate rose with each low point in the 'stop–go' cycles that plagued post-war reconstruction (Glynn 1991). Between 1950 and 1973 the British growth rate had been only half the OECD average and by the end of the 1960s it was being openly touted by Harold Wilson's Labour governments that the political commitment to full employment could not be sustained.

Rates of joblessness at this time were already straining the credibility of claims for managed growth. Under Wilson the general rate of unemployment rose to over the half a million mark (2.5 per cent), a figure that even a few years previous would have been seen as politically unsustainable. But it was the shock waves following the 1973 'oil crisis' that underlined the vulnerability of the British economy, as economic stagnation coupled with rising inflation sent unemployment surging above one million[1] (4.2 per cent) in the summer of 1975; a landmark figure above which it was to stay for the next 25 years. Worse still was yet to come. Under the Labour governments 1975 to 1979, unemployment peaked at over 1.5 million in August 1977, after which it began to decline. Any upturn in employment fortunes were short-lived, however, as the recession of the early 1980s, aggravated by the austerity measures imposed by the first Thatcher government, brought about a doubling of the unemployment rate from 4.4 per cent in 1979 to 8.9 per cent in 1981 (2.5 million). Unlike the earlier recession, this time the rate continued to rise reaching a post-war peak of 11.4 per cent in August 1986 (or 3.3 million according to official estimates), during Thatcher's second term of office. From 1987 onwards, levels did decline again to around 5.2 per cent (1.5 million) in June 1990. But, with the onset of a third recession in the space of 15 years, a further surge in joblessness pushed the official rate well back into double figures, peaking once again at over 3 million in 1993. It is indeed one measure of the profound crisis that characterised these years, that after four successive election victories, 18 consecutive years in power, countless initiatives and huge amounts of public money, the Conservatives left office in 1997 with the official unemployment count of 1.6 million (5.5 per cent), still well above the figure they inherited in 1979.

It is difficult to underestimate the calamitous impact of unemployment upon the young. With the crisis decades came an especially rapid deterioration in the employment prospects of the young, with unemployment for the under 25s doubling and for minimum age school leavers trebling between 1974 and 1975 alone (Ashton 1986). Again employment levels for young people picked up in line with the general increase in the aggregate demand for labour but by 1981, with the economy in the depths of the worst slump since the 1930s, one in six under 25s and one in five school leavers were officially without work. At its peak in 1986, almost one in four 18 and 19 year olds were unemployed and this figure was only slightly improved upon 10 years later with youth unemployment still estimated to be in the region of 15 per cent; or almost twice the national average.

Of course, the impact of unemployment was not evenly distributed. For those leaving school with a reasonable level of qualification jobs still existed, although they were increasingly difficult to secure. Many more took shelter in the rapid expansion of further and higher education (see Chapter 2). But for those young people leaving school with few, if any, qualifications, the likelihood of unemployment greatly increased. In 1979, a young male leaving school with no qualifications was between four and five times more likely to be unemployed than a graduate; for unqualified young women it was double. Twenty years later the gap had widened even further. Unemployment also fell heavily on young blacks. Study after study revealed the scale of the problem facing black school leavers, with general rates of unemployment among both young people of African-Caribbean and Asian descent running between two and three times the level of their white peers (Shire 1997; Skellington 1992; Solomos 1988). Again, the employment gap between young blacks and whites steadily widened. Given that unemployment was further concentrated in particular regions, localities and urban areas, through much of the 1980s and 1990s whole communities found themselves decimated by the absence of any meaningful opportunities for their young to work.

As damning as they are, these figures certainly underestimated the true scale of the problem. On the one hand, calculating unemployment figures from those claiming unemployment benefits, as is the official practice, meant the plight of young women often went unrecorded. It has been estimated that as many as 40 per cent of unemployed women are omitted from the official statistics, since their effective exclusion from a right to benefits because they cohabit with a male partner provides a powerful disincentive to register

(Maguire 1991). On the other hand, consecutive Conservative governments felt little compunction when it came to manipulating the count. After almost two decades of Conservative power, the net effect of more than 30 changes to the accounting procedures ensured major downward adjustments to the headline unemployment figures. Estimates by the Unemployment Unit, an independent research organisation, consistently pointed out that if the unemployment count had remained consistent with pre-1980 methods of collection, then the rate would have been around half a million higher. Even using the more inclusive International Labour Office (ILO) definition of unemployment – which defines the unemployed as all those seeking and available to work, as opposed to the United Kingdom's claimant count which measures all those who can satisfy the administrative requirements for claiming benefit – provides a considerable underestimation (Bivand 2002a). The Unemployment Unit's own measure of unemployment using a broad based definition that includes all those who want to work but who cannot start immediately, perhaps due to caring responsibilities, points to an actual rate 1.5 million above the current claimant count. And if we include in our definition what the Unemployment Unit defines as 'labour market slack' – or all those who want work, are on government schemes and the under-employment of part-time workers who really want full-time work – over 3 million extra people would be added to the official total of around 1 million unemployed in 2001.

No jobs to go to?

There is no consensus on what accounts for this dramatic deterioration in the employment fortunes of the young. Certainly, there was no comparable increase in official rates of youth unemployment during the 'great depression' of the inter-war years. To what extent this was a consequence of the absence of unemployment benefits (i.e. no incentive to register) or the relative cheapness of youth labour (i.e. the substitution of young workers for adults kept youth unemployment low) is the matter of some debate (Whiteside 1991). In any case, during the slump of the early 1980s, the Department of Employment was estimating that an increase of 1 per cent in adult male unemployment was producing a 1.7 per cent increase among teenage males; and that a 1 per cent increase among adult women produced a rise among teenage females of 3 per cent. Reviewing evidence from the Organisation of Economic Co-operation and Development (OECD), O'Higgins (2001) has come to a similar conclusion. Averaged across industrialised nations, a 1 per cent increase in the general rate of unemployment produces a 2 per cent increase in youth unemployment.

In part, this sensitivity to changes in the aggregate demand for labour was an effect of young workers' particular vulnerability to the 'business cycle': the instability in economic activity that defines the history of capitalist development. Employers responded to each slow down in economic activity by curtailing new recruitment and axing training provision in an attempt to cut costs, and by inflating the qualification and experience needed for those vacancies that remained (Raffe 1983). In an effort to protect existing members, trades unions too were guilty of enforcing the principle of 'last in, first out' in aiding management to select workers for redundancy. Statutory redundancy payments linked to length of service also made it both easier and cheaper to sack the young. These factors were further compounded in the early 1980s by unfavourable demographic conditions, as the number of school leavers entering the labour market bulged to a post-war high (Deakin 1996). Nevertheless, the upturns to the business cycle that followed each recession, together with a considerable decline in the size of the youth cohort through the 1980s and into the 1990s, made little notable difference to the continuing scale of youth unemployment, particularly among those with few qualifications. In contrast to the two thirds of young people leaving school to directly enter work at the beginning of the 1970s, 25 years later only 8 per cent were finding work. By the time the Conservatives lost power in 1997, only one in five minimum age school leavers were entering the labour market directly and half of these were still destined to begin their working lives on government training or work experience schemes (Department for Education and Employment 1997).

The sheer scale and persistence of youth unemployment therefore points to something more profound than either fluctuations to the business cycle or demography can explain. As Hobsbawm (1994) makes clear, the three 'quick recessions' of 1973–75, 1981–83 and 1990–93 marked not just a series of downturns but an important shift in the underlying structure of post-war capitalist economies. For the young unemployed, this was marked by an acceleration in the long-term decline of those industrial sectors that had traditionally offered an important source of employment (Maguire and Maguire 1996; Maguire 1991; Ashton 1986). With each recession, the long-term contraction in manufacturing accelerated and employment in UK-based manufacturing sharply declined with 3.5 million full-time manufacturing jobs going in the two decades after 1973 (40 per cent of the total). Between 1980 and 1983 alone, one third of British manufacturing jobs disappeared as 20 per cent of productive capacity was wiped out. With the decimation of manufacturing employment came a sharp reduction in the number of apprenticeship places from 250 000 in 1965 to 150 000 in 1980, and a subsequent halving again in the following four years (Deakin 1996). On top of this, in traditionally labour intensive areas of production the demand for young people to fill semi- and unskilled manual jobs evaporated, either lost in the general 'shake-out' of labour or sacrificed to the economies offered by automation.

Beyond this, the emergence of mass youth unemployment also reflected shifting modes of employer control. 'On their own, structural shifts in industry composition cannot account for the observed aggregate changes in young adults' employment prospects' (OECD 1996: 142). The dramatic decline in the demand for youth labour in manufacturing should, to some extent, have been compensated for by the marked expansion of those other sectors in which the young have also had a strong presence. In the service sector, over 4 million jobs have been created since 1970 and although the hotel, catering and retail distribution sector is currently the biggest employer of youth labour in Britain (Gabriel 1988), relatively speaking, service sector employers continued to shun the young. It was only during the late 1980s and 1990s that the service sector discovered a real enthusiasm for young workers, particularly part-time student labour, and most of the expansion in this sector was accounted for by the employment of adult women workers (Lucas 1997). For employers, the attraction of adult women, many of whom were returning to work once their children had started school, was their perceived stability at work and their apparent amenability to the growing phenomenon of part-time working. Employers had long berated young workers for their irresponsibility, inadequate motivation and lack of reliability, but while the 'long boom' persisted this 'restlessness, their immunity from the constraints of long-term instrumentality' (Frith 1980: 38) was tolerated and even factored into recruitment policies. It was the absence of a clear sense of commitment and discipline, and the failure of young workers to demonstrate 'realism' when it came to the serious business of work, that motivated employers to respond to increased competitive pressures by moving away from their traditional reliance on youth labour, towards the recruitment of what were seen as more 'stable' categories of worker.

Overcoming 'deficient youth'

As well as explaining the declining use of youth labour, criticisms like these also articulated the parameters within which the political crisis of youth unemployment was 'resolved'. It mattered little that there was no compelling evidence to confirm the increasingly popular view that school leavers held unrealistic views about their future working lives or were ignorant about the nature of the work on offer. On the contrary, most minimum age school leavers were all too aware that the jobs on offer were most likely to involve noisy, dirty, physically demanding or routine working practices, and that their work would be performed for scant remuneration and little intrinsic reward (Mizen 1995; Finn 1987). It was the quality of work on offer that accounted for young people's restlessness. Yet as we saw in Chapter 2, by the time of the 'Great Debate' on education, it had become something of an article of faith – among employers, government, civil servants and growing numbers of academics – that it was the deficiencies of the young themselves, rather than a problem of the quality of work on offer, that accounted for the growing numbers of workless youth.

With little evidence that the young unemployed were responsible for their own predicament, the significance of the 'deficiency model' of youth, as Davies (1986) terms it, is to be found at the level of politics and the state. More specifically, the 'deficiency model' became the principle means through which the growing influence of the Manpower Services Commission (MSC) was legitimised, as it was transformed from one of the last expressions of the political commitment to inclusion, and a modest one at that, into a central instrument through which the restructuring of the labour market was enforced. Originally a concession to the long-standing calls for an organisation to oversee a national plan for labour; within the space of a decade after its founding in 1973 few young people over the age of 14 would manage to escape its influence. As Davies remarks, 'as an integral and indeed taken for granted element of its philosophy, the young were characterised as, by their very nature, lacking in appropriate skills, qualities, habits and attitudes' (Davies 1986: 54). Most clearly articulated through the belief that unemployed young people needed a period of vocational preparation as a means to secure employment, through the MSC, responsibility for the deepening political failures of the inclusive strategy was transferred away from the state.

However deeply ideological the deficiency model of youth may have been – after all it purposely left untouched the crucial questions of investment, productivity, the organisations of work, in short where jobs would come from – the growing force of this argument was given strength by changing state practices. During its early years, the MSC clung tentatively to some vestiges of inclusion, even as its purpose became progressively redefined. One of its first acts was to take over the 100 000 places Training Opportunities Scheme launched in 1972, intended to promote the retraining of the unemployed (Lindley 1983). Pressure from the trades unions and widespread concerns about civil disorder led to the rapid expansion of such temporary measures, initially in the form of subsidies to jobs. Beginning in earnest under Labour in 1975, the Temporary Employment Subsidy offered subsidies to employers to defer redundancies; the Job Creation Programme provided subsidised employment in community initiatives to 16 to 24 year olds; and the Recruitment Subsidy for School Leavers gave financial assistance to private sector employers and the nationalised industries for giving preference to recruiting unemployed school leavers. The following year, a new round of job subsidy measures were extended through the Youth Employment Subsidy, this time for the young long-term unemployed (i.e. six months or longer).

Job subsidy measures proved both costly and inefficient. And, with the rate of youth unemployment rising faster than ever, they clearly did not work. In a significant development in 1976, Labour modified the provision of direct job subsidies through the introduction of the Work Experience Programme (WEP). Instead of paying employers to retain or take on a young person in a full or part-time capacity, in effect to use public money to create or preserve a job, WEP paid employers a subsidy to provide an unemployed school leaver with up to six months' work experience, paying an allowance and not a wage. In this respect, WEP marked a terminal point of the political commitment to full employment, by substituting direct attempts to create employment with a limited period of work experience. It was on the terms laid down through WEP's vocationalism, that subsequent special measures for the young unemployed were built. In 1978, WEP was incorporated into a more systematic, significantly expanded and far more costly programme of work experience, in the form of the Youth Opportunities Programme (YOP). Split into two broad categories, under YOP unemployed school leavers were either provided with a short period of structured compensatory education and training, or up to 12 months on Work Experience on Employers Premises. Providing 162 000 places during its first year, by the depth of the early 1980s recession some 550 000 unemployed young people were placed on YOP; or nearly half of all school leavers.

If there was any remaining doubt by 1978, then YOP marked the Labour government's final acceptance that the political commitment to full employment was dead. Through YOP, Labour sought to distance itself from any responsibility for the continuing deterioration in the employment fortunes of the young. In turning to work experience and vocational preparation as the 'solution', however temporary it was hoped it would be, YOP not only constituted a reluctant acceptance that the deepening crisis of youth employment would be settled on terms dictated by the market. It also held out the possibility for government to extricate itself from its previous promises of full employment and security of working life. By putting in place a temporary period of vocational preparation, responsibility for youth unemployment could be shifted away from the interventionist state and on to 'deficient' youth, and the problem of workless youth redefined in terms of the needs of employers and the market.

Consolidating the training state

The election of the Conservatives in 1979 is often regarded as a turning point for youth unemployment, a final break with the supposed post-war consensus and the beginnings of the monetarist revolution proper. For sure, after 1979 the young unemployed were subjected to a more intense and systematic process of restructuring, one that was, moreover, pursued with a callous indifference not seen for 50 years and most likely not replicated elsewhere in the industrial capitalist world. But, as we have seen, by the time the Conservatives came to power, both the political conditions and institutional basis for the consolidation of mass work experience programmes as the basis for the restructuring of youth were already clearly established. One crucial difference was that whereas Labour governments had turned to work experience and vocationalism out of force of circumstance, after 1979 they became a guiding principle of government action. If under Labour it had been conceded that youth unemployment was a problem of supply and of young people's reluctance to 'knuckle under' and accept those jobs going, then under the Conservatives these ad hoc palliatives were judged insufficient. Only through a large-scale expansion of vocationalism backed up by the root and branch re-regulation of the youth labour market, could the employment fortunes of the young be revived.

Under the Conservative governments of Margaret Thatcher, the momentum already achieved by Labour was therefore embraced with something of a missionary zeal. The young, it was argued, were unemployed not because of a lack of demand, failure of investment, the indifferent imposition of technology or, above all, the pursuit of profitability over young people's need for jobs. On the contrary, unemployment among school leavers was singularly articulated in terms of the problems caused by the misplaced interventions of the past. The expansion of state activity under the Keynesian strategy, it was argued, had eroded youth's historical value as a source of willing, cheap and disposable labour. Not only had the comprehensive schools instilled in the young a wanton disregard for the work ethic (see Chapter 2), but the indiscriminate availability of welfare benefits, too easily accessed and paying inflated rates for open-ended periods of time (Marsland 1996; see also Chapters 4 and 5), had corroded the incentive to work. Furthermore, undue trade union influence had distorted market mechanisms and priced young people out of jobs, while restrictive working practices had produced a cumbersome and outmoded apprenticeship system, which compounded the more general inflexibility of labour (Minford 1985). Only by reconstructing the interventionist framework along lines dictated by employers and the market, would the growing army of unemployed young people find their way back into work.

Far from bringing about a diminution of the state, under the Conservatives its power over the lives of the young unemployed in fact underwent a massive expansion. Early ambitions to curtail the influence of the MSC, a body Margaret Thatcher's Conservatives still associated with the discredited inclusive strategy of the past, proved short-lived. Faced with a serious and rapid deterioration of young people's employment prospects, significantly aggravated by the Conservative's austerity measures, evaporating public support and the emergence of deep fissures in the social fabric, the MSC had again become the preferred means of dealing with the young unemployed. Once in power, and despite the rhetoric of curtailing the influence of the state, the Conservatives did little to disturb the by now considerable role played by YOP. But by 1981, plans were already afoot for a new and ambitious programme of training and work experience, the object of which was to, 'move towards a position where all young people under the age of 18 have the opportunity either of continuing in full-time education or of entering a period of planned work experience combined with work-related training and education' (Department of Employment 1981: 1).

The central plank of this 'new deal' (Finn 1987) for unemployed school leavers was the Youth Training Scheme (YTS), a £1 billion replacement for YOP (later rising closer to £2 billion). Launched in 1983 as a 'revolution' in training provision but this time only for the young unemployed, YTS was to provide 450 000 places each year on schemes lasting 12 months. Once on a scheme, trainees would be given a period of structured work experience, either directly with employers or in community settings, alongside a minimum entitle-ment to off-the-job training at a further education college or other recognised training institution. Further expanded in 1988 to provide up to two years' training, the role of YTS was subsequently enforced by the withdrawal of unemployment benefits to all but the most desper-ate. In this new variant, the first year was intended to concentrate on broad-based training, with the second given over to opportunities for greater specialisation. To cement this expansion, greater stress was placed on accreditation. By the end of the decade, such was the scale of YTS that nearly 400 000 young people were beginning their work-ing lives on a government scheme, or nearly two thirds of all school leavers. With the expansion to two years, the previous commitment to jobs for all was finally buried under the government's new-found promise to 'guarantee' all unemployed school leavers a place on a scheme by the Christmas after leaving school.

Far from revolutionising provision, YTS extended many of the prin-ciples already established but pursued them in far more methodical terms. By giving an unemployed young person to an employer for up to 24 months, like YOP the intention was to increase the attractiveness of youth labour to potential employers by allowing young people an opportunity to accumulate knowledge of work and some practical skills to go with it. Again like YOP, trainees on YTS would also be paid a training allowance, with provision for employer 'top-ups', still set well below average rates of youth pay. Like YOP, funding for the scheme would come from the public purse, in effect providing employers with free labour at the tax payer's expense. And like YOP too, the practice of YTS was to valorise divisions within the labour market, as those with better qualifications secured the best schemes (Lee *et al.* 1990); and the structuring influence of gender (Cockburn 1988) and 'race' (Solomos 1988) were further entrenched.

Whereas YOP had perhaps reluctantly conceded the inability of gov-ernments to control levels of youth employment, under YTS this was made into a virtue. Writing at the height of its influence, Finn well recognised that through YTS, 'the government declared its intention of transforming the relationship between working class youth and the labour market' (Finn 1987: 155). In providing a training 'solution' to youth unemployment, YTS sought to undermine the established system of industrial apprenticeships. Its stated mission was to promote the acquisition of transferable skills, one that would not only increase the stock of human capital but also facilitate ease of movement between different tasks and jobs throughout a young person's working life. In this way, flexibility could be promoted, while trainees were exempted from the 'red tape' of bureaucracy imposed by the 'race' and sex discrimination legislation that remained from politically more inclusive times. Trainees too found themselves marginal to the core provision of health and safety protection. Finally, by paying a training allowance at well below the 'going rate' of youth wages, differentials in relative earnings between adults and young people would be restored and young people would be priced back into jobs. Extolling the virtues of YTS to potential employers, the then Chairperson of MSC, Lord Young, was not shy in encouraging employers to avail themselves of, 'the opportunity to take on young men and women, train them and let them work for you almost entirely at our expense, and then decide whether or not you want to employ them' (quoted in Davies 1986: 58).

The 'revolution' betrayed

'Across the industrialised world, and in many developing countries too, the thought is paramount that the way to economic growth is via skill formation to raise labour productivity and hence average living standards' (Ashton and Green 1996: 1). In the United Kingdom, YTS spearheaded the belief that it was the quality of labour and the provision of training and education, which held the key to revitalising not only the employment prospects of the young, but also the fortunes of the nation as a whole. Yet as Ashton and Green also argue, the exact relationship between the stock of human capital possessed by a nation and trends in economic growth are at best unclear. We will return to this theme in more detail in Chapter 7, but it is worth noting here that although wealthier countries do possess a more highly qualified workforce, and those individuals with the highest levels of skills and qualifications tend to benefit in terms of higher incomes, the relationship between skill level and prosperity is one that is difficult to unravel. At the very least, increasing the quality and volume of the supply of skills is no simple answer to the problem of youth unemployment and relative economic decline. In fact, on many indicators the evidence of a simple positive relationship between education and training inputs and economic performance is both weak and contradictory. As Coates (2000) points out, low grade production technologies persist in large parts of the world's manufacturing sectors that have a plentiful supply of well educated recruits, while the labour intensive, low-skilled service sector has been the dominant source of new jobs, both within the UK and across the capitalist world more generally. For these reasons, the growing urgency with which training came to be advocated as a 'solution' to the problems of youth unemployment was more significant for its political force. Through the turn to training and education as the principle means of 'solving' the crisis of youth employment, governments could politically justify the retreat from even the nominal engagement with market forces that had been the hallmark of the Keynesian years.

Thus as far as YTS was concerned, claims that changes to the quality of labour coming into the labour market could enhance employment opportunities for young people were never more than ideological. Practically speaking, however, YTS did facilitate an overt and sometimes highly politicised attack on established training practices, many of which still embodied the more previously inclusive approach. As YTS was launched, the scope of the Industrial Training Boards established during the 1960s, with their tripartite structures and (admittedly weak) statutory powers of intervention, were considerably reduced. Alongside this, craft-based apprenticeship and technician training programmes were attacked as anachronistic, out of touch with the needs of employers and workers, and more concerned with the restrictive practices of the trades unions, than with the genuine skill requirements of the economy. Via YTS, traditional conceptions of skills training rooted in the accumulation of depth knowledge and the acquisition of process-specific skills were replaced by training organised according to notions of work-based 'competencies' (Pollert 1988). Such a 'revolution' in training practices would, it was claimed, bring about the development of both 'portable' skills, transferable within and between occupational boundaries, while enhancing the inflexibility of the old craft system. Through the classification of training into 'occupational families', where each family represented an area of the economy within which individual trainees could acquire sets of generic skills, the intention was also to separate young workers from the idea that skills training would tie them to a specific job for life.

Ultimately, YTS proved a woeful vanguard for the skills revolution, unable as it was to break through the 'low skills equilibrium' that for so long has characterised Britain's relative decline (Finegold and Soskice

1988). The reorganisation of training around 'occupational training families' and 'competencies', in fact emptied the process of skills acquisition
of any depth knowledge content, in favour of the accumulation of lower
level vocational information spread thinly across ill-defined occupational segments (Ainley 1999b). Far from breaking out of this low skills
equilibrium, YTS further locked the provision of training more firmly
into a vicious circle of low skills provision driven increasingly by the
short-term imperatives of employers. The majority of work experience
placements remained concentrated among small employers, providing
trainees with semi- and unskilled labour, with trainees spending most of
their time incorporated into the routine production tasks performed by
existing employees, but on far lower rates of pay (Mizen 1995). Where
employers continued to demand skilled labour – it is a considerable measure of the failure of the Conservative's skills revolution that even during
the deep recessions of the early 1980s and 1990s, in some sectors shortages of skilled workers remained acute – many chose to retain their pre-
existing provision, preferring instead to limit their involvement with
YTS to the creation of separate programmes motivated by some endur-
ing obligation to the communities in which they were located. As one
study of the engineering sector concluded: 'it appears that apprenticeship has influenced the content and quality of the engineering YTS
rather than YTS innovating apprenticeship' (Dutton 1987: viii).

Cheapening youth labour

YTS' pursuit of flexibility further became a euphemism for insecurity,
an attack on working conditions and the cheapening of youth labour.
As Benn and Fairley commented, the scheme set out 'to break people,
especially working class young people, into a life of low wages and
long periods of unemployment' (Benn and Fairley 1988: 3). Increases
to the relative value of youth wages during the 1960s and 1970s had
featured significantly in some explanations of the disproportionate
impact of unemployment on the young, as pressure from the trades
unions and an overly interventionist state had inflated the cost of
youth labour to a point where employers could no longer afford to
take them on (Wells 1983). The evidence to support this was never
more than patchy, with the relative wages of young workers only one
among many factors in decisions over whether or not to hire
the young. Nevertheless, depressing youth wages became an explicit
element of government policy. By using YTS to bring 'about a change in

the attitudes of young people to the value of training and the acceptance of relatively lower wages for trainees' (Department of Employment 1981: 5.8), the intention was to 'price young people back into jobs'.

To this end, the allowance paid to trainees was set well below market rates and then its real value allowed to erode. Between 1988 and 1997, when youth training was finally abandoned by New Labour, the allowance had risen once, for 17 year olds, by 50 pence per week. On top of this, the 1982 Young Worker Scheme and its 1986 replacement the New Worker Scheme, both paid direct subsidies to employers to recruit young people in jobs with a low wage ceiling. The last vestiges of wage protection for young workers was removed with the reform of the Wages Councils in 1985 and their subsequent full abolition in 1993. In 1986 the jurisdiction of the Wages Councils over workers under 21 years old was abolished and their powers limited to setting minimum basic hourly and overtime rates. Together with the erosion of young people's benefits (discussed in Chapter 4), the payment of more 'realistic' levels of youth pay would be encouraged.

The cumulative effect of these measures accelerated the decline in the relative value of youth pay. One dramatic illustration of this is the erosion of the real value of the training allowance. Against an actual YTS allowance of £30 and £35.50 per week in 1997, had the value of the original allowance introduced under YOP kept pace with changes in average earnings, the allowance paid to trainees would have risen to £93.10 and £117.20 for 16 and 17 year olds respectively. Even taking the less generous rate of price inflation as a means of up rating allowances, as is now the case with welfare benefits, the level of allowance in 1997 would have been worth £63.80 and £81.10 (Convery 1998). On top of this, graduates of YTS could also expect lower wages than other comparable groups of young workers who had not been through the scheme (Bynner *et al.* 1997). YTS also encouraged a steady depression of youth wages more generally which, between 1979 and 1994, fell from 42 to 25 per cent of the adult rate for under 18s, and for 18 to 20 year olds from 61 to 49 per cent. By 1994, 46 per cent of 16 year olds and 45 per cent of 17 year olds in employment were earning less than the National Insurance threshold and the number of young workers experiencing low pay increased dramatically across the workforce. As Novak makes clear,

The relative fortunes of young workers on low wages (i.e. those under 25) have deteriorated markedly since the late 1970s, from

being almost 70 per cent of the overall median earnings to just over
half... The relative pay of this group deteriorated faster than
low-paid workers overall. (1998: 19)

Vocational preparation, training, flexibility and lower wages nevertheless failed to bring about any significant revival in young people's
employment prospects. We noted above how, throughout the 'crisis
decades', unemployment rates for the young remained well above both
the national average and rates for adult workers, and that youth
employment levels continued to demonstrate remarkable sensitivity to
economic fluctuations. Whether or not spells on government training
scheme made anything more than a marginal difference to job
prospects is doubtful. Part of the reason for this can be found in the perverse impact of government schemes, where they actually contributed
to unemployment as employers opted to take on trainees at the expense
of existing workers or as substitutes for their normal recruits (see
Chapter 4). Trainees were also forced to bear the stigma of graduating
from schemes which many employers associated with remedial functions. Even supporters of youth training's positive effect on youth
employment levels have been forced to concede that the employment
prospects of trainees depended largely upon wider changes to the aggregate demand for labour (Deakin 1996). Between 1988 and 1990, for
example, during a period of marked economic growth, one in seven
trainees leaving a scheme was returning to unemployment, with the
comparable figure for black young people over twice as high. A little
under two years later, as the economy once again lurched back into
recession, the unemployment rate among graduates of the scheme rose
to one in four. What is probably safe to say is that those leaving youth
training schemes did so with an edge over those struggling to enter
work directly from unemployment. But even during the steady growth
of the mid-1990s, only around one in four leavers was going directly
into work (Department for Education and Employment 1995).

Extending the net

Unemployed school leavers may have been at the sharp end of
the state's restructuring of social relations but in this respect they were
not alone. As unemployment deepened, the growing incidence of
long-term unemployment (i.e. six months or more) among 18 to
24 year olds became a particular source of alarm. By the time that John

Major became Prime Minister in 1991, one third of all claimants were long-term unemployed, of whom one third were aged 18 to 24. By the beginning of the 1990s, official estimates were pointing out that for every 10 people experiencing unemployment, four or five would return to work within six months, two more within 12 months and three more would remain without work for over a year (Morris and Llewellyn 1991). The former – the frictional unemployment caused in the 'normal' course of economic activity – could be left to look after themselves but for the latter, the provision of open ended and relatively generous levels of benefits were held to have compounded their deficiencies, through encouraging a marked deterioration of the skills and motivation needed to get back into work.

For this group of young people, job creation measures continued to be the mainstay of provision well beyond their abandonment for school leavers. The employment subsidy measures introduced by Labour in 1975 survived until a few months before the 1979 General Election and, to many people's surprise, were subsequently revived by the Conservatives in 1981. The Community Enterprise Programme launched that year targeted 18 to 24 year olds who had been unemployed continuously for six months, by enrolling them onto temporary employment projects with a community orientation. The following year this was replaced by the bigger and more ambitious Community Programme (CP), within which long-term unemployed 18 to 24 year olds were again a target group, and which too offered temporary employment on community projects but this time for up to 12 months. Unlike the schemes for school leavers, CP paid a wage (i.e. the rate for the job) to a ceiling of £67 per week, which in effect meant most places were part-time.[2] In 1986, CP was further extended to provide a quarter of a million places, two thirds of which were for those aged under 25, many of whom had experience of previous youth training schemes. Around 70 per cent of CP leavers returned to the dole.

The reasons why job subsidy and temporary employment programmes survived longer for this group than they did for unemployed school leavers, lay primarily in the practical difficulties they posed. Delivering a scheme big enough to deal with the huge increase in school leaver unemployment alone provided quite a challenge, while trades unionists, educationalists, the voluntary sector and employers, all essential to YTS' success, needed convincing of its merits. Fortunately for the government, the slightly lower levels of unemployment among young adults and a more muted sense of public outrage, also tempered the political urgency. Nevertheless, by 1988, with two-year youth training up and running, CP was axed. In its place, came a new programme of Employment Training (ET), offering up to a year, and in a few cases 2 years' work experience and training organised along lines similar to YTS. Within ET's target group of the long-term adult unemployed, 18–24 year olds unemployed for 6–12 months were designated a 'guarantee' group (i.e. they were ensured of a place), a dubious honour which could be exchanged for a mixture of employer-led work experience, supported by opportunities for directed training.

According to King (1995), ET marked the final triumph of neoliberalism over social democracy. Certainly ET represented a significant intensification of the pressure on the young long-term unemployed. The immediate spur for this came from the failure of the 'Lawson boom' of the late 1980s, named after the then Chancellor of the Exchequer, to combine a period of vigorous economic growth with a corresponding decline in unemployment. The practical failures of previous measures, as evidenced by stubbornly high rates of (long-term) unemployment, were taken as a clear indication of the degree to which the young had become separated from the actualities of work. It mattered little that the claims made of the Lawson boom were at best exaggerated, that levels of job growth were inflated and that the creation of part-time jobs was the dominant force (Finn 1988).

Promising to get the 'workers without jobs to do the jobs without workers', ET marked a further phase in the restructuring of young people's relationship to the labour market. Instead of paying a wage as CP had continued to do, however restricted this had been, in a key development participants on ET were paid an allowance equal to their 'benefit plus' a £10 weekly premium. Thus with ET, the spectre of 'workfare' (i.e. work or training in return for benefits – see Chapter 4) long threatened by the Conservatives appeared a reality. ET also further consolidated the low skills, low paid training and work experience provision already institutionalised through YTS. The short duration of the work experience placements underlined the modesty of ET's ambitions, offering little time for participants to achieve anything other than low-grade vocational qualifications. Its success in getting participants into jobs was similarly unexceptional. Tellingly, neither ET nor its replacement by Training for Work (TfW) in 1993, ever achieved job placement rates of greater than 40 per cent. As important was the link between government measures for the young long-term unemployed and the political pursuit of low pay.

The training market

With few signs of the predicted upturn, ET marked one element of a more wholesale turn to market forces. Whereas up to this point, government schemes had sought to effect a 'solution' to youth unemployment through the embrace of vocationalism, by the beginning of the recession in 1990, the whole framework of state provision for the young unemployed was in the throes of further transformation. In 1988, the MSC was abolished and re-designated the Training Commission and then shortly afterwards again the Training Agency. These changes of title reflected an important organisational shift. Throughout the 1980s, the original inclusion of trades union representation on the MSC had been retained, largely a pragmatic response to the inability to run such large-scale programmes without the support of the trades union movement. With ET, however, the position of the trades unions changed. Using the TUC's opposition to ET's package of work for benefits as the pretext, with the formation of the Training Agency the involvement of the trades unions was brought formally to an end. In its place, formal ownership of training provision for the young unemployed was given over more fully to employers.

One measure of this was the replacement of YTS in 1990, by the innovatively named Youth Training (YT). Once again, this was more than a semantic exercise. Like the medieval quack administering an ever-greater number of leeches to the body of a clearly haemorrhaging patient, the government's remedy for its ailing youth training schemes was a further dose of market forces. What little protection YTS offered to the young unemployed in the form of stipulated minimum requirements and an approved structure, were loosened (Ball 1989). And, in the name of flexibility, the stipulated minimum length of training was removed, schemes were reorganised in the pursuit of an ever-greater range of low-level vocational qualifications and training providers were freed from the requirement to ensure a minimum level of off-the-job training. By letting the market decide, quality assurance could be secured by linking a programme's success to the quality of its outcomes and these arrangements were cemented in place by new funding arrangements, delivered through a new network of Training and Enterprise Councils in England and Wales (TECs – Local Enterprise Councils in Scotland).

Two years later, the young unemployed were also subject to a more radical experiment in market forces. Credits for education and training had long been a pet project for many neo-liberals, promising as it did to end state monopoly. By providing each school leaver with a Youth Credit, the intention was to redefine the young unemployed as consumers in the pursuit of their own self-interests, on the one hand, while on the other credits would stimulate the supply of training places as employers and providers competed to attract these newly empowered young consumers. Like many other experiments in the political imposition of market forces, the practical impact of credits was to widen already existing sources of division. As long as a young person was relatively well qualified and white, there were few difficulties in securing those better opportunities for training. Conversely, credits ensured the further corralling of young black people and those with no qualifications into voluntary projects, where opportunities for advancement into jobs were most limited (Mizen 1990). As one review candidly put it, 'Youth Credits have not made much difference to training for young people in the past, and probably will not in the future' (Maclagan 1997: 4).

The political pursuit of market forces found its most developed expression in the national framework of TECs. At the same time the MSC was replaced, a network of 82 regional TECs was put in place to deliver government programmes for the unemployed. Dominated by representatives of local business, each TEC was contracted with the then Department of Employment to promote the training of the young, in ways that it was claimed would be more sympathetic to the needs of local business. Justifying the move, the government's position was that publicly funded training should be countercyclical and therefore primarily confined to periods of recession. During sustained economic growth (such as that during the late 1980s), the financial cost to government should be curtailed. To back up these words with deeds, the creation of TECs was accompanied by significant cuts to per capita funding. In doing so, the government argued that training would become more cost-effective, local employers would exercise greater control and quality would be enriched, as local employers both rejigged and expanded what was on offer.

In fact, the TEC initiative clearly exposed the fallacy of the monetarist 'solutions' to youth unemployed, underlining as it did the failure of the market to deliver any long-term or significant improvement in skills. Imposing market forces made little sense when it was the reluctance of employers to invest in training in the first place that helped account for Britain's relatively weak skills base. As Peck remarks,'... with perverse logic, the government has decided that the best way to respond to ostensible market failure in the training system is to mimic the market itself using public funds' (1991: 4). A further substantial problem was that the assumed continued expansion in economic growth and employment levels was inconveniently dashed, when the economy lurched back into recession in the early 1990s. Barely off the ground, TECs were quickly faced with a by now familiar problem of rapidly escalating rates of youth unemployment. Somewhat predictably, as levels of youth unemployment rose, TECs were rapidly swamped and around 90 per cent of their budgets remained dedicated to fulfilling the contractual obligation to deliver the government's primary programmes for the unemployed: YT and ET/TfW. Consequently, few other opportunities to deliver innovative or original training initiatives were possible, particularly where local labour markets were again teetering on the brink of collapse. The urgency of finding placements for these unemployed young people also compounded the problem of employer's reluctance to train, given that placements were largely vacancy led. Thus TEC's preoccupation with programmes for the unemployed actually exacerbated the more general problem of employer withdrawal from training during a period of recession.

TECs also intensified market discipline over the young unemployed through the introduction output related funding (ORF). Instead of payment linked to the number of training places filled, as under the previous system of funding, TECs were remunerated on the basis of their success in achieving certain predetermined outputs: the number of recruits, placements in a job or education course, or the attainment of nationally recognised qualifications. One direct consequence of this was that TEC provision quickly became skewed towards those most likely to achieve these outputs. Those young people most urgently in need, and therefore least likely to satisfy ORF requirements – the unqualified, those with learning difficulties, criminal records, a history of drug or alcohol abuse, certain groups of ethnic minority youth and such others – were least likely to find support (Rolfe 1996). Another consequence of ORF was to more fully consolidate the role of training provider as a profitable activity, since ORF linked a TEC's ability to generate income to its training throughput, allowing some to generate considerable profits. In 1996 alone, it was estimated that the combined annual surpluses held by TECs above that spent on the training of young people was over £33 million and that their combined accumulated surpluses were in the order of £260 million (TEN 1997). There was little evidence that these surpluses were held on account of likely future investment.

Despite the promise of a free market revolution in skills provision
for the young, the British record remained lamentable. The failure of
market forces to revitalise training provision was acknowledged in
1994, when Modern Apprenticeships (MApps) were launched to boost
the supply of skilled young labour. Initially launched in 40 sectors,
ranging from agriculture, chemicals and childcare through to business
administration, tourism and engineering, government provided
funded opportunities for young people under the age of 25 to undertake training to National Vocational Qualification (NVQ) Level 3.
Typically running for three years, modern apprentices were given a
structured period of training, specified periods of off-the-job training
and a minimum learning period, for which they were paid a wage.
Measures like this could not, however, disguise the continuing relative
decline of Britain's skills base. Internationally speaking, by the time
the Conservatives were defeated in 1997, Britain continued to spend
less on education and produced fewer well educated and trained
young people than most other industrialised countries and languished
at the bottom of OECD tables for the proportion of young people,
both male and female, remaining in education beyond the minimum
school leaving age. Forty per cent of 19 to 24 year olds had yet to reach
NVQ Level 2 or equivalent.

Reluctant youth

Possibly the single biggest failure of the training 'solution' to youth
unemployment, was its inability to win over the young. Those who
had the qualifications, wherewithal or simple good luck to escape its
attention did so, and in large numbers. Most young people saw training
schemes as something to be avoided if at all possible, a last resort in a
desperate situation. By the beginning of the 1990s, youth training's
share of school leavers was already in sharp decline as successive waves
of young people sought alternative 'solutions', mainly in the expansion of further education (see Chapter 2). Indeed, as each new government measure was rolled out to fanfares proclaiming the
beginnings of another 'new deal', the culture of hostility, misgiving
and ambivalence deepened. Few unemployed young people believed
with any conviction the claims of government, ministers and their
expensive advertising campaigns, that these schemes were sympathetic
to their needs, or that they could provide much in the way of genuine
assistance (Murray 1996; Banks and Bryn Davies 1990). Indifference,

suspicion and hostility on the part of trainees pervaded each new initiative and participation was motivated as much by the need to defend benefit entitlements, as an endorsement of what was on offer. Unemployed young people complained that these training schemes were irrelevant to their needs, more often than not provided inappropriate training and work experience placements and that employers were badly prepared to receive them. The suspicion that work experience placements were little more than exploitation, providing employers with cheap or 'slave labour' ran deep and dissatisfaction with placements was rife (NACAB 1994; Durning *et al.* 1990). Trainees did appreciate the opportunity to actually do something in the absence of few practical alternatives. But even these grudging acknowledgements were tempered by a sustained and deeply felt cynicism of the motives of both employers and government.

The young also demonstrated a remarkable propensity to act upon these sentiments. Rates of early leaving from training schemes remained endemic (Durning *et al* 1990; Gray and King 1986), despite the severe penalties that such defiance was likely to invoke (see Chapter 4). Anywhere between one half and two thirds of all participants on government training schemes were leaving early, with rates among black trainees even higher (Usher 1990). For all trainees, reasons for leaving were dominated by criticisms of their scheme's performances, doubts about the quality of training, the lack of advice or support, and the paucity of the training allowance. Admittedly, the single biggest reason for leaving remained the movement into a job, but it is a measure of the abject status of these schemes, that for the majority of early leavers work was likely to mean a 'dead-end' job, probably short-term, most likely low quality, and paying barely subsistence wages. One consequence of this was a growing awareness that many young people were simply 'dropping out' (see Chapter 5).

Conclusion

While the social democratic claims to inclusiveness through jobs for all was always built upon uncertain foundations, its practical limitations were cruelly exposed with the end of the long post-war boom. In its place, the onset of the 'crisis decades', marked by economic stagnation followed by periods of boom and bust, brought with them a significant acceleration in the rate at which the British economy shed labour. Within a generally deteriorating situation, the vulnerability of the young to unemployment was particularly marked, as downward movements in the aggregate demand for labour were transmitted into disproportionate increases in the rates of joblessness among the young. The reasons for young people's new found sensitivity to unemployment lay in a significant change to the structure of work. The shocks following the first recession of the 1970s quickly revealed the fragile nature of manufacturing industry as those semi- and unskilled jobs previously occupied by young people were drastically reduced. The accelerated growth of the service sector, certainly to begin with, further worked against the young. Most of the jobs created by the service sector were part-time and employers preferred to utilise the growing availability of adult women workers to fill their need for low skilled labour. This in turn reflected crucial changes to the nature of employer control. Instead of utilising young workers who were perceived as unreliable and instrumental in their attitudes towards work, employers looked to more 'stable' categories of workers to meet the tougher competitive pressures that they were facing.

The rise in the numbers of unemployed youth presented governments with a major political problem. Under the Keynesian interventionist state, full employment had been a measure of the political commitment to inclusion and concession. Governments may have always exaggerated their ability to manage aggregate economic activity in ways that would guarantee security through work, but escalating youth unemployment ruthlessly undermined the credibility of government when it came to the commitment to jobs for all. The subsequent turn to vocationalism and then market forces as 'solutions' to the problem of workless youth derived their significance not so much from their ability to resolve the underlying lack of demand for youth labour. On the contrary, they provided the state with the political means to disengage itself from any continuing responsibility for the employment fortunes of the young.

This was most clearly evident in the turn towards the 'deficiency model' to explain the phenomenon of workless youth. Always ideological, the power of the deficiency model derived its practical substance from the activities of governments from the middle of the 1970s onwards. Instead of seeking to confront market forces in ways that would have given some substance to their earlier political commitment to jobs for all, the actions of the state acknowledged that the resolution of the problem of youth unemployment would be on terms dictated by the market. Temporary employment subsidy measures were both short-lived and practically ill equipped to deal

with the scale of the problem, quickly giving way to the more permanent solution offered by work experience and training schemes. By
providing young people with a period of vocational preparation, later
expanded into a lengthy structured period of youth training and
employment, the deficiencies exhibited by young people coming onto
the labour market could be rectified. The failure of the training state
to bring about any marked or lasting improvement in the employment
opportunities of the young, became the basis for the subsequent
wholesale restructuring as training provision for the young
unemployed was reorganised along the lines of markets by the
beginning of the 1990s.

Thus the political turn to vocationalism and markets as the 'solution'
to youth unemployment also involved an intense restructuring of
young people's relationship to the labour market. For those who could
not secure a job or who were unprepared or unable to take up a place
in an expanded further education, a training scheme rapidly became
the only viable option. In entering a government programme, the
young unemployed were subjected to a methodical attempt to recompose the very nature of their labour. Through these programmes,
wages were depressed, insecurity was institutionalised and skills training emptied of much of its previous technical or craft content. With
the introduction of full-blooded market forces into training provision
at the beginning of the 1990s, the political transformation of the
terms of young people's relationship to the labour market was as deep
as it was broad. It is the development of a complementary restructuring process through the social security system that we shall turn to in
the next chapter.

CHAPTER 4

The Changing State of Social Security

If the political problem of youth unemployment was 'resolved' on terms dictated by work experience programmes, training schemes and an ideology of 'deficient' youth, then these developments found a complement in the restructuring of social security. Young people's relationship to social security provision has received little systematic comment (cf. Harris 1988) but from the middle of the 1970s, social security emerged as a key site in the political restructuring of youth.[1] Throughout this period, the reorganisation of social security along more exclusive lines arose in response to the deepening crisis of the Keynesian welfare state and its inability to offer a credible 'solution' to the problem of youth unemployment. Far from delivering its ostensible commitment to inclusion, or social security 'from cradle to grave' as it was so famously put, mass unemployment quickly exposed the precarious foundations on which this stood. At the beginning of the 1980s the system was under intolerable pressure. A little more than a decade later, the commitment to social security as the basis of a more inclusive youth was also dead.

That the restructuring of social security took a youthful dimension is evident in two ways. To begin with, as more and more young people found themselves experiencing unemployment, so too did their reliance on social security increase. With little prospect of a secure job and few other chances of an income, growing numbers of young people were forced to look to the state for their only legitimate means of support. Second, that they could do so was itself partly a consequence of youth's progressive recomposition in terms laid down by the post-war welfare state. With the expansion of a state administered system of insurance against unemployment for all workers, young people found themselves progressively incorporated into the structure of social security. Partial coverage, lower levels of benefit, a restrictive test of need and stiff eligibility criteria all ensured that social security continued to provide the basis for integrating young people into the labour market and the family. Nevertheless, the inclusive strategy brought with it tangible concessions for the young through greater coverage under the national insurance scheme, more generous benefit payments and a grudging acceptance of the legitimacy of young worker's entitlement to benefits in their own right.

It was precisely these concessions that ensured young people would be a target within the more general restructuring of social security that gathered pace from the early 1980s. As elsewhere, there was no specific 'youth policy', if this is understood to mean that young people were subject to unique or exceptional treatment in the overhaul of the political means through which the surplus working population was managed. As is the general argument of this book, while none of the developments detailed below were unique to the young unemployed, state policy did involve the (re)construction of clear divisions between young people and adults, as the former emerged as an important 'target' group in the broader process of change. As unemployment exposed young people's fragile grip on the labour market and increased their reliance on the largesse of the state, we find a callous disregard for the needs of the young, as this forced dependency became the basis for their subordination to market forces.

Thus the politics of youth is simultaneously a politics of social security and the politics of social security has involved the creation of more exclusive forms of provision. From the inclusion of young workers through a reformed system of social security we find over the past 25 years the development of a new and far more exclusive strategy for managing the young unemployed. Whereas under the former, young people were treated on the basis of socially determined criteria of need, these have been replaced by new agents of restructuring in the form of money and the market. In the restructuring of social security the scope of provision was curtailed, the value of benefits paired back with little regard for the needs of individual claimants, rules of eligibility have become more exclusive, the means to access benefits more intrusive and degrading, benefit entitlements have become contingent upon further judgements on the willingness to work and for those still able to make a successful claim, the price has been paid in terms of their continuing vilification.

Social security: from pillar to post

We are now somewhat accustomed to the explicit link between social security and the maintenance of market discipline but this should not detract from important historical changes to the form that this relationship has taken. Under the system of social security advanced by Beveridge, the pillar of the welfare state's ostensible commitment to providing social security over the life-course, the commitment to greater inclusiveness was circumscribed by clear anxieties over the implications of providing benefits by right. By insuring all workers against the risk of unemployment (and ill health), Beveridge was mindful that a worker's right to non-means-tested unemployment benefit (UB) could corrode the work ethic and undermine the family form (Wilson 1977). In practice, therefore, the scheme did little to disturb the sanctity of either, modifying rather than revolutionising the system of social insurance inherited from the inter-war years by generalising cover across the entire working population (Addison 1977). Without doubt numerically more inclusive, Beveridge's national insurance scheme thus retained many of the features of the one that it replaced. Rates of benefit for the unemployed never reached subsistence levels and eligibility was governed by the retention of a modified workhouse test of need and a judgement of willingness to work. Entitlement to UB was policed through the requirement that an unemployed worker possessed a satisfactory employment history, while children and women's entitlement to benefits through the working head of household further buttressed the family. For the considerable number of workers unable to qualify for the scheme, the parsimonious, intrusive and degrading system of means-tested national assistance (NA) benefits developed during the inter-war years was retained.

The political commitment to inclusiveness expressed by Beveridge's reform programme did bring more young people within the scope of social security, but at the cost of reconstituting their subordinate status. While the National Insurance Act 1946 extended eligibility for insurance benefits to all young people over the minimum school leaving age (then 15), the advantages remained largely formal since the precarious nature of youth employment and young workers' tendency to 'hop' from job to job, prevented satisfaction of the scheme's requirement for continuous employment. The social insurance scheme also further reproduced young people's dependency upon their families, as the rates at which benefits were paid were purposefully held well below adult levels (Harris 1988). Only if a young person under 21 years old was married or had their own dependent children were they entitled to the full rate of benefit which, for the first time, was paid at the same level for boys and girls. Such divisions were similarly replicated in the extension of NA benefits to the young. These too were paid at a lower level than the full adult rate, although additional assistance was available to those not living at home. In any case, in the context of strong demand for youth labour much of this new-found inclusiveness was academic, as during the initial post-war years strong demand for youth labour meant that young people's claims on the system were minimal. In December 1959, for example, of the 2.1 million NA claims only 27 000 came from the under 20s of which only 6000 were in respect of unemployment (Langan 1996).

This *modus operandi* remained relatively uncontroversial until Wilson's Labour governments of 1964–70, after which social security for the unemployed took on greater importance.[2] As the 'long-boom' slowed and unemployment began to rise, Labour responded by increasing the scope of cover. By making benefits for the unemployed more attractive and by increasing their inclusiveness, Labour hoped to effectively 'buy-off' rising trades union and popular discontent over its stuttering economic policies, while also facilitating worker mobility by removing resistance to unemployment (Sinfield and Showler 1981). Most of these measures had only an indirect impact upon the young but their general effect was to consolidate young people's growing presence within the benefits system. In 1966, earlier moves to replace flat rate payments for UB with graded ones more closely attuned to previous earnings were elaborated (Hill 1991). And within the provision of NA benefits, renamed supplementary benefit (SB) in 1966, moves were also made to soften the stigma that had dogged assistance benefits since the time of the poor laws. Greater support for the short-term unemployed was provided by the move from NA to SB and social security's inclusiveness was further enhanced with the Redundancy Payment and Contract of Employment Acts, which respectively gave statutory support to minimum levels of redundancy payments and workers the right to notice of termination of employment. It was this practical structure of inclusiveness that emerged, albeit under increasing pressure and subject to a more intensive ideological assault, relatively unscathed from Edward Heath's government of the early 1970s.

As we saw in Chapters 2 and 3, however, the reaction of the Labour government 1974–79 to youth unemployment was to endorse the 'deficiency model' as a means of legitimising its resort to work

experience programmes as a 'solution' to youth unemployment. This
approach found a complement in their changing relationship to social
security, although Labour initially trod a careful path. To begin with
there was little option other than to rely on the existing system of
social security as the primary method for addressing the political costs
of rising unemployment. Practical difficulties in generating work experience placements on a scale sufficient to make a meaningful impact
on youth unemployment, coupled with pressure from the trades
unions, a well-organised 'welfare rights' movement and ebbing public
support for Labour's agenda, all made a rapid retreat from an inclusive
system problematic. Parts of the welfare state were for the first time
exposed to real cuts in expenditure in Labour's 1975 budget, but social
security provision for the unemployed emerged relatively intact
(Gough 1979). Indeed, as the political costs of rising unemployment
rose, Labour continued to work towards a reduction in the role of the
means test and, for the first time, established a statutory link between
increases in average earnings and the uprating of benefits.

Nevertheless, after 1976 rapidly rising unemployment, a stagnating
economy and the need to see through its commitment to public expenditure cuts saw Labour embark upon a significant change in tack
(Ginsburg 1979). While benefits for some were protected and even
enhanced, Labour stepped back from its previous political support
for universalism in social security by encouraging greater selectivity and
discretion, and by exacerbating long-standing divisions between
the 'deserving' and 'undeserving' unemployed. For the latter, this meant
the greater use of discretion in judging claims and more emphasis on
social security as a deterrent through, for example, the more aggressive
application of the 'not genuinely seeking work' test. Labour was also
willing to pander to the enthusiastic search for the much maligned but
rarely spotted 'scrounger'. For the young too, developments were far
from encouraging. Concern over whether unemployment benefits provided sufficient incentive for young people to look for work had already
surfaced at the beginning of the 1970s, in response to growing concerns
over unemployed youth in tourist areas (a scare that emerged once
again a decade later – see Chapter 5). And, as youth unemployment continued to rise, the independent Supplementary Benefits Commission,
a quango created by Labour in the 1960s to advise on social security
matters, suggested in 1976 that payment of benefits to unemployed
school leavers could be delayed until the end of the summer vacation
following their departure from school. This issue was further explored
two years later by the then Department of Health and Social Security.

By all means necessary

As far as social security for the unemployed is concerned, Labour's change of tune became the chorus line for successive Conservative governments. As we shall see, the central tenets of the monetarist critique of social security adopted by the Conservatives in power had little basis in the reality of young people's lives. Nevertheless, the strains placed on the social insurance system by what was now mass unemployment, combined with Labour's partial retreat from its previous commitment to inclusivity, appeared to give practical substance to the monetarist critique of welfare. State expansion, it was claimed, had actually accelerated the decline of Britain's international competitiveness and was responsible for the failure of manufacturing industry to compete on the global stage (Bacon and Eltis 1976). The growing proportion of gross domestic product consumed by the welfare state and its burgeoning cadres of 'unproductive' workers, meant that fewer resources were available to the private sector, the supposed engine room of growth. Such a swollen, parasitic public sector could only be funded at the cost of higher taxation, both personal and corporate, or by excessive government borrowing. Either way, both were damaging for the economy. The former sucked valuable resources away from the investment necessary for economic growth and the latter's emphasis on deficit funding stoked the fires of inflation.

One way to remedy this was to reduce expenditure on welfare, as a precursor to a more methodical restructuring programme. This importance of the latter stemmed from its identification with disincentives to work, in which 'the rich don't work because they don't get enough money, while the poor don't work because they get too much' (Clarke and Langan 1993: 52). For the wealthy on the one hand, the high rates of personal taxation needed to fund the public sector were seen to inhibit the culture of risk taking necessary for dynamic market capitalism, since in exercising its claim over an individual's earned income the state corrupted the relationship between effort and reward. For the poor, on the other hand, the growth in public spending on state benefits had succeeded in divorcing the relationship between work and income, effort and reward, so central to the maintenance of free markets. Through the provision of open-ended and relatively generous unemployment benefits as of right, the welfare state had removed the means for self-reliance necessary if workers were to meet the needs of themselves and their families. It was the perverse incentives of the inclusive strategy that had, according to one critic, demoralised the British working class by turning a once-industrious population into a 'sub literate, unskilled, unhealthy and institution-alised proletariat hanging on the nipple of state maternalism' (Barnett 1986: 304).

Deploying these arguments freely as their justification, the Conservatives set about reorganising social security along more exclusive lines. Instead of the political commitment to social security as a means to young people's incorporation into an expanded citizenship, provision was reconstituted more explicitly on terms dictated by employers and the market. While there was nothing youthful about this in the sense of a unique set of policies for the young, the young unemployed did consistently emerge as a 'priority' or 'target' group within the broader strategy of change. The reasons for this are not simply that the young were regarded as 'easy targets', although it is certainly the case that the welfare rights of the young enjoyed little vocal or organised support. Jones and Novak point out that by singling out young people it was possible to establish as violable those 'basic benefits once considered inviolable, not only for the young but also for the rest of the poor' (1999: 66). More than this, however, as relative beneficiaries in the more general expansion of social rights, the young were also prime targets for their withdrawal. It was the relative advantages bestowed under the Keynesian welfare state's strategy of an inclusive youth that ensured young people would be at the forefront of change, not least because the disproportionate rates of youth unemployment was taken as one of the clearest vindications that the monetarist critique was right.

The immediate impact of the Conservative's general election victory in 1979 was, therefore, to give greater clarity and focus to elements of the restructuring already introduced by Labour and to fur-ther intensify the ideological harassment of the young unemployed. Prominent to this was the acceleration of an already well-established trend away from social insurance-based benefits as the major source of relief from unemployment and the move towards the greater use of means-tested alternatives. As already noted, in generalising the social insurance system across the whole of the working population, the inclusive strategy sought to formalise the right to unemployment benefits as a means of overcoming resistance to the restructuring of labour markets from those most likely to experience short periods of unemployment. In this way, UB could avoid the deeply entrenched and popular hostility towards the arbitrary and intrusive means-test, through establishing unemployment benefits as of 'right'. In encour-aging a return to the means-test, therefore, a more transparent connection could be made between the labour market and the family as sources of support for the unemployed (Ginsburg 1979). Although in practice the distinction between insurance and means-tested unemployment benefits is often a fine one, particularly given that the low rates of insurance benefits means that the majority of claimants have to rely on means-tested ones as well, the greater element of contingency involved in the administration of the latter underlines its importance as a method of deterrence. In subjecting themselves to a means-test, claimants undergo a more intrusive and degrading process of assessment, must generally satisfy stiffer eligibility criteria and are more open to the negative operation of discretionary powers possessed by the benefit authorities, while they also open themselves more fully to the criticism that they are somehow less deserving than other categories of claimants (Dean and Taylor Gooby 1992). This deterrent effect is clearly apparent in the low take up of means-tested benefits like income support (IS – formerly supplementary benefit) (81 per cent of all those entitled make claims), Family Credit (51 per cent) and Housing Benefit (80 per cent); relative to those benefits provided by right, for instance, take up of the state pension and child benefit is almost universal (Department of Social Security 1992). As Titmus well recognised, 'the fundamental objective of all such tests of eligibility is to keep people out: not let them in' (1968: 134).

Excluding the young through the means-test gathered pace as youth unemployment rose. During the 1960s, around one in four of all claims for unemployment benefits were reliant on means-tested NA but around 30 years later it was closer to three quarters. By the middle of the 1990s, the proportion of the working population enjoying coverage against unemployment under the social insurance scheme was around only 20 per cent, down from 40 per cent two decades earlier. Between 1973 and 1995, the number of all unemployment claimants reliant on means-tested benefits rose by a staggering 675 per cent and by the time the Conservatives lost power in 1997, approximately 70 per cent of all unemployed claimants were to some extent reliant on income support (Evans 1998).

One reason for this was that an insurance-based system designed to address low levels of short-term unemployment was simply unable to cope with the slump in the demand for labour. As the level of joblessness rose, not only were more and more workers making claims, but the growing frequency with which some workers experienced unemployment made the contributory requirements for insurance benefits more difficult to satisfy. In addition, the increased incidence of long-term unemployment further undermined insurance-based benefits, as unemployed workers exhausted their time-limited UB entitlements. For the young, the return to mass unemployment swept away any remaining pretence the social insurance system may have had to extending the possibility of inclusion. Marginal to the practical operation of the social insurance system at the best of times, escalating levels of unemployment not only excluded large numbers of young workers from entry to the scheme in the first place. But even many of those fortunate enough to get a job found that it did not last long enough nor pay well enough for them to build up the necessary contributions.

As rising unemployment stripped social insurance of much of its practical value, governments proved eager to encourage this trend. High on rhetoric but with few concrete proposals, the Conservative victory at the 1979 General Election was nevertheless followed by two social security acts in 1980, which among other things aimed at restricting the coverage of social insurance. By axing the earnings related supplements to UB introduced by Labour 20 years earlier, payment levels were returned to a flat rate, the lower level of UB available for those with only a partial contributions record was abandoned and UB for students in the short vacations was abolished. More fundamental still was the Social Security Act of 1986, following the much-vaunted 'Fowler Review' published the previous year. Even at the 1983 General Election, the Conservative's clear hostility towards the existing social security system did not foreshadow the way in which social security would become a central aspect of government policy. Yet the 1986 Act marked the beginnings of a more fundamental reorganisation of social security provision for the young unemployed. '[D]esigned primarily at nil cost and to isolate and stigmatise the poor' (Andrews and Jacobs 1990: 288), the Act further codified the earlier turn to means-testing as a generalised method of administering mass youth unemployment. Purposefully eschewing the need to address the collapse of the social insurance system, and using the pressing need to simplify the system as its justification, the 1986 Act replaced SB with IS and formalised the system of administration (Novak 1998).

Under IS, scope for discretion in response to individual needs was curtailed by the more systematic operation of the means-test, in which previous rights to additional or single payments were abolished in favour of a standardised structure of premiums 'targeted' at particular groups (for instance, for dependent children, lone parent families, a disability etc.). Two years later, the 1988 Social Security Act further codified the importance of means-testing for the young by overhauling their place within the system. To begin with, the extension of the contribution requirements for insurance benefits hit young people particularly hard, given the difficulties already encountered in building up the necessary contributions record. The impact of this change alone was to exclude 350 000 people from entitlement to UB (Andrews and Jacobs 1990). In addition, via the introduction of a new system of payments that calibrated rates more closely to age, IS for 16 and 17 year olds was abolished for all but those in the 'severest hardship' (a measure formalised the following year in response to the intense difficulties the abolition of IS meant for some of the most vulnerable groups of young people); and for those aged between 18 and 24, payment was at the reduced rate of 80 per cent of the adult level.

Means-testing was further strengthened by the Jobseekers Allowance (JSA). Introduced in 1996, JSA did away with the distinction between IS and UB and replaced it with 'contributory' and 'noncontributory' variants of the JSA. With this change in name came an even greater exclusion of the young unemployed from what remained of the insurance system. A dramatic reduction from 12 to six months in the maximum period for which 'contributory' JSA (formerly UB) could be paid, meant around a quarter of a million unemployed people were immediately forced into sole reliance on the means-tested element (Unemployment Unit 1994). JSA also further extended the principle of age-related levels to the payment of those contributory benefits that remained. Unlike young people receiving IS, the 1986 Social Security Act left untouched the rates at which UB was paid and under 25 year olds continued to receive the same amount as adults. Under JSA, however, the rate at which contributory JSA was paid to 18 to 24 year olds was brought into line with IS, representing an instant 20 per cent reduction in the value of payments to this group. For young women, the consequences of this were especially punitive. As more women entered the labour market during the 1980s, so the proportion earning coverage under the social insurance scheme had grown. With the reduction of contributory JSA to six months, many young women who had previously been entitled to protection against unemployment in their own right lost their entitlement to insurance-related JSA and, in doing so, were forced back on to dependence on partners.

Re-stating incentives: actively seeking work?

Exclusion through the means-test was also reinforced through what was euphemistically referred to as incentives. Making benefits contingent upon a judgement of willingness to work has been a central method through which social security has operated to reintegrate unemployed workers into the labour market. The ability to manage labour in this way is a well-documented feature of modern systems of poor relief, as Ginsburg makes clear:

> Poor law authorities have historically used the threat of withdrawal of relief to bring pressure to bear on the unemployed to find wage work. Essentially the withdrawal of relief functions as a punishment for those claimants on the employment register who fail to find work and also serves as a warning to others who might eventually be in that position. (1979: 73)

Incentives like this are evident in the requirement, institutionalised during the inter-war years, that receipt of benefit be conditional upon the ability to satisfy some assessment of work readiness. Such a judgement serves to regulate the behaviour of those in employment, either by deterring workers from leaving their jobs in anticipation of an automatic right to benefit or by pressurising the unemployed to relinquish their claims. In practice, this judgement has operated through the requirement that a claimant must be 'available for' and 'genuinely seeking work' in order to qualify for benefits and that 'refusing suitable employment without just cause' can lead to their subsequent disqualification. Similarly, the incentive for workers to remain in the labour market has been maintained through the right to refuse benefits on the grounds that unemployed claimants have made themselves voluntarily unemployed 'without good cause' or because they have been dismissed due to 'industrial misconduct'.

It was not until the mid-1980s and the development of an 'active benefits' regime that the conditionality rules governing the receipt of benefit were significantly modified. Important changes to the details of the conditions for the receipt of benefit did take place under Labour when, in 1976, it reinstated in areas of labour shortages the previously discarded 'four week rule' that time-limited benefits for unemployed single adult males between 18 and 45. In 1982 moves were again made to tighten the availability for work test through the introduction of new administrative procedures designed to probe more fully a claimant's availability for work. But it was not until 1986 that the rhetoric of policing the 'workshy' was matched by more substantive changes, through the imposition of significant alterations to the availability for work test.

The reasons for this new-found urgency in turn derived from the failed promises of the first two Thatcher governments. As already argued in Chapter 3, economic growth during much of the 1980s had been accompanied by stubbornly high levels of unemployment particularly among the 18 to 24 age group. This was taken as clear evidence that the incentives to search for work were insufficient and by the end of the 1980s government was unequivocal in its belief that, 'unemployment … could be considerably reduced and many vacancies filled if unemployed people looked more intensively and effectively for work' (Department of Employment 1988a: 57). Ministers were also at pains to point towards evidence of significant fraud (see below) and estimates suggested that as many as one in five of all long-term claims for unemployment benefit were failing to satisfy the requirements for availability for work. Ignoring both the modifications already made and the fact that most of the jobs being created were part-time and/or low paid manual work, the supposedly existing 'passive' system of entitlement was to be transformed into one promoting the 'active' search for work. Instead of the payment of benefits on an open-ended basis where claimants had to prove that they were available for work, social security would be reconstituted in ways that would up the ante on claimants to return to the labour market as quickly as possible, backed upon by new and extended powers of sanction.

The first significant moves in this direction took place in 1988 with the further strengthening of the availability for work criteria. These new criteria stressed that a claimant must be ready to take up a job offer within 24 hours, further limited the restrictions that claimants could place on the nature and conditions of the jobs they were prepared to accept and required proof of 'actively seeking work'. Further modifications appeared the following year when the 1989 Social Security Act formalised the requirement that claimants must engage in an ongoing 'active' job search as a condition for benefits and demanded that they produce evidence of their efforts (Bryson and Jacobs 1992). The Act also subjected claimants to a more intense and frequent process of review, through the production of 'Back to Work Plans'. Formulated when first registering, the Plans provided an additional standard against which the satisfaction of these new eligibility conditions could be judged through a review process after three and six months of unemployment.

The 1989 Act also removed references to the previous concession that allowed claimants to refuse the offer of work on the grounds of 'suitability' and restricted the 'good cause' for refusal to a far narrower set of criteria. The clear intent was to force the young unemployed to take up low skilled job opportunities, through the requirement that a young person made redundant after the completion of a craft apprenticeship, for example, could in an area of high unemployment now be required to accept the offer of a job in a fast-food outlet. To complement this new emphasis on 'active' job search, after 1991 resources were shifted from the large-scale training and work experience programmes outlined in the previous chapter, towards the creation of new short programmes aimed at counselling and job-search techniques (see below). As enforcement, the maximum of six weeks for which a claim for benefits could be reduced on the grounds of failure to satisfy the availability criteria, originally instigated in 1911, was first extended to 13 weeks in 1986 before doubling again in 1988.

Perhaps there would have been more justification for these measures had there been evidence of widespread transgression. Yet in the year before IS for 16 and 17 year olds was removed, of the 30 000 young people who declined places on youth training, a sure fire way to demonstrate that they were 'actively seeking work', only 700 had the voluntary unemployed deduction applied to their benefit. Between the start of youth training proper and 1987, only 2244 school leavers had the same deduction made to their benefits (Mizen 1995). More generally, by the end of the 1980s one estimate was claiming that around 400 000 claimants each year were being affected by these tighter availability for work tests alone (Andrews and Jacobs 1990). Where these tests had more success was in their rarely articulated but nonetheless important objective of reducing the claimant count, as we have already examined in Chapter 3, by some 5–7 per cent. In addition, evaluations of pilots of the actively seeking work criteria showed that 3–4 per cent of claimants did not pursue their claims and a further 3–6 per cent of claims were disallowed.

Exclusion was also pursued through the more intensive supervision of the young long-term unemployed. First introduced for those unemployed for two or more years, by 1986 Restart was developed into a national programme of six monthly interviews within which the growing number of young long-term unemployed people (i.e. six months or more) aged between 18 and 24 years old were identified as a 'priority' group. Presented as an opportunity for claimants to obtain much needed counselling and guidance, in reality Restart worked to more thoroughly police the 'actively seeking work' criteria. Through the notorious Restart 'menu' presented to claimants at interview, unemployed people were offered a number of 'options' ranging from a job through to a government-training scheme, work experience programme or short-term counselling and re-motivation course. Although few of the menu options were explicitly compulsory, at least in Restart's earlier phase of development, taking one was viewed as clear proof of a claimant's efforts to actively seek work. Indeed, since we shall see below that the prospects of Restart leading directly to a job remained extremely unlikely, its primary impact was to intensify the pressure on target groups like the young long-term unemployed to leave the unemployment count.

If the harassment of the unemployment through the 'active benefits regime' failed to bring about any significant improvement to the fortunes of the young unemployed, this was not taken as a measure of its limitations. On the contrary, once again the sharp deterioration in the demand for youth labour and the surge in youth unemployment during the early 1990s was followed by a further turn of the benefit screw. 'Changes are needed to make clear to unemployed people the link between the receipt of benefit and the obligations that places upon them' (Department of Employment 1994: 10), argued John Major's more 'caring' Conservatism. True to his word, these sentiments were forcefully institutionalised in 1996 with the Jobseekers Allowance. JSA further codified the job search activities required by claimants through an obligatory Jobseekers Agreement. A 'contract' in which the state was clearly the dominant party, the Agreement stipulated the day to day activities required from a claimant and underpinned this through new formal powers of instruction in the form of the Jobseekers Direction. Through the Direction claimants may be 'directed to improve their employability' by undertaking a specific job search activity, attending a specified course or by 'taking steps to represent themselves in ways acceptable to employers' (ibid.: 20), if their demeanour is considered to compromise their chances of finding a job. As well as finding themselves punished for their clothing, hairstyles, choice in jewellery, even their manner, JSA also effectively abolished any rights that claimants may have retained to refuse the offer of a job on the grounds that it was inappropriate to their skills or experience. To support this new regime, the range and duration of sanctions available for non-compliance were once again expanded, including for the first time the possibility that certain categories of claimants such as young single people could have the payment of benefits completely removed for a period of up to six months.

Pernicious in the extreme, exclusion through the 'active benefits regime' was also imposed in a number of more subtle ways. In 1994, the Employment Service introduced a new operational framework which set annual performance targets, among which was the requirement that the benefit authorities disallow a pre-specified number of claims each year. Not unsurprisingly perhaps, two years later the number of disallowed claims for unemployment benefits had risen threefold, from 76 000 in 1993/94 to 238 000 in 1995/96 (Murray 1997). At the same time, the number of sanctions imposed on claimants for refusing or failing to attend compulsory job-search and motivation programmes doubled from 37 000 to 79 000 and by the final year of John Major's Conservative governments in 1997, many of these annual targets were being exceeded. As the independent Unemployment Unit was forced to conclude, 'it is clear from this ... that a positive outcome [from the active benefits regime] is a reduction in the claimant count, rather than a positive outcome from the unemployed person' (Bivand 1998: 13).

A workfare state for the young unemployed?

One further aspect of this 'active' regime were moves to make benefits contingent upon some sort of reciprocal activity. Calls for a return to a system of 'workfare', whereby an unemployed person is required to undertake some form of compulsory work experience, training or job search activity as a condition for the receipt of benefits, became a more urgent feature of political discourse throughout the 'crisis decades'. For some sections of the New Right, the appeal of workfare came from its role in moral regeneration, as a method for instilling in those corrupted by the misplaced philanthropy of the welfare state a sense of obligation and self-responsibility; a sentiment now echoed by elements of the centre–left (Field 1997; Etzioni 1993). For 'New Right' demagogues such as Charles Murray (1990), the young long-term unemployed had become key members of an emergent 'underclass', a quasi-separate class of indigent, criminal and promiscuous beings threatening to tear asunder the social fabric (see also Marsland 1996). Such was their impact that King (1995), for example, views this new morality as the driving force in returning social security for the unemployed back to the liberal principles of self-reliance embodied in the nineteenth century poor laws. Manifest in the creation of an interlinking network of 'work–welfare', throughout the 1980s and 1990s the attack on 'dependency culture' succeeded in supplanting the rights-based structure of social security rooted in Beveridge, by one demanding a 'work or training requirement in exchange for receiving their benefits' (*ibid.*: 217–18).

As tempting as it may be in theory, workfare's practical appeal remained less apparent. Notwithstanding the general shift towards greater compulsion, successive Conservative governments remained ambivalent about workfare, especially in its 'harder' forms. This uncertainty was neither the result of a new-found compassion nor a renewed sense of social responsibility for the young unemployed. Governments throughout the 1980s and 1990s indeed continued to invoke the spectre of workfare as one means of disarming opposition – from trades unions, the Labour Party and the unemployed – to many of the measures already examined above. On the contrary, government circumspection over 'harder' forms of workfare arose primarily from its practical, cost and economic implications (Deacon 1997). Establishing mass work experience and training schemes during the 1980s had involved a huge bureaucracy and considerable cost implications for the Treasury. Also, the experience of youth training suggested that finding sufficient employers to live up to the 'guarantee' of a place meant considerable logistical problems, thus risking a situation where the state would be forced into the position of employer of last resort. Governments also recognised that workfare would actually distort market mechanisms as the large-scale measures introduced during the 1980s had been accompanied by substitution (i.e. where employers take on the unemployed at the expense of existing workers), deadweight (i.e. where unemployed workers would have been employed regardless), and displacement (i.e. where employment declines among workers not subsidised by such measures).

Such problems were not so pressing for 'softer' forms of workfare. The relative growth in the long-term unemployed, something particularly marked among 18 to 24 year olds, was taken as further proof that a supposedly generous and 'passive' social security system could generate severe labour market detachment. The implications of this were not just limited to the fact that long-term unemployment was held to seriously corrode the motivation, personal skills and moral character necessary to find and hold down paid work, as theorists of the elusive 'underclass' would have it (Murray 1992). The pressing need to tackle long-term unemployment was also necessary if its role as a barrier to the operation of free markets was to be removed (Glynn 1991). One of the perverse effects of social security, according to monetarist orthodoxy, had been to create a semi-permanent category of marginalised workers whose detachment from the labour market acted to inflate wage pressures and apply a brake to industrial performance. By getting this category of worker to compete more effectively for jobs, wage demands could be held in check and productivity improvements brought about as more workers competed for the available jobs (see Chapter 7).

It is worth noting here that the equation of long-term unemployment among the young with labour market detachment and the deterioration of their so-called 'employability' is a tenuous one. As Murray, Marsland (1996) and others sought to continually demonise those young people struggling with the consequences of long-term unemployment, their attempts to portray them as a population physically separate and socially removed from the rest of the working population have little substance. The experience of long-term unemployment cannot be separated from the experience of unemployment in general because once time lags are factored for, rates of long-term unemployment closely mirror changes to the aggregate level. If trends in long-term unemployment thus mirror broader changes in the demand for labour, 'it cannot therefore be true that the experience of unemployment makes people less employable or that the availability of unemployment benefits has created additional long-term unemployment' (Webster 1997: 10).

Nevertheless, issues of fact often proved incapable of halting the momentum behind the restructuring of social security. By the beginning of the 1990s, the young were constituted, once gain, as a 'priority group' within a more general turn towards the greater selective use of compulsion as a means of tackling long-term unemployment. Moves to give what was then the Secretary of State for Employment powers to designate as compulsory 'approved training schemes' were effected by the 1985 Social Security Act and once designated, the refusal to take up the offer of a place on such a scheme without 'good reason' could expose a claimant to considerable sanctions. Although this power was never exercised – the compulsion that became associated with youth training was a consequence of the removal of income support from school leavers and not its status as a designated programme – the willingness to enter a work experience, training or motivation programme became an important benchmark against which eligibility for benefits was judged.

It was not until 1990 that the first compulsory programmes were introduced and even here this was initially limited to mandatory attendance at Restart courses for those claiming unemployment benefits for two or more years. By 1994, this had been expanded into a portfolio of short-term programmes which for 18 to 24 year olds unemployed for more than six months meant Workwise and 1-2-1 Interviews: short and intensive re-motivation and job counselling sessions. Dressed up in the language of personal responsibility, confidence building, re-motivation and self-appraisal, failure to attend without good cause exposed young claimants to a reduction in benefits of up to 40 per cent for the period courses ran. As Finn (1998) further notes, once bedded down these provided a springboard for additional experiments with 'softer' forms of workfare as a means for imposing limits on the duration of claims. The supposedly open-ended nature of benefit entitlement for the unemployed proved a constant source of irritation to those who equated long-term unemployment with over-generous social security. In 1993, pilots for Workstart offered financial incentives to employers to take on a person unemployed for two or more years and this was further expanded in 1995. However, in 1996 Workstart was replaced by pilots for Project Work which required all those aged between 18 and 50 who had been unemployed for two years to undertake 13 weeks on a range of Employment Service programmes, followed by a further 13 weeks compulsory training. This subsequently became the model for the New Deal for Young People introduced by New Labour (see Chapter 7).

Compulsion isn't working

The turn towards greater compulsion was a disaster for the young unemployed. Such measures were in no small way responsible for the removal of large numbers of young people from the official unemployment count, so contributing to the de-politicisation of the problem. We have also noted above how the re-composition of the benefits regime for the young unemployed led to increased number of claims being disallowed or withdrawn, the cost of which has undoubtedly contributed to many of the considerable hardships for young people discussed in the following chapter. The experience of Restart is illuminating here, as estimates suggest that its impact upon the claimant count was a net reduction of around three quarters of a million (Finn 1998). Like many of these measures, the primary 'success' of Restart was in compressing the duration of claims for benefits but with few leaving unemployment to enter a job. From the 17 827 000 Restart interviews that took place between 1990 and 1997, the percentage of claimants placed into jobs as a direct outcome never exceeded 1.7 per cent (or 54 900 in 1996) until the final year, when the jump to 4.7 per cent largely followed from administrative changes (i.e. changes to the way in which a 'positive' outcome was recorded) (Murray 1997). Measures like Restart have further been responsible for the production of something analogous to a 'revolving door' for the young unemployed, as greater pressure to take up a government scheme or one of the now numerous insecure or casual jobs, quickly leads back to the dole queue where the cycle begins again.

Lack of success on this scale has not been limited to Restart. Evaluation of two of the largest mandatory programmes for the long-term unemployed, Jobplan Workshops and Restart Courses, both of which targeted the 18 to 24 year old long-term unemployed, revealed that only 4 per cent of participants were moving into a job and up to three quarters were leaving without any form of 'positive' outcome whatsoever. Pilots for Workwise, with their four-week regime of intensive assistance and motivation, revealed job placement rates only slightly higher (9 per cent), with nearly two thirds leaving without any outcome at all (Murray 1996). Two government evaluations underlined the practical limitations of Workstart, with its net impact on job creation (i.e. its ability to generate new jobs) restricted to around one in six of all subsidised places (Finn 1988).

Failure to provide any significant upturn in job prospects alone is a damning enough indictment of the 'active benefits system', but the cost of this has further added to a now deeply entrenched culture of hostility among those whose needs these measures were supposed to serve. Like youth training and work experience schemes (see Chapter 3), Restart for example was dogged by indifference, suspicion and defiance since its introduction as a national programme. Evaluations consistently illustrated that claimants felt the practical value of interviews to be low, hostility was commonplace and participation was motivated primarily by the need to safeguard benefits (Banks and Bryn Davies 1990; Durning et al. 1990). Few participants on short-term re-motivation courses placed any real value on the programmes as a means to a job, tended to view them as the actions of a predatory government intent on victimising the unemployed and many were ready to act upon these sentiments. Once referred to a programme, the failure to begin a Restart Course (45 per cent), Jobplan Workshop (51 per cent) or Workwise (56 per cent) programme ran at spectacular levels and rates of early leaving were endemic (15, 7 and 28 per cent respectively) (Murray 1996). The significance of young people's active willingness to step outside of these new institutional forms designed to keep them in should not be underestimated, given that non-compliance without 'good reason' could expose them to severe and lengthy benefit penalties.

Tackling the fraudsters

Social security's reconstitution according to more exclusionary principles was further pursued through the search for the young welfare scrounger. The image of the welfare scrounger is a powerful one in British history and when equated with unemployed youth makes for a potent mix. As unemployment rose, concern about the impact of social security on the moral fibre of Britain's young people intensified, as depictions of unemployed school leavers leading comfortable lives on unearned incomes, with unlimited leisure time, taking drugs and drinking – all at the tax payer's expense – while making fraudulent benefit claims, became a powerful legitimating force in the neo-liberal ideological armoury (Mungham 1982). Hardened by repetition into something taken as given, governments felt able to claim with relative impunity that investigations, 'have unearthed evidence of fraud on a massive scale' (Department of Employment 1988b: 34); allegations subsequently repeated in an alarmingly casual fashion by prominent figures in the first New Labour government (Field 1996). Government estimates point out that 2 per cent of all social security claims are definitely fraudulent, that there are grounds for suspecting fraud in another 3 per cent of cases and that there is a low degree of suspicion in another 2 per cent. Translated into cash terms, this suggests that to anywhere between £2 billion and £7 billion are lost on fraud from an annual social security budget of over £100 billion; incidentally, this is against Inland Revenue estimates of the tax free 'hidden economy' costing between £45 billion and £60 billion in lost revenue to the Exchequer. Yet as Spicker[3] points out, even the starting figure of 2 per cent has no rational basis, as it is derived from the estimates of large retail organisations, which assume a loss of between 1 and 2 per cent through theft. Other methods of calculating the cost to social security fraud are equally suspect, since their focus is on 'detected' fraud. Here the total cost of fraud is arrived at by multiplying by 32 the amounts involved in every detected case, on the suspect assumption that if such claims had gone undetected this is the average length for which they would have run.

In any case, the measures put in place to detect social security fraud most likely inflated these estimates. Early in the 1980s, the first Thatcher government established the Specialist Claims Control Unit to target abuses of the system. Disbanded in 1986 after allegations of intimidation and harassment, the experience of the Unit did not prevent the imposition of further measures giving benefits staff financial incentives to root out fraud. Criteria to evaluate the efficiency of the Benefits Agency included the detection of a specified number of frauds, performance related pay for 5500 fraud investigators was linked to the number of cases detected and local authorities were provided with financial incentives for their anti-fraud successes (Jones and Novak 1999). By the time the Conservatives lost power, pressures to overestimate levels of fraud pervaded the entire system of administration, as evidenced by the findings of a National Audit Office report which questioned the validity of 30 per cent of claimed cases. Nevertheless, in 1995 the Department for Social Security launched what was claimed to be a self-funding £1 billion Five Year Security Strategy – savings from the non-payment of fraudulent payments would, it was argued, cover the costs of the programme – to tackle the problem. This was followed a year later by the creation of a free phone benefits 'cheatline', backed up by an extensive advertising campaign encouraging the public to inform on those they suspected of cheating. In 1997 another supposedly self-funding Benefits Integrity Project was targeted at the alarming rise in claims for long-term invalidity benefit and the Social Security Administration (Fraud) Act the same year further tightened the screw. The Act sought to bring the full force of the law on the young unemployed suspected of fraudulently claiming, by creating several new offences such as dishonestly making a false statement and failing to report a change in circumstances, both of which have the potential to lead to long prison sentences and/or a large fine.

Undoubtedly some of the young unemployed, like their older unemployed siblings and parents, do make fraudulent claims as they struggle through on benefits. With low wages, insecurity and exploitation often the only alternative to benefits paid at barely subsistence level, we should not be too surprised if more young people find themselves defrauding the social security system to avoid the hardship and misery that otherwise awaits them. In any case, even where fraudulent claims are made these are far more likely consequences of ignorance, chance and pressing need rather than of any sophisticated manipulation, systematic planning or 'life-style' choice. As one study of fraudulent claiming found, 'combining minimal social security benefits and informal employment was neither a rewarding experience nor a preferred life-style: it wasn't something to be planned' (Dean and Melrose 1999: 128). Other studies too illustrate how claimants who also work, do so in order to supplement insufferably low rates of benefit, while risking the dangers of employment in an informal economy dominated by low wages, exploitation and the absence of effective health and safety protection (Jones and Novak 1999).

Money as incentive

The resort to such desperate measures is one consequence of the systematic erosion of expenditure on social security provision for the unemployed over the last quarter of the twentieth century. The young people in Dean and Melrose's (1999) study (19 to 25 years old) were more likely than older age groups to justify their fraudulent activity in terms of hardship and deprivation. This is not surprising given that the restructuring of social security excluded or marginalised large swathes of young people from the receipt of unemployment benefits, pressed those who remained into intrusive and degrading tests of eligibility and subjected those still fortunate enough to pursue a successful claim into an impoverished means of existence. From the middle of the 1970s onwards, governments sought to contain the aspirations of the unemployed within increasingly tighter financial constraints through a relentless relative decline in the value of benefits: a downward trend, which was to continue for the next 20 years (Evans 1998).

What Labour began in the 1970s, the Conservatives adopted with conviction. Shortly after coming to power, the two Social Security Acts in 1980 first cut the real value of unemployment benefits by 5 per cent, the first real decline in value since the inter-war depression, and then exposed the receipt of benefits to income tax liability. The same Acts terminated the earnings-related additions to unemployment benefits, as already noted, and in a move whose consequences have been incalculable, the annual uprating of benefits in line with increases to the standard of living was ended. In its place the annual uprating of benefits each April was linked to increases in inflation, which over the long-term has risen at a much slower rate than average earnings. The result has been a sharp drop in the relative value of unemployment benefits. Measured at 1995 prices the real value of unemployment benefits actually rose by £1.06 per week between 1974 and 1996, but over the same period their value relative to average earnings suffered a dramatic decline. Even without taking into account the fact that young people aged 18 to 24 were paid lower benefit levels with the introduction of IS and then JSA, for a single adult unemployed person the value of benefits declined from 20.3 per cent of average earnings in 1971 to 18.4 per cent in 1979; by 1994 this had further declined to 13.8 per cent (Oppenheim and Harker 1996). For a (young) couple with children, the decline was even more marked as the level of IS proportionate to average income dropped from 77.2 per cent in 1979 to 28.7 per cent in 1990 (Kumar 1993; see Chapter 5).

Containing expenditure on social security has served a double purpose. On the one hand, in providing a guaranteed income at a reasonable level, monetarists argued that social security benefits degraded the discipline of wage labour and thus had an important role to play in maintaining high levels of unemployment through the provision of disincentives for an expeditious return to work (Minford 1985). By containing social security for the unemployed within sharply bounded monetary constraints, political or administrative discretion could be removed and the aspirations of the unemployed more closely reconciled with what the labour market had to offer. On the other hand, the effects of this would not be limited only to the unemployed. By depressing the level of benefits, a brake would also be applied to wage pressures more generally since it would remove, or at least significantly modify, the role of the social security system in providing a 'floor' for wages (i.e. a level below which they could not realistically fall) that acted to keep them artificially high. In effect, wage determination could also be returned more closely to market forces. In this respect, as in so many other areas, reality quickly intruded. Expenditure on social security for the unemployed continued to rise throughout the 'crisis decades', as real spending increased by 109 per cent between 1974 and 1996, an average of 3.4 per cent each year (Evans 1998). At something approaching 15 per cent of the total, expenditure on unemployment benefits constitutes a relatively small proportion of the social security budget, but across the same period the outlay on unemployment benefits showed the single biggest increase, a massive 320 per cent.

Conclusion

The political restructuring of social security provision for the young unemployed has therefore brought about a remarkable change in the nature and form of youth. Under the Keynesian commitment to inclusion, young people were progressively incorporated into a more benign and expansive structure of social security. Provision may have been far from generous, the maintenance of labour discipline and reintegration into the family form never far from view, but the inclusive strategy did bring with it significant concessions for the young, in the form of greater coverage under the social insurance system, more generous benefit provision and some recognition that an unemployed young person had access to welfare resources in their own right; however hesitantly or grudgingly these may have been bestowed. The rise of mass youth unemployment was to change all this. In explaining young people's peculiar vulnerability to the re-composition of social security along more exclusive lines, Andrews and Jacobs comment that, 'it is hard to escape the conclusion that the young have been deliberately selected as easy targets in the assault against benefits' (1990: 74). As far as it goes this is undoubtedly correct, but convenience is only one side of the story as it was young people's relative prominence within the broader framework of a more inclusive system of social security, which explains their relative prominence within the subsequent restructuring programme.

Undoubtedly ideological, the monetarist-inspired assault on the inclusive strategy for social security nevertheless derived what practical value it possessed from the continuing high rates of unemployment among the young. The monetarist critique of state welfare in general and social security in particular, stressed the malign impact of both upon free markets. Benefits by 'right', generous rates paid for an unlimited duration and a passive system of administration had disconnected effort from reward, undermined self-reliance and prevented free markets from achieving high employment levels of growth. Young people's especially advantageous position vis-à-vis access to social rights was therefore held to account, initially for the disproportionate impact of unemployment on the young and, more latterly, for the emergence of significant levels of long-term unemployment among young adults. In addition, the hesitant turn towards a more restrictive benefits system for the unemployed by Labour during the 1970s gave further impetus to the monetarist critique. What Labour had adopted perhaps somewhat reluctantly in its final years in power, was nevertheless elevated to a point of principle by successive Conservative governments during the 1980s and 1990s. From shaky beginnings in which the attack on young unemployed benefit claimants was more significant for its invective than its practical content, by the late 1980s it was becoming increasingly obvious that young people's relationship

to the social security system was undergoing a profound and fundamental change.

The purpose of this restructuring process has been to reconstitute
unemployed young people's relationship to the social security system
according to the more exclusive principles of the market. In doing so,
governments were eager to politically disengage themselves from the
previous responsibilities they had assumed for the direct condition of
young people's welfare. Whereas the inclusive strategy offered some
rational basis for reconstituting young people's need for work and
subsistence within politically and socially determined notions of need,
provision subsequently sought to confine these aspirations within
what the market has to offer. Restructuring was therefore directed
towards excluding young people from the benefits system by
physically removing major areas of provision to which they were once
entitled, by reconstituting what remains within the discipline of the
means-test, narrowing eligibility criteria, making judgements on the
willingness to work harder to satisfy, returning to a system of benefit
levels governed by what is effectively the principle of 'less eligibility',
extending sanctions and greater surveillance. And by making access to
benefits for the young long-term unemployed contingent upon an
intensive regime of short courses, motivation programmes and job-
search programmes. In place of the political commitment to social
security as the means for young people's integration, a situation was
created in which governments tied young people's survival more
closely to a labour market increasingly populated with low quality
jobs, and upon families themselves struggling with the costs of social
and economic change. The personal, financial and social costs of this
new and more exclusive state of youth are difficult to quantify but we
shall achieve some measure of their impact in the following chapter.

CHAPTER 5

The Changing State of the Family

Social security is certainly one of the most direct and visible elements of youth's political restructuring but this is by no means the end of the story. As we argued in Chapter 1, the Keynesian strategy went well beyond narrow fiscal techniques for managing demand but articulated a much more expansive relationship between state and civil society. On the one hand this involved a marked expansion in the influence of the state to the point where few corners of society remained immune, while on the other hand the guiding principles of this expansion were the political commitments to conciliation and concession. The repudiation of the Keynesian strategy and its replacement with money and the market as the key agents of restructuring therefore also necessitated a similarly expansive process of change. Just as the process of monetarist restructuring redefined the lives of the young in terms of their relationship to schooling and education, the labour market and the social security system, so too did it have important implications for young people's relationship to the family.

As this chapter considers, a key component of the Keynesian strategy of compromise and conciliation had been to bolster the nuclear family. An issue of the state and the political in ways rarely appreciated, under Keynesianism the family was elevated into a key unit of social administration. Through the welfare state the structure of the family was progressively redefined, as governments sought to both support and reinforce family life through a series of material concessions that ranged from the direct transfer of money and resources, through to the granting of in kind benefits like health and social care. This was also backed up by an intensive ideological programme that emphasised the sanctity of the family, in what Wilson terms 'the state organisation of domestic life' (1977: 9; Williams 1989). The monetarist repudiation of Keynesianism was therefore simultaneously expressed in terms of the reconstruction of this relationship, involving as it did both an 'increased use of money as a means of control and *the new emphasis on the family*' (LEWRG 1980: 122, original emphasis). Through the turn to money and the market as the basis of their approach to the political management of social relations, governments also redrew the terms upon which they had previously sought to organise the family.

For women both the implications and consequences of this have been well documented but what has been less remarked upon are its implications for youth. As the family was subject to new forces and as new disciplines and tensions emerged, so too was young people's relationship to the family – as both dependents and in terms of their own aspirations for independent living – similarly recomposed. In particular, the cost to the family of young people's protracted dependency, itself a result of young people's progressive removal from the labour market and confinement in longer and longer periods of compulsory education, had to some extent been off-set by new forms of state support and, more significantly, full employment and rising living standards. With the political turn towards the market, however, the terms of this dependence were redefined as governments sought to withdraw previous sources of support, make others available on a much more selective basis and set about redistributing an even greater proportion of the costs of the social reproduction of the young back onto the family. As we shall see, the implications of this for young people were extensive.

The changing relationship between state and family also impacted significantly upon young people's own aspirations for independence. Just as 'there was *no* explicit Tory policy to return women to their homes' (Wilson 1987: 204, original emphasis), neither did the turn to monetarism involve a simple strategy of returning young people to the family. Policies directed at reintegrating young people into the labour market on the basis of training and work experience schemes, the depression of youth wages and a more punitive social security system are, as we have seen, clearly testament to the determination of governments to reconstitute youth as a cheap and flexible source of labour; but what resulted from the restructuring of the relationship between state and family was in many ways far worse. In making young people's aspirations for independent living more fully contingent upon market forces and access to money, governments also ensured that young people's desires to establish families of their own were subject to formidable barriers. In changing the state of the family, the consequent hardships, deprivations, lack of resources, greater conditionality of state support and the absence of affordable and secure accommodation all constituted considerable obstacles in the quest for independent living.

The benefits of children

Within the terms set down by the Keynesian strategy young people's relationship to the family changed markedly. Longer-term trends towards children's expulsion from the labour market were further underwritten by the extension of compulsory secondary education, and both served to reinforce the family as the primary means of support for the young. The costs of this newly created dependency were considerable. Whereas pre-war children could to some extent ease the burden of their social reproduction through full-time employment by age 13 or 14, the terms of the post-war settlement institutionalised a much greater reliance upon the family. With all children required to undergo secondary schooling to age 15 and then 16, parents found themselves faced with an additional set of costs. To put things into some sort of perspective, one recent estimate has placed the cost (at 1997 prices) to the family of rearing a child until their 17th birthday at around £50 000 (Middleton *et al.* 1997).

The limits to the family's capacity to sustain such a burden was to some extent acknowledged by the introduction of family allowances. Following the Family Allowances Act 1945, by paying a weekly sum in respect of dependent school age children it was anticipated that some of the worst hardships and privations could be avoided and the dependent young reconstituted as a site of social and economic investment. This commitment to the welfare of the young nevertheless stood alongside an additional set of imperatives. Family allowances would also provide mothers with sufficient incentives to fulfil their 'historic' role as guardians of both the future supply of labour and the integrity of the British 'race' (Williams 1989; Wilson 1977). And such subsidies would help to alleviate the anticipated wage pressures resulting from full employment. By socialising an element of the costs of dependent children to the family, the hope was to forestall inflationary pressure generated by adult workers seeking higher wages as compensation for the costs of their dependent children. As Daniel and Ivatts remark, 'certainly any analysis of post-war benefit levels for children makes it apparent that they had been set at levels designed not to meet the needs of children but rather preserve the incentives of adults to work' (1998: 69).

As inclusive as the principle of family allowances ostensibly were, of far more importance to the welfare of the young was the strength of the post-war boom. With family allowances set well below the level recommended by Beveridge, and with their value uprated only twice between 1948 and 1967, the dependent young's well-being remained closely wedded to the fortunes of their parents. 'One reason for teenagers' good times from 1950 to 1970 was that their parents were employed and relatively well off', writes Frith (1984: 200). Full employment coupled with rising wages ensured that the growing costs of dependent children could to some degree be sustained by the 'family wage'. These 'good times', however, were not enjoyed by all. As every student of British social policy surely knows, by the middle of the 1960s the 'rediscovery of poverty' pointed clearly to the practical limits of both the social democratic welfare state and the ability of the family to meet the needs of its young. In an era of universal plenty, evidence emerged that inequalities were actually widening and that some 2.5 million children were living in poverty (Abel Smith and Townsend 1965). Pockets of unemployment and the persistence of low pay, aggravated by such factors as ethnicity and lone parenthood, underlined how a significant minority of dependent children and young people remained insulated from the benefits of the 'long boom'.

Evidence of continuing child poverty clearly contradicted the welfare state's claims to have created an inclusive childhood. Politically sensitive and the object of well-organised campaigns (the Child Poverty Action Group was created as an immediate response to these findings), Wilson's Labour governments of the 1960s nevertheless did little of any substance to disturb the terms of young people's dependence upon their families. It was not until 1971 that a new benefit, Family Income Supplement, was introduced by Heath's Conservatives as a means of providing state support for children living in working families on low incomes. In line with Heath's other unsuccessful attempts to politically disengage his government from the inclusive strategy the Conservatives had previously supported, the introduction of Family Income Supplements epitomised tentative moves away from universal welfare provision in favour of more selective (and thus exclusive) forms of support for the dependent young.

'Perhaps the most important success of poverty campaigners, however, was the transformation of Family Allowances into a new universal child benefit' (Alcock 1999: 209). Launched in 1975 by Labour, its inclusiveness and egalitarianism appeared to mark out child benefit (CB) as an important development in addressing the needs of dependent children. Its universal coverage, availability for all children up to age 16 (19 for those still in full-time education) and high rates of take-up seemed to give substance to Wilson's initial radicalism as far as tackling low income, poverty and inequality were concerned. By ensuring all families enjoyed a minimum level of financial support for their children, CB indeed opened up the possibility of constructing a platform from which the needs of all children could be addressed in a rational manner. For both Labour and the Conservative government that followed however, the status of CB remained uncertain. Never more than a contribution to the costs of child care, and a minor one at that, Labour had at least sought protection of its value by index-linking the annual uprating to changes in the level of inflation. Under Conservative governments of the 1980s and 1990s, however, this concession was removed and although the universalism of CB survived its importance was steadily reduced. Payment levels were regularly frozen, its universalism continued to attract much hostility and CB's value was steadily eroded as governments sought actively to shift further the cost of dependent children back onto the family. Where state support remained in the form of income support and family credit, its purpose was progressively redefined within the more general retreat from universal welfare provision through targetng and the means-test (see Chapter 4).

In the context of sharp increases in unemployment, greater job insecurity and growing wage inequalities, the withdrawal of state support for children and young people was nothing short of disastrous. At its most extreme, dependent young people were thrown into poverty on a massive scale to the point where, 'over the past 20 years, children have replaced pensioners as the poorest group in UK society' (Brewer and Gregg 2002: 4). As governments sought actively to confine aspirations for work within the limits set by the market (reinforced by a more regressive system of taxation), the surge in general unemployment produced a big increase in the number of children living in workless households. In 1968, at the height of the political commitment to inclusion, 4 per cent of children were living in workless households, that is those households with at least one person of working age but no employed adult. In 1979 this figure had risen to 7 per cent and by 1996 one in five of all children were living in households without a working adult. The greater prevalence of low paid and insecure employment also saw the number of children of the working poor double (Howard *et al.* 2001) and those children living in families reliant on IS increased from 7 per cent in 1979 to 26 per cent in 1993.

When the Conservatives were elected in 1979, around 1.7 million (14 per cent) children were living in poverty, defined as households with incomes of at least 60 per cent of the median income after housing costs (Brewer and Gregg 2002). By the time they lost power 18 years later, the corresponding figure was one in three, or 4.2 million children, with rates of poverty particularly acute among those from minority ethnic groups.

As well as boasting one of the highest rates of child poverty in the industrialised world, the shifting status of dependent young people brought immense benefits to a few. As more and more children found themselves living in families undergoing a sharp deterioration in their relative ability to meet their young one's needs, the relative divisions between those young people dependent upon their families widened to gaping proportions. In 1995 an influential study commissioned by the Joseph Rowntree Foundation stated that, 'for most of the post-war period until the late 1970s there was a trend towards greater equality of incomes. Since then, this trend has been decisively reversed' (Hills 1995: 21). For 20 years after 1978, the income and wealth of the richest 20 per cent of the population underwent a sustained improvement and, by the late 1990s, the top 1 per cent of the United Kingdom population owned nearly a quarter of all marketable wealth. At the same time, the income of the very poorest declined in real terms and many of those on supposedly 'middle incomes' experienced only stagnant or modest growth. According to the Child Poverty Action Group, between 1978 and 1999/2000 the top 20 per cent of earners saw their share of income grow from 43 per cent to 52 per cent of the total, while for the lowest 20 per cent the increase was barely half a percentage point, up from 2.4 to 3 per cent (Howard *et al.* 2001).

Labouring to learn

Such a sharp and sustained deterioration in the terms of large numbers of young people's relationship to the family, also worked to some degree to actually qualify their dependent status. Far from returning responsibility for children to their families as governments during the 1980s and 1990s proclaimed (Marsland 1996), the combination of an elongated education and the decline of opportunities for full-time employment reinforced young people's growing status as a source of flexible labour. Faced with longer periods of dependence upon parents and guardians increasingly unable to meet their needs, many young people responded by actively seeking out and taking up the growing opportunities for part-time working. In a trend repeated throughout much of the industrial capitalist world, during the period 1984 and 1995 the number of young men aged 18 combining education with employment rose from 15 to 22 per cent, while the comparable increase for young women of a similar age jumped from 18 to 33 per cent (OECD 1996). Driven primarily by the requirements of an expanding service sector, by the middle of the 1990s the number of young people seeking to cushion the costs of their protracted dependency through part-time work was exceeding those in full-time employment.

Less immediately visible but no less significant were patterns of school age working. During a period in which the young have been vilified for their 'deficiencies' as workers, it is somewhat ironic that the majority of children and young people have sought to qualify their dependence upon the family by undertaking paid employment *before* they reach the minimum school leaving age. In more than passing echoes of the 'half time' system that encouraged children to combine work and schooling around the turn of the twentieth century (Horn 1994), the changing status of young people to the family was further expressed by routine levels of school age working (Mizen *et al.* 2001). 'There is [now] overwhelming evidence *that employment is a majority experience* for children. The onus is on anyone who wishes to suggest that child employment in Britain is trivial or marginal to present evidence that this is indeed the case' (Hobbs *et al.* 1996: 16; original emphasis). A growing number of studies reported that at any one time, between one third and one half of all secondary school age young people could be found in paid employment, and that between two thirds and three quarters of children would work before leaving school. Notwithstanding problems of definition, translated into 'hard' numbers anywhere between 1.3 and 1.7 million secondary school age children can be found working at any time.

Typically, much of this working stood outside stereotypical ideas of children's employment. Delivering newspapers still constituted the single biggest source of paid work for school age children, but patterns of working extended into a range of employment situations more usually associated with adult workers. As the service sector continued to create more part-time employment opportunities, children found jobs washing up, serving in shops, preparing food and waiting tables on the one hand, and door to door selling or working as carers or cleaners on the other (Mizen *et al.* 1999). Most of this employment was illegal, either transgressing limitations on permitted hours or involving prohibited jobs, and the vast majority of these young workers remained unregistered. Poor quality and atrocious levels of pay were also endemic. In coming to a judgement about the nature of this employment, it is difficult to disagree with the sentiments of US researchers that 'only academics, policy makers, or nostalgic parents would glorify the meaningless and manual work performed by most teenagers' (Steinberg *et al.* 1981: 420).

The reasons why these children worked remained complex. It was simply not the case that 'children's jobs' remained as a structural hangover from an earlier phase of capitalist development, in the way that some sought to explain the situation (Lavallette 1994). Most of the jobs characteristic of children's employment were also among the most important sources of work for part-time adult (women) workers. Even in relation to newspaper deliveries, children and young people often found themselves in competition with other categories of marginal workers, such as state pensioners, the unemployed or those reduced to employment in the informal sector. Furthermore, given that most of these jobs could be found in the same sectors dominating the employment of school leavers – hotel and catering, wholesale and retail – it appeared that dependent children had been caught up in employers' greater use of part-time youth and student labour more generally (OECD 1996). For employers looking for an additional source of flexible labour, particularly those desperate to pare back costs in under-capitalised, labour intensive and hugely competitive areas of the service sector, the relative cheapness of school age labour, its disposability and young people's relative tolerance of boring and unrewarding tasks took on a greater prominence.

Lucas is certainly correct in arguing that 'the increased participation of students in part-time and other flexible forms of employment has clearly been driven by government politics aimed at increasing the availability of flexible workers, especially young people' (1997: 597). Alongside this, demand among school age children for these low quality and exploitative part-time opportunities remained strong. Necessity and hardship featured only fleetingly in explanations of why school age children worked in such large numbers and even where such factors were introduced, it was often only simply to exclude them. Others argued that work for children was more likely a preserve of the relatively affluent, to the point where 'these "enterprising" children contradict the stereotypical view of children who work as "exploited victims", and they may be advantaged over their less well off peers, not only by their relative affluence but also … when it comes to competing for jobs later on' (Morrow 1994: 141). With little supporting evidence, however, the realities of deprivation, poverty, stagnating family wages and the anticipation of a protracted dependence, provided some of the most acute examples of the cost that dependence upon the family entailed for young people (Middleton and Loumidis 2001). It is certainly the case that very few children entered work in order to pay the rent, utility bills or buy food for their families. But the growth of family deprivation and poverty, the widening of inequalities and a leisure time increasingly commodified and dependent upon access to money, provided a powerful source of pressure for children to make themselves available for any opportunities for part-time employment (Mizen *et al.* 1999).

Zeroing-in on the disaffected

The reconstituted nature of young people's relationship to the family was further expressed in other ways. Faced with the choice between no job, no unemployment benefits, a government training or work experience programme and remaining in full-time education, a growing number of young people simply put on hold their aspirations for independent living by simply 'dropping out'. As early as 1991, the independent Unemployment Unit had identified that around 100 000 16 and 17 year olds were neither in employment, education or training. They had, in effect, simply disappeared from official view. Around a decade later, estimates of 'status zer0',[1] as these young people were termed initially, had risen to around 135 000, or nearly 10 per cent of the age group (Bivand 2000). Estimates from the OECD claimed that by the middle of the 1990s, the number of young people not in education or out of the measured labour force in the United Kingdom was around one in four. A similar picture emerged from local studies where, in South Wales for instance, it was found that at any one time between 16 and 23 per cent of minimum age school leavers were status zer0 and that even this was most likely an underestimate, relying as it did on incomplete records supplied by the careers service (Williamson 1996). Once they had dropped out, two thirds of this group of young people were likely to remain status zer0 for six months or more, some of which was intermittent as young people moved in and out of various institutional settings and some of which was near continuous after completing compulsory education. Turbulent family histories, contact with unsympathetic welfare professionals and hostility towards government programmes and education had generated in many a strongly held sense of suspicion and indifference to the institutional alternatives now on offer in the changing state of youth.

In performing such a disappearing act, so to speak, this group of young people may have unwittingly provided government with a convenient 'solution' to the political problems stemming from the rising tide of visibly excluded youth. For the young themselves, however, the prospect of a spell as status zer0 held a more substantial set of problems as far as any aspirations for independent living were concerned. The distribution of status zer0 young people mirrored closely local concentrations of adult unemployment, deprivation and poverty, and this relationship was further accentuated among African-Caribbean or Asian youth (SEU 1999a). Status zer0 also appeared as a significant predictor of future unemployment or insecure working, and was strongly related to exclusion from intermediate and higher levels of qualifications and skills later in life. If this was not enough, resort to status zer0 held further potential problems in the way of the drift into offending behaviour and substance abuse (see below).

The 'problem' of the never-married young mother

Another group of young people whose relationship to the family was altered significantly by status zer0 were single young mothers. Unlike status zer0 young people in general, the growth of lone parenting across the 'crisis decades', particularly among never-married young women, did prove a constant source of public irritation to government. As a means to berate the welfare state, these young women were identified as symptomatic of all that was wrong with the social democratic commitment to support for family life, in what constituted a sustained attempt to shift the blame for the growth in lone parenting away from the political withdrawal of those substantive sources of support the family had previously enjoyed. In its place, responsibility for the sharp contraction in opportunities for working class girls and young women was laid squarely at the feet of 1960s 'permissiveness', the erosion of parental discipline brought about by a liberal education, a culture of welfare dependency and, ultimately, the fecklessness of the young women themselves. For neo-conservative champions like Charles Murray (1992), teenage lone parents were one of the clearest manifestations of the growing problem of the British 'underclass', with their deficit of responsibility, lack of shame and utilitarian approach to welfare.

That Murray's mix of anecdotalism and selective use of evidence, whipped up by a good dose of invective at the expense of some of the most marginal groups of young women in the United Kingdom, need not detain us here. Others have already exposed in admirable detail his many failings (see MacDonald 1997). Unquestionably ideological, the bitterness of his attacks on these young women nevertheless did capitalise upon important changes in young people's relationship to the family and to those processes through which they sought to establish families of their own. The basis of these changes were not be found in the permissive liberalism of the welfare state and its denigration of the traditional family form, however. On the contrary, with the political pursuit of unemployment, low wages, flexibility and insecurity came a marked acceleration of longer-term changes to the ways in which young people went about trying to assert their own independence. As Smith argues, 'almost certainly the fall in marriage rates and rise of single parenthood is not just associated with a change in young people's life-styles' (1997: 190). For her, trends like these were more a visible consequence of the new costs of being young. It was unemployment, government programmes, low wages and part-time working that accounted for increased rates of poverty among young heads of household aged 20 to 29 years old; a rise from 13 to 15 per cent during the 1980s alone. Austerity had also contributed towards reversing the fall in the average age of marriage for both young men and women that characterised the 1950s and 1960s (Irwin 1995). The average age of marriage for males had risen from 24 in 1970 to 26 in 1986, a trend mirrored for young women but with marriage occurring on average 2 years earlier than men. More young women were also opting for cohabitation and the average age of leaving home crept up throughout the 1980s and 1990s. At the same time, fertility rates declined and the age of first birth within marriage rose steadily from the mid-1960s onwards. For increasing numbers of young people, therefore, aspirations to form families of their own had to be progressively deferred.

Even if the considerable practical difficulties facing young people's desires for independent living and families could be successfully negotiated, difficulties in holding these families together took on a new importance. Similar pressures of work, welfare and insecurity lay behind the decline in the family form of two married parents living with their natural offspring, which had for a while at least appeared to define convention during much of the initial post-war period. By the end of the twentieth century, such were the stresses on family life that the nuclear family was now a minority, characteristic of only around one quarter of all families. As its significance declined, at least numerically speaking, the number of households containing children and headed by one parent rose from 2 to 7 per cent, 90 per cent of which were headed by women. Today, of all households with dependent children just over one fifth are headed by lone parents and there are approximately 1.5 million lone parent families rearing 2.3 million children (Daniel and Ivatts 1998). In a clear indication of the problems now confronting family life, the single biggest cause of lone parent families was marital breakdown.

There was also a notable increase in the number of never married teenage mothers, the particular object of Murray's considerable opprobrium. The incidence of birth outside of marriage increased throughout the post-war period, from around 5 per cent in the 1950s to around 35 per cent at the end of the century. Ninety per cent of all teenage births are now outside of marriage and, as if often repeated, Britain has the highest rate of unmarried teenage motherhood in the world (SEU 1999b). What is often conveniently ignored, however, is that the rate of live births to teenage mothers reached a peak at the end of the 1960s, during the height of the post-war political commitment to an inclusive youth, before undergoing a significant decline into the 1980s. Since then, small fluctuations notwithstanding, the figure has stabilised well below its earlier levels. What changed was the prevalence of 'shot-gun' weddings, which had forced many pregnant young women into marriage, often with disastrous outcomes (Selman 1996). Together with the rise in cohabitation, often as prelude to later marriage, the number of births to women of all ages outside marriage increased fourfold between 1971 and 1996. Even here, however, the spectre of the feckless unmarried mother remained a misnomer. Despite increased numbers of births outside of marriage, in 1996 around four fifths were jointly registered by both parents, of whom three quarters were living at the same address. Only around 8 per cent of all live births outside of marriage were solely registered.

Despite intensive efforts to assert the contrary, there is also no reliable evidence to support the often-repeated statement that many young women become pregnant with a view to taking advantage of welfare support (Kiernan *et al.* 1998). In fact, at the time of becoming pregnant teenage mothers are much more likely to be ill-informed about those sources of state support that remain available (Allen *et al.* 1998; Phoenix 1991). Indeed, early pregnancy is much more likely a manifestation of the new costs to being young, strongly related as it is to poverty, disaffection with schooling, stressed families and delinquency. Describing these young women as feckless, amoral or cynical in their approach to welfare may provide a convenient ideological diversion from the real nature of the problems that they face. It also serves to obscure the possibility that bearing a child may provide some of the most marginal groups of young women with a sense of control, purpose and agency to lives otherwise unlikely to be punctuated by meaningful alternatives.

Somewhere to live?

Problems of independence and family formation were further compounded by changes to state support for housing. Always a precarious exercise at the best of times, the Keynesian welfare state had provided some means of material support for young people's aspirations for independent living. Council housing offering young working families a source of safe and affordable long-term accommodation, buttressed by a system of rent rebates and housing benefits, did provide tangible opportunities for some measure of security of housing; at least for some (Anderson 1999). For childless young couples and single young people, however, housing aspirations remained closely tied to the private rented sector. Without access to social housing and usually shunned by the banks and building societies as bad financial risks, private renting constituted the principle means of securing independent accommodation for most young people. That is, provided they were willing to tolerate endemic poor quality, predatory landlords and the insecurity of lets that made up much of what was on offer (Ginsburg 1979).

With the retreat from the inclusive strategy came marked changes to the form of support available for independent living. Up until the 1980s no age criteria were applied to the administration of support for housing costs, which was still rooted in some notions of individual need. It was only with the turn to austerity that age emerged as a criterion for rationing support for housing costs. Warning signals were already apparent as early as the mid-1970s, surfacing in the alarm over whether the board and lodgings payments available to unemployed young people were a licence to indolence (see Chapter 4). It was not until a decade later, however, that these concerns were given a greater focus. The immediate stimulus for this was a doubling of expenditure on board and lodgings payments following the slump of the early 1980s, as more and more young people were forced to rely on the welfare system to buttress the costs of living away from home (Rugg 1999). From 1985 local discretion in setting the rate of board and lodgings payments was removed in favour of nationally imposed ceilings and time limits to claims for young people under 26 were introduced. Justified in terms of the need to combat unemployed young people's cynical use of the benefits system to holiday at tax-payers' expense, claims for board and lodgings were time-limited to two, four or six weeks depending upon locality, with the shortest claims applied to coastal areas.

Subsequently withdrawn for hindering labour mobility, these attempts to restrict support for board and lodgings for the young were followed by more radical changes. As part of the more comprehensive restructuring of social security introduced by the Conservatives towards the end of the 1980s, the administrative distinction between householder/non-householder was removed. The importance of this was that the distinction embodied some notion of individual need in its assumption that certain categories of claimants incurred higher living costs than others. For example, a young person claiming support for housing costs and living independently would take on greater expenses than a young person of the same age living at home or in shared accommodation. Just as age assumed a greater significance as a source of conditionality in relation to benefits for the young unemployed (see Chapter 4), so too was the householder distinction replaced with a system of age-related payments. Thus denying notions of individual need, all young people under the age of 25 were placed onto a lower rate of benefit than someone 25 or over and living in exactly the same conditions. This was in spite of the fact that well over half of all 24 year olds were householders or joint householders.

This same review process also created the Social Fund as a replacement for one-off social security grants to meet cases of 'exceptional need'. For some of the most desperate groups of young people, these grants had provided something of a life-line, no matter how fragile, by allowing for non-reclaimable payments in the absence of other means to secure necessities such as a bed, second-hand cooker, cot or children's clothing. Even here, however, such payments were only made on the judgement that a serious risk to health or safety would result from their absence. Nevertheless, in an act of craven parsimoniousness grants were replaced by loans from the Fund, repayable on a weekly basis. In what has been described in terms of 'a nightmare from Alice in Wonderland' (Jones and Novak 1999: 62), the distribution of loans was made contingent upon the solvency of locally administered and cash-limited funds and, in a bitter twist, an assessment of an individual's ability to repay, rather than any assessment of their need.

As the introduction of the Social Fund subordinated young people's housing needs to rigidly imposed financial constraints, regulations linking the level of support for housing costs to age were subsequently replaced by even tighter arrangements. A year before losing power, Conservative amendments to the housing benefit regulations in 1996 set out to restrict directly the degree of state support available for young people renting, by limiting Housing Benefit payments to local average rents for single rooms. Continued by New Labour, the 'single room rent' denies young people those previous opportunities for obtaining state support for self-contained accommodation, by paying housing costs based upon the occupation of one room in a shared dwelling. All young people under 25, without dependents and living in private rented accommodation now have their Housing Benefit paid at the same level regardless of individual circumstances or personal need. As Rugg concludes,

> Thus it can be seen, that the history of assistance with private rental costs is essentially one of gradual restriction, to a degree that it is now the case that young single people in the private rented sector are only likely to have their rent fully covered by benefit if they live in very basic rooms in shared housing. (1999: 55)

The impact of these changes was especially vindictive, coming at a time when young people's reliance on the private rented sector assumed even greater importance. Throughout the 1980s, governments had sought to redefine the basis of state support for housing by introducing market forces more fully into the public provision of housing. The result was a significant constriction in the housing functions of local authorities and a marked contraction in the social rented sector, as council building programmes were halted and the best quality local authority-owned housing sold off through the 'right to buy'. Much of what remained in public sector ownership was subjected to a centrally imposed policy of neglect and under-investment, as the fabric of much council-owned housing stock underwent a significant deterioration, while rents were brought progressively into line with the private sector (Ungerson 1994). With the inability of other providers of social housing to meet the demand, and with the costs of owner occupation spiralling upwards, the consequence was a further aggravation of the already acute shortage of affordable and safe accommodation for those young people seeking a degree of independence.

Stepping over the young homeless

The result of these changes were clearly evident in the deepening crisis of youth homelessness. In something of an understatement, Please and Quilgars note that 'while the inability of some people to manage to live independently is clearly a key factor causing youth homelessness, it is also important to consider the causal impact of political decisions and changes in society' (1999: 94). The changing state of youth indeed found one of its most visible expressions on the streets of many major cities in the United Kingdom.

Reliable estimates of the scale of homelessness are by their nature difficult to arrive (Hutson and Liddiard 1994). What is certain is that the official statistics compiled by government for all intents and purposes serve to exclude large numbers of the young homeless. Parsimonious at the best of times, statutory definitions of homelessness have operated on the assumption of functionality (Anderson 1999) so that dependent children and people considered vulnerable receive assistance, with the remainder left to fend for themselves. In practice, and reaffirmed in the 1985 and the 1998 Housing Acts, meaningful notions of homelessness are restricted to those judged not to have made themselves intentionally homeless and are deemed to be in 'priority need'. Satisfaction of this considerable hurdle has important implications, since once accepted as homeless local authorities are placed under a statutory obligation to make attempts to find a person secure and permanent accommodation; although the link between homelessness and the right to permanent accommodation was broken by the 1996 Housing Act.

It is from these criteria that the official homeless statistics are produced. What they show is that the number of people accepted as homeless increased significantly throughout the 1970s and that between 1978 and 1991, when official estimates reached their peak, there was a threefold increase from 58 000 to 170 500. The number averaged 150 000 between 1993 and 1995 (ONS 1996) and by the beginning of 1997 there were still 117 000 cases of official homelessness in England and Wales. By the 1990s, it was widely accepted that the United Kingdom had the highest rates of homelessness in Europe.

Importantly, these figures referred to households and not individuals. Undoubtedly, many young people would have found themselves 'hidden' within these statistics, since one of the ways of satisfying the 'priority need' criteria was the possession of dependent children. Shelter points out that by disaggregating these figures into individuals, official estimates of homelessness would most likely triple, around half of whom would be children and young people under the age of 16.

Official estimates therefore need treating with caution, as by definition they exclude the bulk of people experiencing various types of housing and accommodation problems. Of the two in three applications to local authorities for housing support rejected, at one end of the spectrum could be found the street homelessness and rough sleepers, while at the other end there existed the various categories of 'hidden homeless' that make up the bulk of the homeless population. This latter group included prisoners released from custody, care leavers, those sleeping on the floors of friends and relatives, involuntarily living in shared accommodation and those able to find only temporary housing. In 1992, for instance, it was estimated that there were 63 000 people in temporary accommodation and another 11 000 in bed and breakfast. At the peak of the crisis in 1992, Shelter's own estimates suggested that around 1.7 million people could be described as in some way homeless. Included in these figures were single people living in hostels and lodgings, 317 000 insecure tenants and around 1.2 million 'hidden homeless' (Diaz and Coleman 1997).

Apart from those children and young people still dependent upon a parent or guardian (i.e. under the age of 16), official estimates generally exclude the young. Few single young people ever satisfy the requirements for statutory homelessness. Without being deemed at severe risk or having dependents of their own to care for, young people are de facto excluded from official classification and thus access to statutory forms of support. A Social Exclusion Unit (1998a) report into rough sleeping estimated that there were 2400 people sleeping rough in London alone, with another 10 000 sleeping rough across the nation each year. A quarter of these were estimated to be aged 18 to 25. National estimates of youth homelessness range from around 33 000 among 16 to 21 year olds to around a quarter of a million among those aged 16 to 25, with the highest concentration in London. Shelter points to the fact that around 17 000 young people go through the Centre Point hostel each year, 50 000 young people are living in temporary accommodation, another 2000 can be found in the capital's squats and another 45 000 are living in 'inappropriate conditions' such as sleeping on a friend's floor. It is among this latter 'hidden homeless' that young women and young black people are most heavily represented, since their vulnerability to sexual, physical and racial abuse means that living 'on the street' is not a practical option (Boulton 1990). It is also important to note that there is compelling evidence that youth homelessness is not just an urban phenomenon but that it is widespread in rural areas too (Carlen 1996).

Some government Ministers were content to dismiss the explosion in youth homelessness in terms of 'those one stepped over on the way to the opera'. Yet as the problem of youth homelessness deepened and the ferocious assault on these young people as criminal and feckless (Carlen 1996) proved incapable of obscuring the evermore visible presence of the young homeless on the streets of British cities, government did act. In their rapid and enthusiastic conversion to the French practice of Foyers, John Major's Conservative governments looked to new forms of transitional accommodation as one prominent means to address the problem. In a complement to the 'deficiency' model of unemployed youth, the expansion of a network of Foyers linked the provision of short-term accommodation to participation in training and job-search activities, in a sort of 'housingfare' to accompany the 'workfare' and 'learningfare' introduced to deal with crisis of youth elsewhere (Lund 2000). '[A]n expensive diversion unlikely to make a substantive contribution towards overcoming the housing problems young people encounter' (Gilchrist and Jeffs 1995: 1; cf. Quilgars and Please 1999), Foyers marked the triumph of short-term market-led solutions to some of the most fundamental problems of youth.

From the margins to the centre?

We shall deal with the costs of crime in the next chapter, but it is important to note here that the political pursuit of austerity also saw many families struggling to cope with the costs of their children's increasing resort to illegal drugs. Throughout the 'crisis decades' a mass of evidence built up consistently pointing to the growing presence of drugs in the lives of the young. Evidence from the Home Office's British Crime surveys (BCS) of 1994, 1996 and 1998 (see Chapter 6 for more details) for instance, regularly illustrated that although drug taking was relatively rare among the general population and that periods of drug use tend to be confined to short-lived experimentation, the highest incidence of drug taking occurred among those in their mid to

Table 5.1 Drug use among young adults aged 16–29 (as a percentage)

	Ever used	Within last year	Within last 6 months
Cannabis	42	23	14
Amphetamines, LSD, magic mushrooms, ecstasy, poppers	28	10	5
Heroin, crack cocaine and cocaine	6	3	—

Source: Home Office 1998.

late teens. As Table 5.1 shows, nearly one in two young people between the ages of 16 and 29 were admitting experimenting with illegal drugs at some time during their lives and with one in seven reporting recent drug use. As the table also shows, the drug of choice was cannabis, followed by amphetamines and ecstasy, with use of class A drugs like opiates a minority activity.

Across the 1990s, rates of illegal drug use among secondary school age children also rose to significant levels. The numbers of 14 and 15 year olds using illegal drugs increased sixfold in the 10 years after 1987 and by the time the Conservatives left power, around one in four boys and girls had experimented with illegal drugs before leaving secondary school – Table 5.2. As Balding (2000) points out, the percentage of 12 to 13 year olds who tried drugs in 1996 was actually higher than the percentage of 15 to 16 year olds who had tried drugs in 1987. The average age of initiation into drug taking also declined significantly throughout the 1990s, while the emergence of 'poly-drug' use – the use of different drugs, either simultaneously or within short periods of time – became increasingly common. Boys may be using illegal drugs in larger numbers than girls but the gap narrowed over time, with girls increasingly moving towards the consumption of 'harder' substances (South 1997).

Among others, Parker (1998) has argued that findings like these point to a 'normalization' of drug-consumption among the young. By this, they do not mean that drug-taking became routine for most young people, although statistically speaking increasing rates of usage do point to experimentation with illegal drugs becoming a majority experience in the near future. Rather, their claim is that analogous to teenage smoking and earlier sexual experimentation, over the past two decades or so we have witnessed 'the spread of deviant activity

Table 5.2 Trends in drug use among 11 to 15 year olds (as a percentage), 1987–97

	1987	1988	1989	1990	1991	1992	1993	1994	1995	1996	1997
Boys											
11–12	1	1	1	2	—	7	4	2	—	—	3
12–13	2	2	4	3	7	8	7	6	9	9	5
13–14	3	3	8	7	12	14	16	13	—	16	14
14–15	4	6	13	13	19	23	24	27	32	33	26
15–16	8	8	11	22	22	—	35	36	39	—	—
Girls											
11–12	1	1	1	2	—	3	2	2	—	—	2
12–13	1	2	2	2	5	6	5	5	8	7	4
13–14	3	3	9	6	10	13	14	13	—	15	12
14–15	5	6	13	10	19	23	22	23	28	31	24
15–16	6	6	9	15	21	—	28	31	34	—	—

Source: Balding 2000.

[i.e. illegal drug use] and associated attitudes from the margins *towards* the centre of youth culture' (152). Greater availability, earlier initiation, more frequent use, a more 'streetwise' attitude and the mainstreaming of dance culture (Redhead 1993) all brought about a significant shift in both attitudes and behaviour towards illegal drugs and their use, compared to as little as 20 years ago. By the turn of the twenty-first century, illegal drugs had in some respects become a more 'normal' aspect of young people's lives and perhaps a 'rite of passage' (Coffield and Grafton 1994; Measham *et al.* 1994).

As Parker freely concedes, there were distinct limits to this growth in young people's consumption of drugs. As we have also noted, despite their widespread use, consumption remained sporadic and/or usually confined to the use of 'softer' drugs. Most young people continued to limit their experiments with drugs to one-off or occasional use, or restricted their consumption to 'recreational' drugs such as cannabis or ecstasy. These patterns were reinforced by a strongly held set of values when it came to the possession and use of 'harder' drugs. The attitudes of young people were far from unequivocally liberal or permissive, with most continuing to view 'harder' drugs like opiates and cocaine with the type of suspicion and hostility that has long defined popular attitudes. As Shiner and Newburn testify,

> The young people who participated in our qualitative study and who had not used drugs commonly subscribed to a restrictive set of views, characteristic of the 'adult world'. This was clear in the associations they made between drug use, crime and other forms of

deviant behaviour. Surprisingly, perhaps, the attitudes of those respondents who had used drugs were, in many respects, similar to those expressed by non-users. (1997: 526)

Much more alarming was the steady rise in the use of 'hard' drugs, albeit from a smaller base. Research evidence through the 1990s was consistently pointing to a small but nevertheless relentless rise in the number of young people reporting use of crack cocaine and heroin, for instance, so that by the end of the century somewhere between 3 and 6 per cent of all young people had experimented with this category of drug. For cocaine, rates of usage among the young were much higher, perhaps in double figures, as significant reductions in price and greater availability saw its increasing incorporation into young people's leisure pursuits (Economist 2001). For opiates, however, the backdrop was not just a reduction in price and better quality of supply, but also the decaying inner cities that increasingly defined the parameters of their lives. Both prolonged drug use and the use of 'harder' drugs were generally the preserve of some of the most disadvantaged groups of young people living in the major urban centres. The decimation of their communities through unemployment, the absence of regular or stable incomes and the physical deterioration in housing and community resources provided the setting for a significant increase in opiate use throughout the 1980s. Around one third of all new Home Office notified drug addicts were under 25 years old, around two in five were under 21 and twice as many males as females were making up all new notifications (Auld *et al.* 1986). Gender appropriate notions of behaviour may have prevented 'good girls' from using 'harder' drugs like opiates to the same extent as males, but drug use among young women in many inner city areas also embarked upon a similar upward trend (Taylor 1993).

These shifts in the structure of young people's lives were thus paralleled by a new enthusiasm for drugs. As Pearson (1987) argues, as the 'crisis decades' rumbled on the bohemianism that heroin use once signalled was overwhelmed and then replaced as the drug of choice by an increasingly desperate young white male working class. Rates of opiate use among this group soared during the 1980s in some cities like Liverpool, Manchester, Leeds, Bristol and London, that had all possessed a long-standing culture of intravenous drug use. Not only did rates of use increase sharply but important changes in the form of use were also evident. The growth of an informal economy – one beyond official view and centred on 'the street' and the housing estate where thieving, drug dealing and handling stolen goods became routine – was also articulated in terms of a new set of 'irregular' pleasures (Auld *et al.* 1986), in which long-term intravenous use of heroin was replaced by a culture of intermittent sniffing and smoking.

Conclusion

Thus the political turn to austerity marked the onset of a significant process of change for both young people's position as dependents upon their families and in terms of their aspirations for independence and families of their own. As dependents, the decoupling of the Keynesian welfare state from the family and the reconstitution of the relationship in terms of money and market relations had extensive implications. The progressive withdrawal of universal benefits for children and their redefinition in terms of greater selectivity and exclusivity, saw a marked alteration in the relationship between young people and their families. With the re-regulation of labour markets the impact on large numbers of young people was profound. For some, this meant considerable benefits as governments encouraged a huge shift in the holding of wealth and the generation of income away from the poor to the rich. For many more, however, the marked growth in inequalities of income and wealth fed through into a sharp deterioration in the relative fortunes of large numbers of children and young people still dependent upon their parents. At its most extreme, by the end of the twentieth century Britain possessed one of the highest rates of child poverty in the industrial capitalist world, with more than one in three children living in conditions of poverty.

One further cost of this was the increased urgency that paid employment took on for the dependent young. In a vivid counter to those eager to paint school leavers as 'deficient' workers, paid employment became the 'norm' for the majority of secondary school students, as these young people responded to the likelihood of a protracted dependence by seeking out and taking up paid work. Employers' demand for part-time young workers also gave those beyond the minimum school leaving age some means of managing their enforced dependence, while others responded to the new post-16 landscape by dropping out altogether. By the beginning of the 1990s, a significant minority of school leavers were forced into 'status zer0' in preference to the new institutional routes of work-based training or continuing in education. For some young women, this was often combined with early motherhood. Much maligned, a slowly growing number of young women responded to the new constraints they faced by shunning what may have once been an accepted route to marriage and motherhood and initiating families on their own.

Aspirations for independent living were similarly redefined. Never adequate, previous forms of support for young people's housing costs generated during more politically inclusive times were first undermined and then progressively reorganised along new and more punitive lines. For the young, notions of individual need were replaced by arbitrary calculations undertaken on the basis of age and these were quickly superseded by even more parsimonious provision, which limited state support for housing costs to a single room in shared accommodation. Combined with the steady erosion of social housing provision, to which single young people had always been marginal, a marked change in the demand for youth labour and more restrictive benefits for the young unemployed, the end of the 1980s was witness to a huge escalation of youth homelessness. Alongside this, the increased cost of being young was further expressed in terms of young people's turn to illegal drugs. While much of this remained sporadic and confined to experiments with 'softer' drugs, trends in the use of 'harder' drugs also underwent a notable rise. In a little over a decade, use of opiates went from being the preserve of the bohemian few into the near-exclusive preserve of a marginalised and dispossessed white working class youth. Indeed, as the end of the twentieth century approached successive governments had done much to withdraw or significantly erode those sources of support that had previously buttressed young people's relationship to the family. As a consequence, many were now forced to confront a series of formidable barriers to a satisfactory family life, both as dependents and in relation to their own aspirations for independent living.

CHAPTER 6

The Changing State of Law and Order

Government's pursuit of youth as a cheap and flexible source of labour certainly provides one of the most telling expressions of the changing state of youth, but the upward spiral in youth crime musters a close second. Over the period under consideration in this book, there was a dramatic increase in overall rates of recorded crime and within this the presence of the young loomed large. While it is beyond doubt that criminal youth served an important ideological and discursive function for governments, the changing state of youth was nevertheless also expressed in terms of the practical criminalisation of young people. Trends in young people's offending behaviour broadly mirrored the steady increase in both the volume and rate of offending more generally characteristic of the last decades of the twentieth century, to the point where offending became well established as a majority activity among the young. At its high point, those aged between 10 and 20 years accounted for four in 10 of all convicted offenders, with some groups, notably the very poor and young black people, facing acute levels of criminalisation.

The political dimensions to this were extensive. At one level it is true that the criminalisation of youth cannot be accounted for in simple terms of state restructuring. Even though it is now openly recognised in some quarters that the criminal justice system, particularly incarceration in young offenders' institutions, is an effective way of cementing latent delinquency into something more tangible, the state continues to exercise very little direct influence over young people's criminal and delinquent behaviour. It is a fact of modern social life that despite the sharp intensification of the means to identify, apprehend, convict, supervise and punish young transgressors, large numbers of primarily working class young people have remained steadfastly immune from the attempts of successive governments to curtail their delinquent activities. At another level, however, youth crime and delinquency remain profoundly political. This was not just an aspect of youth's importance as a political expedient, where the demonisation of young people provided a powerful way for governments to justify their adoption of punitive 'solutions' to deeper problems of social order. Nor is it solely a product of the attempts of governments to achieve a degree of separation from any responsibility for increasing levels of youth crime, no matter how concerted their attempts to achieve this. The criminalisation of youth that occurred during the last quarter of the twentieth century was also political, because it stood as one of the most prominent monuments to the crisis of the commitment to an inclusive youth and the adoption of market-led 'solutions'. It is in the growth of unemployment, the degradation of young people's relationship to the labour market, rising inequalities in income and wealth and the active withdrawal of substantive sources of welfare support, that a further political dimension to the problem of youth crime can be found.

That in managing the general problem of crime and delinquency, the state differentiates young people from the population of adult offenders is further testament to the political importance of criminal youth. For over 150 years now, the state has separated out the young delinquent from adult offenders through the construction of specific and distinctive methods of administration. As far as the post-war period is concerned, the forms that this has taken are sometimes described in terms of competing models of 'welfare' and 'justice' (Goldson 1997a). Such a typology certainly captures the broad contours of recent changes, but equally the changing state of law and order is well expressed in Young's account of the rise of the 'exclusive society',

> from a society which both materially and ontologically incorporates its members and which attempted to assimilate deviance and disorder to one which involves a great deal of both material and ontological precariousness and which responds to deviance by separation and exclusion. (1999: 26)

Young's purpose is to illustrate how the social democratic commitment to effecting rational solutions to the problem of crime, turned on the principles of inclusion. What was needed for the majority of young offenders was guidance and support rather than punishment and sanction, expressed through more inclusive structures of administration. The adoption of 'treatment' programmes, for example, literally sought to resolve the growing problem of offending through the more effective incorporation of young offenders into mainstream society, most explicitly through the re-engineering of their family and community life. The 'separation and exclusion' of more recent approaches have, in contrast, involved a reversal of these principles. 'Solutions' to youth offending, such as they exist, were subsequently sought in the development of new forms of provision whose purpose was to confine young people within the rule of law and, increasingly, to effect their physical removal – from families, homes, communities, jobs, schools and friends – to places of incarceration.

That this has been politically driven is clear and the restructuring of youth justice provision according to these principles of 'separation and exclusion' is the second main theme of this chapter. Unlike Young, however, the process of restructuring examined here does not resort to an underlying functionalism; one where Fordist standardisation required the absorption of the delinquent 'other' and post-Fordist de-standardisation their exclusion. While this undoubtedly has the merit of locating crime and criminal justice provision within the framework of post-war capitalist development, its functionalism fails to grasp the importance of deeper political forces. It is argued here that the changing state of law and order and the restructuring of youth justice that it involved, developed in the wake of the practical failures of the strategy of inclusion and incorporation. Through resort to justice and punishment, and by subordinating young people's behaviour to the anonymous discipline of the law, successive governments sought to disengage themselves politically from both the direct responsibilities for managing youth offending that they had previously assumed. At the same time, the resort to the rule of law allowed governments the capacity to politically distance themselves from the consequences of the policies we have already examined in earlier chapters, and which they had self-consciously chosen to pursue.

Sign of a misspent youth?

That the changing state of youth has been expressed simultaneously as a crisis of youth criminality is certain. There is more than a grain of truth in the claim that, 'probably the most important single fact about crime is that it is committed mainly by teenagers and young adults' (Smith 1995: 395). Like all statistics, official records of offending come with several caveats, not least among them an awareness of how the collection of crime statistics is the outcome of a complex and shifting pattern of legal (i.e. changes to the law), interpretative (i.e. what is subjectively acknowledged as crime) and interactive (i.e. police recording practices) factors (Maguire 1997). Keeping these in mind, Home Office figures on convicted offenders nevertheless provide both a useful guide and compelling picture of the extent of youth's criminalisation. For example, the year before the Conservatives lost power in 1997, for every five offenders cautioned or convicted of indictable offences, two were under 21 years old, one in four were under 18 and, of almost 5 million convicted offenders during the year, nearly 2 million were between 10 and 20 years (Table 6.1). Furthermore, during a period in which young people's claim to the ownership of property has decreased inversely to its centrality to social life, so too have offences against property emerged as the biggest source of youth offending. Much of this is petty offending, opportunist theft, shoplifting

Table 6.1 Offenders found guilty of, or cautioned for, indictable offences for England and Wales: by gender, type of offence and age, 1996

Age	10-13	14-17	18-20	21-34	35+	All 10+ (100%) (000s)
Males						
Theft and handling stolen goods	7	24	16	38	16	153.7
Drug offences	—	12	23	54	11	72.8
Violence against the person	4	22	15	42	17	43.9
Burglary	8	31	20	36	5	40.5
Criminal damage	8	24	16	39	13	11.7
Sexual offences	4	14	7	30	45	6.4
Robbery	6	38	22	30	5	6.0
Other	6	8	16	56	19	70.1
All	4	20	17	44	15	405.1
Females						
Theft and handling stolen goods	10	26	12	34	18	54.5
Drug offences	—	9	18	57	16	8.7
Violence against the person	8	34	10	34	14	7.9
Burglary	15	39	14	25	6	1.8
Criminal damage	7	29	10	37	17	1.2
Sexual offences	10	18	11	32	29	0.1
Robbery	8	51	17	20	4	0.5
Other	1	11	15	54	20	11.5
All	8	23	13	39	17	86.3

Source: ONS 1998.

and pilfering and this must be underlined. However, in recent terms, young people have also accounted for a growing proportion of violent crime, burglary and robbery offences, while drug offences have also risen significantly (Newburn 1997; see also Chapter 5).

As some contend (Brown 1998; Griffin 1992), it is possible that statistics like these tell us a more about the operational assumptions of the police and criminal justice system, than they do about underlying rates of crime and delinquency. Ready connections between delinquent youth and the decomposition of social order have a long and 'respectable' history and one that has, of course, produced a rich vein of enquiry (Pearson 1991). Nevertheless, the conclusion that young people have been disproportionately criminalised as the crisis of youth unfolded is one generally endorsed by self-report studies; although this too is a methodology not without its limitations. Broadly consistent with other self-report surveys (cf. Maguire 1997; West and Farrington 1977), one relatively recent and widely quoted Home Office survey found that one in two boys and one in three girls admitted to ever having committed a criminal act; one in four boys and one in eight girls had committed a criminal act in the previous year; and that in both cases offences against property dominated.

These conclusions are further supported by recent findings from the Home Office's Youth Lifestyle Survey (Flood-Page et al. 2000). From a self-report study of nearly 5000 12 to 30 year olds, 57 per cent of males and 37 per cent of females had committed at least one offence in their lives; and among the 19 per cent of young people who admitted to a crime in the previous 12 months, males were twice as likely as females to offend. Once again, most of these offences appear trivial and criminal activity quickly recedes as young people take on new responsibilities. Yet as the age of peak offending has risen (18 for boys and 15 for girls), evidence also shows how young people's involvement in crime became more protracted. 'If it is true that young people grow out of crime, then many will fail to do so, at least by their mid twenties, simply because they have not be able to grow up, let alone grow out of crime' (Graham and Bowling 1995: 56).

Both the Home Office figures on convicted offenders and the findings from self-report studies, also underline how this process of criminalisation has taken a gendered form. It has also been claimed that 'the most significant fact about crime is that it is almost always committed by men' (Newburn and Stanko 1994: 1) and as far as the official statistics are concerned (Table 6.1) only 20 per cent of convicted offenders in 1996 were female. When young offenders[1] are considered, however, the gender ratio narrows considerably to 3.3:1. For certain categories of offences such as burglary, criminal damage and drugs, however, the ratio is over 10:1. It does appear that the gap between rates of male and female offending has been narrowing over time, although the overall disparity continues (Newburn 1997), and self-report studies consistently show a much lower difference in rates of offending between boys and girls. Campbell's (1981) pioneering study of delinquent girls found only slightly different ratios of male to female criminal activity and roughly parallel patterns of offending. These findings have been broadly replicated in Bowling and Graham's study (1995; see also Flood-Page *et al.* 2000), although they make the important point that the gender ratio is also heavily contingent upon age and seriousness of offence. Among 14 to 17 year olds the ratio of male to female offenders is 1.4:1 but this rises to 11.1:1 for those aged between 22 and 25; a trend in line with the earlier peak and quicker cessation of offending among girls and young women. It is also the case that for expressive offences the offending ratio between males and females aged 14 to 17 is less than 2:1, for property offences 2.5:1 (although there are significant variations between specific types of property offence e.g. theft of and from cars) and for violent offences 3.5:1. These still show important and enduring differences in rates of offending between boys and girls, but ones which are significantly below those manifest in the official statistics.

Black youth in crisis: crime, law and order

Rates of criminalisation appear particularly marked among young black people. The disproportionate presence of black people in the crime statistics raises possibly one of the most contentious issues when considering the changing state of law and order: does this overrepresentation express higher rates of criminal activity among ethnic minority youth, particularly for young black African-Caribbeans, or does it tells us more about the assumptions that the police, courts and legal system bring to bear upon the regulation of young black people?

What is beyond dispute is how the crisis of youth crime has contained a striking 'racial' dimension, one most evident in the identification of street crime with the presence of young African-Caribbean males in Britain's major urban centres. For Gilroy (1987), this was the culmination of a more or less deliberate ideological process during the early 1970s, in which black communities in general and young black people in particular, were redefined as innately criminal. Through a sustained process of ideological vilification, the apparent growth in black criminality was attributed to the pathological or fragile nature of cultural practices, clearly evident in the problem nature of black youth. In redefining the ideological terrain, the responsibility for deepening social and economic decay was partly shifted onto the structure of black communities, especially the African-Caribbean 'family type', while also providing a buttress for beleaguered police forces practising colonial-style containment methods in many of Britain's inner cities (see Solomos 1988). Consequently, the depiction of black young people as the epitome of 'threatening youth' became a self-fulfilling prophecy, as the spectre of the young black criminal generated increased surveillance, in turn bringing more young black people into a criminal justice net being cast ever wider (see also Hall *et al.* 1978).

From this position it is perhaps to be anticipated that the threat of criminalisation is far more significant for black people than it is for white people; a view forcibly voiced over a decade ago by the then Director of the Prison Reform Trust, Stephen Shaw:

> Black people are more likely than their white counterparts to be stopped by the police. If stopped, they are more likely to be arrested. If arrested, more likely to be charged. If charged, more likely to be remanded in custody, and if convicted, more likely to receive a sentence of imprisonment. (Quoted in Skellington 1992: 107; see also Reiner 1989)

The consequences of this criminalisation are readily apparent in recent Home Office data (Home Office 2000). While 2 per cent of the population aged 10 and over are black, 3 per cent Asian and 1 per cent are categorised as 'other' non-white ethnic groups, minority ethnic groups are overrepresented at every stage of the criminal justice process. Of the 800 000 stop and searches carried out in 1999–2000, 8 per cent were on black people, 4 per cent Asian and 1 per cent 'other' non-white; of the 1.3 million arrests for notifiable offences, 7 per cent were black people, 4 per cent Asian and 1 per cent 'other' non-white (black people were four times more likely to be arrested than white or other ethnic groups); of the 180 000 people given police cautions for notifiable offences, 6 per cent were black people, 4 per cent Asian and 1 per cent 'other' non-white; for the male prison population 12 per cent black people, 3 per cent Asian and 3 per cent 'other' non-white;

and for the female prison population 19 per cent black, 1 per cent Asian and 5 per cent 'other' non-white.

Once again the young feature disproportionately within these figures. Although elements of this overrepresentation may be explained by the relative youth of the non-white ethnic minority population, Table 6.2 shows that young black people under the age of 20 are significantly overrepresented in both the arrest and, to a lesser degree, caution figures (between two and five times the presence in the population aged over 10). Among those young people found guilty of an offence, Table 6.3 shows that the overrepresentation of young black people under 20 years old receiving prison sentences is particularly marked (between six and eight times their representation in the population aged 10 or over). Indeed, of the 10 345 young people between the ages of 15 and 20 serving prison sentences in 1999–2000, 1419 (13.7 per cent) were young black people and, once imprisoned, these young black convicts were significantly more likely to receive sentences of 12 months or longer.

Figures like these undoubtedly express the power of ideological manipulation and the discriminatory practices of the criminal justice system, but they do not preclude the likelihood that the crisis of youth has been expressed through real increases in rates of criminal activity among young black people. The stereotyping of black youth and the communities in which they live as inherently criminal, however

Table 6.2 Arrests and cautions for indictable offences by age and ethnic appearance 1999–2000, England and Wales

	Ethnic appearance of person arrested/cautioned as percentage					
	White	Black	Asian	Other	Not Known	Total (100%)
Arrests						
under 14	87.8	7.8	2.8	0.6	1.0	51 627
14–17	86.2	8.6	3.6	0.7	0.9	240 980
18–20	85.8	7.3	5.4	0.7	0.8	203 981
21 and over	87.5	6.9	3.8	0.9	0.9	781 673
Total	87.0	7.3	4.0	0.8	0.9	1 278 261
Cautioned						
under 14	88.0	6.0	3.0	1.0	2.0	26 149
14–17	87.0	6.0	4.0	1.0	2.0	59 212
18–20	86.0	5.0	6.0	1.0	2.0	24 176
21 and over	87.0	5.0	4.0	1.0	2.0	70 672
Total	87.0	6.0	4.0	1.0	2.0	1 80 209

Source: Home Office 2000.

Table 6.3 Prison population by ethnic group, age and sentence length 1999–2000, England and Wales

	White	Black	Asian	Other	Not Known	Total (100%)
By age group						
15–17	79.7	15.4	2.0	2.8	0	2 437
18–20	80.9	13.2	3.0	2.8	0	7 908
21–24	80.7	11.8	3.8	3.7	0	11 448
25–29	82.0	10.8	3.6	3.6	0	12 896
30+	81.2	13.0	2.5	3.5	0	29 867
Total	81.2	12.5	3.0	3.5	0	64 529
By sentence length for young offenders*						
Up to 12 months	89.2	5.9	2.5	2.6	0	2 012
Over 12 months	78.8	15.8	3.1	2.3	0	6 317
All young offenders	81.3	13.4	3.1	2.3	0	8 329

* The term young offender has no legal definition but generally refers to a young person between 10 and 20 years old who has been found guilty of an offence.

Source: Home Office 2000.

invidious, like all powerful ideologies contains an element of practical truth but one, it must be emphasised, that has nothing to do with 'racial' characteristics, criminogenic cultures or pathological family structures. Talk of 'black' crime too is a misnomer. Rather, the acute criminalisation of young black people represents one particular aspect of the political pursuit of austerity directed at the young in general.

That this response should involve a turn towards crime is not an inevitable consequence of hardship or discrimination, since there is certainly no simple or mechanical relationship between deprivation, prejudice and youth crime. Clear indication of this is provided by the obvious fact that not all black young people are criminal, rates of self-reported criminal activity among young black people are often not much higher than those for whites and, historically, Asian young people display lower rates of criminalisation, despite experiencing similar levels of discrimination and social stress (Smith 1997). For young Asians in particular, the experience of austerity is often mediated in ways that help preclude delinquent solutions; although this too may now be unravelling. Nevertheless, for many the turn to crime represents a more or less rational response to the specific experiences of second and third generation immigrants from Africa and the Caribbean. Their high degree of institutional, cultural and formal assimilation has actually underlined the persistence of deeply entrenched exclusionary practices in British society, ones that have consistently confined aspirations for a good education, decent jobs, affordable housing and responsive public services within discriminatory forms. Thus the rise in rates of criminal activity was neither an inevitable nor necessary expression of the crisis of black youth. It was as Lea and Young argue, the 'creation of those black youths who had assimilated, yet at the same time seen themselves rejected by British society through racial discrimination and deprivation' (1984: 129).

The rise (and rise?) of the young criminal

It must also be emphasised that the criminalisation of black young people is one specific manifestation of a much more generalised recomposition of youth. As we have noted earlier, increased rates of criminal activity among black young people initially made their presence felt, albeit in a highly distorted form, during the early 1970s but the first significant increase in the number of known young offenders during the post-war period predates this by over a decade. This increase in rates of juvenile offending, in turn mirrors more general patterns in recorded rates of offending which, from the middle of the 1950s onwards, demonstrate a remarkable capacity for growth; one incidentally replicated throughout most of the developed capitalist world (Young 1999). Between 1955 and 1964 the total rate of recorded offences doubled, then doubled again over the following decade and from 1974 to 1990 doubled once more. Taken together, this represents about a tenfold increase from half a million to 5 million recorded crimes per annum across a period of 35 years, with average annual increases running at about 8–10 per cent (Maguire 1997). Changes to recording procedures and to public perceptions of crime undoubtedly explain elements of this increase but it is generally accepted that crime grew significantly throughout most of the post-war period. Further support for this also comes from the study of victims. The British Crime Survey (BCS) shows a broadly similar trend since its inception in 1982, although at a gentler rate of increase of around 4 per cent per annum.

The pattern of recorded youth crime shown by official estimates generally mirrors the aggregate trend, at least until the middle of the 1980s. Prevalence rates among young males – that is recorded rates per 100 000 of the population aged between 10 and 17 years old – increased significantly from the middle of the 1960s to the middle of the 1970s, after which they dropped a little before rising again to earlier levels by 1985 (Newburn 1997). After this period we witness a significant drop in rates of offending between young people aged 10 and 17, from a total of 172 700 males and 40 700 females in 1985 to 100 200 males and 29 300 females by 1993. These later reductions need qualification, since they are more likely a consequence of changes to policing practices than an indication of significant changes in behaviour (see later). As Farrington argued at the time, given the significant increases in general rates of recorded crime across the same period, it 'seems likely that real juvenile offending has continued to increase since then [1985], despite the decline in official figures, which is almost certainly an illusion caused by changes in police policies' (1992: 157).

This pattern of steadily rising crime rates throughout most of the last half of the twentieth century underlines the complex relationship between social change and youth crime and delinquency. Clearly, the first steep rises in recorded crime predate the state imposition of austerity by around 15 to 20 years, thus limiting the value of explanations that reduce youth crime to a simple effect of unemployment. Of course, youth unemployment defines the context: one simply has to consider how the incarcerated, those deemed to have offended seriously enough to warrant a custodial sentence, 'are overwhelmingly young, male, socially and economically disadvantaged, repetitive property offenders' (Morgan 1997: 1151) to recognise this. Studies of young offenders also consistently show the experience of acute levels of social and economic deprivation, usually accompanied by intense family and personal distress: 'As soon as faces and histories are given to the young people who are steadily filling our prisons, one is left with an overwhelming sense of hopelessness and wretchedness of their prospects' (Helena Kennedy, quoted in Goldson 1997a: 82). It is also clear that youth unemployment has brought clear public order implications, since it is marginalised youth who have featured most heavily in both the inner city riots of the early 1980s (Kettle and Hodges 1982) and the disturbances on peripheral council housing estates during the early 1990s. As one study of the latter concluded, 'the places where disorders happened in the early 1990s were most often large, marginal and low income council estates with a poor reputation, high unemployment and extremely large populations of children and young people, often with lone parents' (Power and Tunstall 1997: 12). But it is in its role as the most acute demonstration of a much broader series of shifts in the distribution of income and wealth (see Chapter 5) that unemployment remains of central importance (e.g. Crow et al. 1989; Box 1987; Lea and Young 1984).

For Young (1999), an understanding of the dynamics of relative deprivation is central to explaining the apparent paradox of rising crime rates in periods of both relative affluence and austerity. On the one hand, the promise of inclusivity offered by the social democratic commitment to full employment and an expanded citizenship not only proved illusory, but also intensified the contradiction between working-class aspirations and the limits to these imposed by post-war development. The continuing inability to satisfy such aspirations not only brought into sharp relief the profoundly ideological claim that capitalism could be humanised, but also fuelled the resort to crime and delinquency as a more frequent means for their satisfaction. On the other hand, Young argues that this heightened sense of relative deprivation was transformed as boom turned to bust. New forms of social exclusion – in the labour market and community, through divisions of class, age, ethnicity and gender – combined with the emergence of an aggressive individualism, to further intensify levels of working class discontent and frustrated aspirations in the context of an aggressive consumer capitalism. As Downes and Rock astutely note, 'rising aspirations for consumption combined with falling expectations of productive employment lead to a particularly corrosive sense of exclusion' (1995: 177).

Welfare and the inclusion of the young offender

Notions of exclusion also have value as a means of understanding the restructuring of youth justice that accompanied this criminalisation of youth. Radical accounts often tend to locate the restructuring of youth justice within a process of ideological conflict, in which the emergence of a 'welfare' model after the Second World War gradually gave way during the 1970s to an approach based upon the restoration of 'justice'. As Goldson points out, 'the constructs of "welfare" and "justice" have served to delineate the conceptual space within which policy and practice relative to juvenile crime has traditionally been located' (1997a: 58). However, the 'space' articulated by each was not so much a product of the conceptual world but of deeper political forces. As Young (1999) asserts, the 'welfare' approach expressed the development of a complex array of institutional means for the management of offending, at whose centre were attempts at inclusion and assimilation. Through newly created cadres of technocrats and welfare professionals, the causes of crime could be identified, problems of family and community addressed and young delinquents brought within an administrative framework geared towards a greater degree of support and rehabilitation. It is in part the political costs incurred by such a strategy that explains its subsequent demise. Evident in the growing rates of offending examined later, the practical failures of the inclusive strategy saw governments increasingly keen to remove themselves politically from the direct responsibilities they had assumed for the management of young people's behaviour. Expressed in terms of justice and the neutral rule of law, the previous search for the aetiology of crime was abandoned, deterrence and punishment replaced reform and rehabilitation, cost-effectiveness and efficiency were brought to the fore and young offenders were subject to a growing range of institutional measures increasingly directed at their physical separation and exclusion.

Despite its deepening crisis, the inclusive strategy for young offenders did embody the basis for a rational response to youth offending. Criminality was to be addressed through a planned response that acknowledged some relationship between the costs of capitalist development and the persistence of crime in the 'affluent society' of the 1960s. Young delinquents were viewed as a problem of progress, one that could be solved through managed full employment and rising standards of living, and through the provision of legitimate means of upward social mobility via an expanded education. For those unable or unwilling to keep up with the pace of social and economic change, an eclectic and ill-defined group of youth professionals, ranging from youth and social workers, teachers, educationalists through to career officers, civil servants, sociologists, psychologists and criminologists, were given responsibility for identifying problems and implementing 'solutions'. As Pitts (1988) points out, however, in line with the broader thrust of social democratic thinking these 'solutions' ultimately rested upon notions of a culturally retarded working class. As with the debate about education (see Chapter 2), it was working-class conservatism, the preference for immediate gratification, low expectations, a constricting fatalism and the failure to adequately socialise offspring that took the blame for rising youth offending. If young people could thus be provided with the personal means and professional assistance necessary to transcend the limits of their constricting family circumstances, then the accompanying status frustration which was seen to underpin much criminal behaviour could be channelled through lawful means.

This inclusive strategy was most fully expressed through the 1969 Children and Young Person's Act (CYPA), which became law in the final year of Harold Wilson's Labour Government. The lasting importance of the CYPA 1969 lies in its attempt to blur the boundaries between the young offender as criminal and as someone in need of care and support. At its heart was a rise in the age of criminal responsibility to 14, a measure that if implemented would have immediately decriminalised a significant proportion of youth offending. It also sought to end custodial provision for young people through the development of a comprehensive system of non-criminal care proceedings. Juvenile Courts, first established 60 years earlier, were retained as a last resort for a minority of the most persistent and serious young offenders, but the Act intended to replace the majority of criminal proceedings with new structures based upon principles of care. The circumstances under which a young person could be brought to court were restricted and the Act aimed to replace incarceration in detention centres, borstals and attendance centres, with new programmes of Intermediate Treatment (IT) in the community. If implemented in full for young people under 14 years old, the CYPA 1969 would have effectively abolished criminal prosecution in all cases except for homicide, placed extensive restrictions on the use of court proceedings and placed the majority of young offenders aged 14 to 16 under the care and supervision of social workers.

The CYPA 1969 has been described as both 'the high watermark and exhaustion of social democratic reform' (Pitts 1996: 256). That it embodied elements of a rational and progressive attempt to address the growing problem of youth offending is certain, even if the Act never enjoyed widespread support. 'Even when welfarism's influence was at its height, therefore, the basis for a counter offensive against it, and in favour of a much harsher and more regressive response to young offenders, continued to exist' (Davies 1986: 75). In fact, the Act signalled not just the end of the line for the strategy of inclusion, it also marked the beginning of its retreat. In the decision to retain a residual role for Juvenile Courts, the Act actually recoiled from proposals contained in a White Paper published four years earlier, in which Juvenile Courts were to be replaced with more consensual Family Councils. Furthermore, with the victory of the Edward Heath's Conservatives at the 1970 General Election, only parts of the Act were ever implemented. Indeed, Heath was quick to drop the most developed welfare elements contained in the Act, by rejuvenating notions of justice as the means to both deter and penalise the most serious young offenders; retaining many of the powers of the police and magistracy; maintaining the age of criminal responsibility at 10 years old; and by reprieving the anticipated demise of detention centres, borstals and attendance centres (Brown 1998).

Restating the rule of law

When explaining the demise of the strategy of inclusion, considerable importance is often given the politicisation of crime that gathered pace throughout the late 1960s and early 1970s. In particular, the progressive erosion of the link between social conditions, 'need' and youth offending and the growing clamour for law and order, are then interpreted as evidence of the power of neo-Conservative ideology over social democratic pragmatism (Pitts 1988); or of the beginnings of a concerted (and largely successful) effort to shift popular anxieties over crime in a more authoritarian direction (Goldson 1997a; Hall *et al.* 1978). In respect of both, however, the undoubted increased ideological importance attached to youth crime to emerge around this time provided not so much the dynamic for change as confirmation of practical failures. On the one hand, attempts to assimilate young offenders had become less tenable as the upward trend in youth crime accelerated in the context of faltering growth, crisis and recession. On the other hand, the growing ideological power of the turn to justice, law and order derived its power from the practical changes to the administration of young offenders already set in motion. Even at its height in 1969, a social democratic government was already looking to extricate itself from the most pronounced welfare aspects of its policy for young offenders.

Initial steps in this direction were limited. To begin with, governments confined themselves to extending the capacity to punish through criminal sanctions aimed at the 'hardcore' of persistent and/or serious young offender, those deemed unable or unwilling to respond to welfare-based initiatives or whose crimes were considered grave enough to merit detention. In doing so, the return to court proceedings and the resurrection of strategies of punishment and custody as the core principle of youth justice, represented the official abandonment of one of the fundamental principles of the 1969 CYPA: ending custodial provision for all offenders under the age of 17. Moreover, what the Conservatives under Edward Heath initiated gathered further momentum with the re-election of Labour in 1974.

Not only was Labour prepared to dance to tunes emanating from the right wing of the Conservative Party and more populist sections of the media, 'although there was a change in government in 1974 the policies and initiatives of the Heath administration were not seriously modified by the Labour administrations of Wilson and Callaghan in the period of 1974 to 1979' (Pitts 1988: 32). Indeed, on returning to power Labour's refusal to implement its own legislation passed five years earlier clearly signalled that the commitment to addressing welfare needs as the basis for a rational programme for young offenders was dead.

As a broad-based strategy the commitment to the assimilation of young offenders was clearly in its death throes, but this did not mean a complete repudiation. In a process of bifurcation, welfare-based responses not only survived but were consolidated into the principal means for managing young offenders, certainly as far as their coverage and scope were concerned. Those parts of the CYPA 1969 that were implemented actually extended the power of social services departments over young offenders, as the use of care orders, supervision orders and IT programmes became more frequent. As a consequence, not only did the influence of the youth justice system undergo a marked expansion, but also young people found themselves drawn into a more finely graded net of surveillance and control. Social workers in particular were given considerable discretion to undertake preventative work with 'pre-delinquents' (i.e. those deemed 'at risk' than convicted of offending) and their families, carry out invasive investigations and influence court disposals (which often had the impact of accelerating a young person's progress up the tariff of sentencing options). In summarising the expansion of IT programmes during the 1970s, Haines and Drakeford comment how 'the zealous pursuit of treatment and of young people to treatment programmes was a major defining characteristic of this period' (1998: 39).

The implications of this were especially severe for girls and young women. In extending the influence of the state beyond a straightforward concern with criminality, welfare became the basis for enforcing 'gender-appropriate' forms of behaviour, particularly in cases of supposed 'moral danger'. The need to 'protect' through early preventative 'treatment' meant that more girls found themselves under formal supervision, often for minor offences or simply for non-conventional forms of behaviour (Worrall 1997). Girls thus became more susceptible to criminal justice proceedings for offences that if committed by boys may have been ignored or dealt with informally. Custody was also often given for conviction of less serious offences and with the possession of fewer previous convictions. Girls were also more likely to be taken into local authority care or committed to approved schools in the name of their care and protection, often before it had been proved that they had fallen into criminal ways.

Exclusion, justice and law and order

To view the general election of 1979 as a 'turning point' for youth justice is therefore something of an overstatement. The election of Margaret Thatcher's first Conservative government, often regarded as the dawning of a new populist and more belligerent phase for youth justice, in reality initially extended the framework put in place during the decade before. The Conservatives did up the ante through their cynical exploitation of popular anxieties over youth crime and ideological conversion to the rule of law. But to equate this conversion with the final triumph of a reactionary media or the misguided theoretical proclivities of a few doctrinaire academics and 'crank' politicians is to ignore its deeper political roots. Indeed, Thatcher's conviction on law and order signalled not so much its ideological coherence or ability to redefine popular aspirations around a new authoritarian agenda (cf. Hall *et al.* 1978). On the contrary, this growing ideological power was a *consequence* of the deepening crisis of the previous strategy of inclusion, expressed most immediately through rising crime rates as the economy lurched deeper into recession. Moreover, it was also the case that the law and order die had already been cast. By the time Thatcher assumed governing power, greater resort to the rule of law was already an established practice as governments looked to distance themselves politically from the previous responsibilities they had assumed for directly addressing young people's offending behaviour.

It may have been the case that Labour had been unenthusiastic converts to a law and order agenda, but it was within this framework that Margaret Thatcher's government intended to operate. As one contemporary commentator observed, 'the dominant feature of narrow Conservative "law and order" policy is its basic continuity with the policies of the last Labour Government, even while masquerading as a tough new broom' (Kettle 1983: 220). The much trumpeted 1979 General Election pledge to get tough with young offenders by creating harsher regimes in detention centres was limited to an 'experiment' in two institutions. Through a short but intensive spell of hard work, discipline, respect for authority and physical exercise, the aim was to both punish and deter the young delinquent. Both 'short, sharp shock' experiments were nevertheless rapidly exposed as failures by the Home Office's own research (Newburn 1997). Even so, this regime was extended to all detention centres after 1985 before its ignominious abandonment three years later. 'Amidst a growing chorus of complaint about ineffectiveness, excessive cost, ill-treatment, self injury and inmate suicides from penal reform organisations and most significantly from the Magistrate's Association, the experiments in "short, sharp shock" were formally abolished in 1988' (Muncie 1997: 294).

In any case, detention centres had become less important and by the middle of the 1980s were operating with considerable excess capacity. Accelerating the by now firmly established policy of bifurcation – custody for the 'hardcore', community service for the remainder – the Conservative's first attempt to legislate on law and order, the 1982 Criminal Justice Act (CJA), had given magistrates further discretion in sentencing. In what has been described as, 'the most rapid growth in the custody of young people in British history' (Pitts 1996: 266), far from endorsing the 'short, sharp shock', magistrates took government at its word by using new powers to by-pass the detention centres in favour of imposing the longer sentences available in youth custody centres, the successor to the borstal. At the same time, the 1982 CJA also consolidated the place of diversionary measures. The Act strengthened powers of caution and placed limits on the conditions under which magistrates could impose custody or residential care on first time offenders. Following the Act, custody could only result if a young offender was a threat to public safety, had committed a serious offence or where s/he was unwilling or unable to respond to non-custodial alternatives. This was strengthened the following year, when new funds were made available from the then Department of Health and Social Security for the extension and development of new programmes of intensive IT.

Bifurcation continued over the following decade, albeit in a modified form. The 1988 CJA further tightened the criteria under which custodial court disposals could be implemented and diversionary measures were again strengthened. The Act also formalised much existing practice through implementing a sentencing policy of 'just deserts'. Through just deserts, serious young offenders were to be subject to the 'neutral' rule of law, in which the sentence would 'fit' the crime. The rule of law was further imposed upon welfare provision the following year, when the Children Act 1989 replaced the application of potentially indeterminate care orders with a new policy of determinate sentencing, while responsibility for civil care proceedings were removed from the criminal

court (Muncie 1997). By the time of the CJA 1991, the policy of bifurcation had culminated with the open acknowledgement that prison did
not work as a general response to youth crime. The Act reinforced the
move away from custodial provision for all but the most serious offenders, re-emphasised and formalised the role of police cautioning (even for
repeat offenders) and replaced the Juvenile Court with the Youth Court[2]
for young offenders and the Family Proceedings Court (for young
people subject to welfare interventions) (Goldson 1997b).

The 1991 CJA also modified non-custodial provision. If young offenders were to remain in the community, it was argued, then their punishment, supervision and policing needed to be more effective. Already, the
1984 Police and Criminal Evidence Act strengthened the powers of the
police to stop and search suspected criminals and the Public Order Act
1985 gave the police new powers to deal with public disorder. The 1991
CJA added further possibilities for community-based punishment, formally re-designating them 'community sentences', and sought to extend
the principles of diversion from custody for the majority of young
offenders to young adult offenders aged 17 to 21. The Act also gave magistrates greater influence in specifying the detail of community disposals
by allowing the imposition of such conditions as electronic monitoring,
curfews, community service orders and residential requirements.

This period, especially between 1985 and 1993, is sometimes
referred to as a 'quiet' or 'successful revolution' in youth justice, in
which pragmatism was ultimately the winner (e.g. Newburn 1997).
Pragmatic they certainly were, but these developments also contained
a good deal of opportunism and expediency, and any successes were
more likely a consequence of good fortune than a result of rational calculation. Recorded rates of youth crime certainly fell during the late
1980s and early 1990s, and the proportion of young offenders aged 14
to 17 years old sentenced to immediate custody fell steadily between
1983 and 1990 (Muncie 1997). But the Conservatives were greatly
aided in this by a significant decrease in the youth cohort and changes
to methods of policing (as noted earlier). Of course, the merits in keeping as many young people out of custody cannot be denied, but this
was primarily an expedient, where 'prosecution is costly and the
juvenile justice system unpredictable' (Brown 1998: 67).

Imposing the rule of law

Like all expedients, the strategy for young offenders rested on shaky
foundations, which by the end of the 1980s, were already looking

precarious. The bursting of the 'bubble' created by the 'boom' of the late 1980s and the third-deep recession within a period of 15 years, further aggravated well-entrenched popular anxieties over delinquent youth (see Chapter 3). To some degree there was good reason for this concern. The surge again in youth unemployment, the ossification of long-term unemployment into something of a characteristic feature of late twentieth century British capitalism, and greater job insecurity all contributed to the sharp increase in levels of recorded crime between 1989 and 1992 alone. In addition to this, the spectre of the 'hardcore' young offender once again loomed large over youth justice and the severe deterioration in the prospects of many young people were most dramatically evident in widely publicised shows of youthful disobedience. In spite of never matching the ferocity of the inner city riots a decade earlier, between 1991 and 1995 there were at least 28 serious outbreaks of violence and civil disorder in British towns and cities. Hard-pressed council estates suffering decades of neglect 'made for a dangerous combination of large numbers of out-of-work young males with no stake in society, living in low income, work-poor households, in areas suffering from high social stigma' (Power and Tunstall 1997: ix).

This lurch upwards in recorded crime presented a number of practical problems. One central difficulty was how to reconcile the significant increase in youth crime with the turn towards the rule of law. The answer to emerge from the beginning of the 1990s, sought to locate the problem not in the withdrawal of substantive sources of support, most clearly evident in widening divisions between young and old, rich and poor or black and white. Rather, blame was apportioned to the administrative structures of the state. Expressed through an amalgam of social Darwinism and cycle of dependency arguments (Murray 1992), both of which had long been discredited (see also Chapter 5), the cause of youth crime was more firmly identified with the malign influence of the interventionist welfare state. Reform and modification were thus not enough. Now only the root and branch restructuring of youth justice and the resort to a more unequivocal role for the law, could the problem of youth offending be contained and the conditions for law and order re-established.

The importance of arguments like Murray's underclass thesis (cf. MacDonald 1997) thus lies not so much in its role as harbinger of change, but in the ideological coherence it gave to a number of emergent themes. By the time the 1991 CJA was implemented, bifurcation was clearly under pressure and was then eclipsed by a further CJA in 1993. Through the Act, the rule of law was consolidated through a range of new custodial sentences, the criteria around which custody could be imposed were loosened and new powers introduced to deal with the 'hardcore' of (very) young offenders. In a statement of intent, the then Home Secretary Michael Howard claimed that 'prison works' to the Conservative Party Conference in the autumn of 1993. The following year, the Criminal Justice and Public Order Act (CJPO) 1994 marked a sharp intensification of the legal regulation of youth, most notoriously through its attempts to criminalise rave culture (McKay 1996). The Act also accelerated the use of custody for younger offenders, through announcing a new secure training order for 12 to 14 year olds and the construction of five new centres in which to house them. Powers were also given to the courts to detain children aged 10 to 13 in custody for longer periods, a recommendation only previously available for 14 to 17 year olds, and increased the maximum sentence available for 15 to 17 year olds. Conditions on which a young person could be released on bail were tightened, the requirement for pre-court social inquiry reports loosened and provision was made to bind over the parents of persistent offenders. Although rates of youth crime fell once again from the middle of the 1990s, this time there was also a sharp increase in the use of custody for young offenders (NACRO 2000).

The marked intensification of the exclusionary potential of youth justice provision, defined the Conservative's last three years in power. In 1994, the 'short, sharp shock' for young offenders was once again disinterred only this time in the form of the 'boot camp': US-style young offender institutions run according to a harsh regime of military-style discipline and physical exercise. There were also proposals, later enacted by New Labour (see Chapter 7), to literally militarise the detainment of some groups of young offenders by placing them in military 'glass houses'. The consolidation of the exclusionary strategy was also evident in another American import, the much-publicised policy of 'zero tolerance'. By emphatically rejecting low spectrum quality of life offences like graffiti, petty vandalism, incivility, begging, busking or rough sleeping, it was argued that the resulting culture of intolerance would lead to a virtuous circle that would eventually embrace much more serious types of offending. Superficially plausible, zero-tolerance in the United States in fact proved inconclusive, with no discernible relationship between its adoption and changes to the crime rates of a number of US cities (Young 1999). Nevertheless, it was ostensibly to support such an objective that one of the Conservative's final legislative pieces, the Crime Sentences Act 1997, introduced mandatory sentences for certain offences, extended the use of electronic tagging, introduced curfew orders and allowed the naming and shaming of persistent young offenders.

Conclusion

Thus the changing state of youth was simultaneously expressed in terms of a crisis of youth crime. Against the backdrop of the political endorsement of deepening unemployment, the re-regulation of the youth labour market and the political pursuit of inequality, more and more young people found themselves excluded from participation in the mainstream institutions of social and economic life. With opportunities for meaningful work scarce, the experience of periodic or long-term unemployment endemic and aspirations repeatedly confounded by deeply engrained sources of discrimination, young people's resort to crime and delinquency expanded to an unprecedented degree. For young working-class males, young black people and for growing numbers of girls and young women, the self-conscious decision of successive governments to withdrawn significant elements of their previous access to and command over meaningful sources of support, expressed itself in a sustained and expansive process of criminalisation.

Alongside this process of criminalisation came significant shifts in the relationship between the state and the young delinquent. Under the social democratic commitment to progressive reform and a humane capitalism, the state took on a greater deal of direct responsibility for the administration of young offenders, most clearly embodied in the political commitment to their inclusion and assimilation. Expressed through a practical strategy of reform, guidance and support, it was hoped that the imperatives of post-war development could be reconciled with continuing demands for social order, through the rehabilitation of young offenders. We thus witness throughout the first decades after the Second World War, a steady expansion of state activity into the lives of young people directed towards the treatment, support and welfare of young delinquents and, increasingly, those deemed 'at risk' of offending behaviour. Through attention to the causes of youth crime, problems of family and community life, the propensity of the young to offend could be tackled at root source in a rational and co-ordinated programme of action. As we have also seen, however, this strategy of inclusion proved ultimately unsuccessful. Not only did rates of youth offending continue to rise to the point where they were approaching crisis levels, in undertaking such an interventionist strategy governments were also faced with a deepening series of political problems. By taking direct responsibility for the youth offending, governments were also faced with the potential costs of failure.

In response to the political problems posed by the inclusive strategy, governments sought to repudiate their earlier commitments to the welfare of children and young offenders. Expressed through a progressive turn to the 'anonymous' rule of law as the principal means to manage the political problem of youth offending, from the middle of the 1970s governments set about the destruction of the institutional forms of the inclusive strategy and their reconstruction around new modes directed at exclusion. Through justice, punishment, law and order, the state set about systematically recomposing young people's lives through new forms of state activity directed towards confining young people's behaviour more fully within the rule of law. Of course, in the same way that the re-regulation of the youth labour market was an inherently political act, so too was the resort to the rule of law. Initiated by a Labour government facing rapidly escalating levels of youth crime, by the time of the Conservative's election in 1979 the framework for managing young offenders through a strategy of exclusion had already been put in place. It was not until over another decade later, however, that a more fundamental assault on the structure of youth justice began. The continuation of welfare-based provision in the form of community-orientated programmes was progressively curtailed and then re-designated as community sentences. As significantly, the capacity of the criminal justice system to punish the young through incarceration and exclusion, from an ever earlier age, was greatly strengthened.

Both the welfare and justice strategies were profoundly ideological, although the former did embody the basis for rational and planned response to the problem of youth offending. That the justice model is profoundly ideological is without doubt; the return to a supposedly law and order agenda, harsher sentencing options and more punitive non-custodial forms of 'treatment' and punishment have provided even less of a rational foundation for addressing rising levels of youth crime than the policy of inclusion and assimilation it replaced. Evaluated on its own terms the return to exclusion, law and order has been a spectacular failure. Crime rates continued to rise, expenditure on youth justice and policing increased and the fear of crime deepened.

CHAPTER 7

A New State of Youth?

In returning to power after 18 years in opposition, the first New Labour government (1997–2001) made much of its 'youthful' credentials. Promising to tackle the neglect of the Conservative years, Tony Blair committed a Labour government to renewal and regeneration by quite literally rejuvenating a country grown weary under the disastrous impact of nearly two decades of neo-liberalism. With the relative youth of its leading figures on the one hand and the youngest Prime Minister for nearly 200 years on the other, New Labour's stated aim was to remould Britain into a 'young country', one confident in its own vitality and secure in its ability to compete with the best.

Youth was also significant for New Labour in another, more substantive way. Contra the assertions of the post-modernists, and their misplaced proclamations of youth's demise, between the general election victories of 1997 and 2001 New Labour attributed to youth a new-found political importance. A priority from the outset, youth repeatedly featured in a number of distinctive and sometimes interrelated initiatives that appeared to give youth a previously unseen political coherence. It is no small irony that what Davies (1986) warned (prematurely?) as the beginnings of a 'national youth policy' in the ascent of the New Right, only perhaps began to take on something deserving such a description with the return of Labour to governing power.

As well as displaying a readiness to acknowledge the divisions that had opened up between the young and the old, and *between* different categories of young people, New Labour also appeared willing to consider the problems of youth in innovative ways. A case in point has been the work of the Social Exclusion Unit (SEU), or what Coles dubs a 'surrogate Ministry for Youth' (2000a: 202). Set up within a few weeks of the 1997 General Election and answerable directly to the Prime Minister, the activities of the SEU within the first Blair government had a distinctly 'youthful' orientation. Four SEU reports – on truancy and school exclusion (1998), teenage pregnancy (1999), Status Zer0 (1999) and young runaways (2001) – were explicitly directed at pressing problems of youth, and two more – rough sleeping (1998) and community renewal (1998) – possessed a clear youthful theme. In line with New Labour's commitment to rejuvenation, the Unit's brief was to promote an understanding of the key characteristics of social exclusion, to generate solutions, encourage cooperation, disseminate best practice and, where necessary, make recommendations for practical interventions. For the young, its novelty appeared to lie in the power to innovate and to step outside of the conventional preoccupations of 'youth policy', to overcome the bureaucratic constraints and limited horizons of government departments and, above all, to promote 'joined-up' solutions – across ministries, local government, voluntary organisations and the private sector – to the 'joined-up' problems of English[1] youth (Mizen 2003a).

Early comment on the work of the SEU was often positive. In a sober and broadly sympathetic analysis Coles concluded that, 'if the SEU is indeed a "rough beast" set loose on government departments to produce coherence in youth policy ... then the government is to be given at least two-and-a-half cheers' (2000b: 107). Plaudits like this are in one sense well directed. Labour's determination to take seriously the sometimes devastating problems faced by the young – whether manifest in unemployment, poor skills and qualifications, housing problems, dependence upon benefits, family disintegration, drugs or crime – certainly marked a notable point of departure with the past. Through the SEU, New Labour underlined its broader programme of moving beyond the monetarists' political reconstitution of youth within the meticulous pursuit of market relations. In New Labour there has been the clear view that markets alone are neither equitable nor efficient and that when pursued with the conviction of the zealot, inevitably lead to levels of social dislocation extending well beyond the private sorrows of the few.

These concessions notwithstanding, New Labour's politics of youth has not been 'new' in the way that those such as Coles believe. For sure, New Labour rejected the blind faith in markets, conceded that the naked pursuit of market relations wreaked damage upon individuals, families and communities, and accepted a degree of culpability on the part of (previous) government in the creation of this new and exclusionary state of youth. But the political strategy that gained ascendancy within the Labour Party towards the end of the 1980s and which culminated with Blair's accession to Party Leader in 1994 (Hay 1999), marks a distinctive expansion of the exclusionary strategies that have now dominated the politics of youth for over a quarter of a century.

Under New Labour, as this chapter argues, young people's rights over and claims to key sources of support continued to be eroded.

Such a conclusion is not a self-evident one, particularly when promises to heal the divisions scarring British society were central in securing New Labour its huge parliamentary majority at the 1997 General Election. Whatever else it may have signified, New Labour's victory did capitalise upon the considerable popular discontent generated by two decades of monetarist restructuring. Cuts to unemployment, tackling inequalities, creating skilled jobs, pursuing decent wages, improving education, raising living standards, improving public services and reducing crime and delinquency, where all high-profile elements of Labour's election campaign. Moreover, aspirations like these would not have been out of place in the programmes of previous Labour governments. Harold Wilson's faith in education as a means to unlock the potential of technological innovation (see Chapter 2), for instance, would sit comfortably with what Thompson has termed New Labour's conversion to 'supply-side socialism' and its determination, 'to increase the flow, enhance the quality and improve the use of factor inputs; the primary objective being to increase productive efficiency, reduce unit costs and, crucially, to enhance Britain's international competitiveness' (Thompson 1996: 39). The principle difference, however, emerges from the extent to which this supply-side socialism reproduces the monetarist faith in markets as the principle method for organising social relations, to the point that Labour's traditional commitment to inclusion and concession as a prime motivation for capturing state power has been displaced. Themes of social justice, co-operation and cohesion all have a legitimate place in the political lexicon of New Labour. A number of important palliatives, as we shall see, have been forthcoming. But the motivation for tackling the costs of social dislocation are not to be found in terms of a political programme that sets out to reclaim and rejuvenate the social democratic commitment to concession, incorporation and inclusion. Rather, it is the political pursuit of market efficiency that articulates the terms of New Labour's governing programme. Or as champions of the so-called 'Third Way' would have it, '... investment in human capital wherever possible rather than the direct provision of economic need. In place of the welfare state we should put the social investment state, operating in the context of a positive welfare society' (Giddens 1998: 117).

Put another way, the neo-liberal 'austere competitiveness' that sought to reconstitute social relations within criteria governed by money and the market, has been replaced with the 'progressive competitiveness' of the Third Way (Coates 2000). In this respect, New Labour's Third Way seems to have incorporated important lessons from the past. If the substance of supply-side socialism carries with it palpable similarities with many of the policies developed during the 1980s and 1990s, the Third Way nevertheless constitutes a new and powerful strategy for the political management of social relations (Burnham 2001). On the one hand, it has served to distance New Labour from its own political inheritance and the realisation that the politics of inclusion, expressed most forcibly through the Keynesian welfare state, was inherently unstable. A return to the social democratic politics of inclusion it is not. On the other hand, it has also allowed Labour to develop new ways of legitimising its own distinctive brand of market-led 'solutions' to the problems of British capitalism. The Third Way's critique of the social consequences of free markets, for example, rests ultimately upon an acceptance of the legitimacy of free markets. The problem is reduced to a series of technical issues concerned with tackling waste and promoting efficiency. Furthermore, New Labour's rejection of the pursuit of untrammelled market relations as the sole object of governing power runs quickly into an insistence on the inevitability of globalisation, while all the time failing to concede the active role of government in the restructuring of social relations on terms more favourable to market forces (Levitas 1998). For reasons like these, like monetarism before it New Labour's Third Way is profoundly ideological. But, like monetarism too, the considerable power of this ideology lies in its ability to capitalise on changes to the form of the state and to practical developments in policy.

Seen in this light, New Labour's apparent 'youthfulness' is not as benign as it makes out. Neither is it quite so new. To return to the example of the SEU, it was not just its skeleton staff or the absence of new resources that marked off the modesty of its aspirations, nor a *modus operandi* that demanded all new initiatives produce a net decline in public expenditure over the long-term. Rather, the SEU provided one focus for Labour's more general determination to re-frame youth and its attendant problems within the terms dictated by supply-side socialism and the politics of the Third Way. The importance of youth to the SEU was not a consequence of youth's dubious honour of being one of the biggest categories of losers under the previous politics of exclusion. If need was a determining factor, we should have expected to see in the work of the SEU a comparable interest in the plight of the pensioner poor or the chronically sick and disabled.

No such comparable interest was evident. Nor did the government's 'youthfulness' provide an example of the belated discovery of the urgent need to support young people's 'transitions to adult life'. On the contrary, such a conspicuous absence underlined New Labour's determination to redefine the problems of youth within its own political strategy of 'progressive competitiveness'.

Another New Deal

A case in point is New Labour's 'flagship' first-term policy, the New Deal for the young long-term unemployed (NDYP). While it may be convenient to see in the SEU a ministry of youth in waiting, the guiding force behind what perhaps may be seen as the defining 'youth policy' of the first New Labour government came from more the familiar sources of the Treasury and then Department for Education and Employment. One of New Labour's key pledges for the first term and the government's only commitment to new expenditure, from April 1998 its choice of four options for young people aged 18 to 24 and unemployed for six months or longer sought to differentiate the programme from the failed mass palliatives of the past. Its Gateway period, lasting up to four months, offered entrants a combination of personal advice and counselling designed to promote 'job readiness' (Department of Social Security 1998a) and preferably direct entry into a job. Failure to find a job through Gateway meant a New Deal option: a subsidised job usually in the private sector and for which employers receive a £60 per week government subsidy; a place on the newly created Environmental Task Force or in a voluntary sector organisation, paid at benefit plus £15 per week; or for the unqualified a place on an education or training course leading to qualification at National Vocational Qualification (NVQ) Level 2. Famously, there was no 'fifth option' of remaining unemployed.[2]

NDYP certainly enjoyed considerable and widespread support and it is easy to see why. Initially funded to the tune of £2.6 billion, later revised downwards to £1.5 billion, drawn from over £5 billion raised by a 'windfall' tax on the huge profits generated by the privatised utilities, meant NDYP had an undeniable redistributional quality. Such relative generosity also underlined the drive for much needed quality, an objective further supported by the substance given to its guidance and counselling function rather than the 'processing-by-numbers' approach characteristic of its predecessors. Participants on one of the four options were guaranteed mandatory training, full protection under health and safety legislation and later, where appropriate, inclusion in the National Minimum Wage (NMW). To cap it all, NDYP was subject to the most extensive system of monitoring and evaluation hitherto put in place: a comprehensive programme of qualitative and quantitative research, the creation of a New Deal Evaluation Database and internal ES analysis of management data (Hasluck 2001).

As significant, however, were NDYP's omissions. The continuing absence of any parallel commitment to a direct government role in job creation, as emphatically signalled by the conspicuous absence of any macroeconomic content to Gordon Brown's 1998 'welfare to work' budget, highlighted the problem of where the jobs for these New Dealers would come from. In line with its attention to competitiveness and investment, the government underlined NDYP's value in promoting 'employability'. By 'holding' the young unemployed more closely to the labour market, NDYP was to overcome the corrosive influence of long-term unemployment and the corresponding detachment from work (Peck 2001). That the blueprint for this was, as Finn (1998) reminds us, the Workstart and Project Work initiatives of the early 1990s, and their experimentation with time limits on benefit claims (see Chapter 4) not only revealed its Conservative lineage, but also exposed a similar preference for blaming the young by reproducing in a somewhat different form the deficiency model of the past. In renouncing its previous political commitment to full employment for one of employability, '[i]nsecurity [for New Labour] had ceased to be presented as a structural feature of labour market. Rather job security had become something that individuals achieve ... a question of individual deficiency' (Levitas 1998: 120). Thus, through its concern with employability, NDYP endorsed the ideological claims of its predecessors: the culpability of individual unemployed young people for their own plight and the moral failings of young people, their parents and communities.

Recourse to employability also provided the government with a degree of insulation from the implications of pursuing New Deal. Publicly New Labour set its face against the Conservative's predilection for a low wage, low skills economy. Privately, the logic of NDYP was very different. By time-limiting the duration of claims for unemployment benefit and requiring mandatory work experience in exchange for continuing payment, not only was there the moral satisfaction of making the young unemployed do, 'something rather than nothing', it would also restore the young to the, 'universe of employable people'

(Layard 1997: 336). Getting the young to compete more effectively for available jobs was important because for Layard, appointed as an adviser on welfare to work shortly after the 1997 General Election, 'unemployment benefits are a subsidy to idleness, and it should not be surprising that if they lead to an increase in idleness ... [and because] unemployed people often adjust to unemployment as a different life-style' (*ibid*.: 334–5). By compulsorily reintegrating the young back into the labour market, not only would the unemployed 'gain in psychic well-being' (*ibid*.: 338) and reacquire the work habits that the 'uni-verse' of long-term unemployment is (self?) evidently supposed to lack. Compulsory re-integration would also increase the stock of employable people in the labour market and thereby intensify the competition for jobs:

> employers will [thus] find there are more employable people in the labour market and that they can more easily fill their vacancies. This increases downwards pressure on wages, making possible a higher level of employment at the same level of inflationary pres-sure. (*Ibid*.: 337; see also Glover and Stewart 2000)

To begin with, the likelihood of lower wages and the intensification of work provided no insurmountable obstacles to success. Throughout the life of the first Blair government, NDYP certainly enjoyed healthy levels of support, not least from among many of the young unem-ployed themselves (Hasluck 2001). Whether or not this can be sus-tained remains uncertain, however, given that the drive towards employability has threatened to hollow out the commitment to qual-ity training that NDYP professed to contain. Early evaluations noted a significant training gap between what was received by young partici-pants and the benefits extended to already employed staff (McIlroy 2000). Also, despite the payment of a £750 training subsidy, one in five participating employers had no plans to offer any kind of training and the majority of those participants working towards a qualification were training for NVQ Level 2. The same evaluations also noted that the unexpected popularity of the education and training option, par-ticularly among better qualified young recruits and ethnic minorities, had led to a bizarre situation where the majority of participants on these options were working towards a lower level qualification than that already possessed. In a parallel with previous schemes, recruits to subsidised employment and the Environmental Task Force were clear in their assessment that these were little more than 'make work' schemes, dominated by a familiar diet of short-term employment, poor quality work experience and training and few meaningful long-term prospects.

From welfare to where?

Final judgement on NDYP will ultimately pass on its success in leading to jobs. However, once we get beyond the grandiose claims made by ministers details of NDYP's performance saw it, 'join a long list of moderately effective programmes, yielding modest outcomes' (Peck 2001: 13). At the beginning of New Labour's second term, of the 731 900 young people who had entered New Deal, 652 800 had left and 79 200 were still participating. Of those who had left, 262 400 (36 per cent) had left to subsidised jobs, 74 900 (11 per cent) had moved onto other benefits, 128 500 (20 per cent) had gone into other known destinations such as further training or a return to Jobseekers Allowance (JSA), while the destination of 186 900 (29 per cent) was unknown (Bivand 2002b). Following up those leaving for unknown destinations revealed that over half had left for jobs but most of these were short-lived, with only two thirds still in jobs three months after leaving (Kalra *et al.* 2001); the (not particularly exacting) criteria against which success in finding 'sustained' employment is measured. More generally, a government-commissioned evaluation tentatively estimated that during its first year NDYP brought about a net reduction in youth unemployment of only 30 000. In subsequent judgements it was estimated that all but 45 000 of placements would have occurred *without* the programme (Riley and Young 1999). More recently still, a damning report by the government's financial watchdog, the National Audit Office, concluded that net job creation was only between 8000 and 20 000 new jobs. Given the level of expenditure involved, this amounted to a cost to the Exchequer of around £5000 for each new job,[3] so that large sums of money have been paid to employers who, it seems, would often have taken on these young people in any case.

Performance like this underlines that it is not NDYP as such that shapes young people's employment prospects, but the general strength of economic growth. Here New Labour has been particularly fortunate, inheriting as it did a relatively buoyant economy and an unemployment level that had started its decline in 1993. After the recession of 1989 to 1992, where the United Kingdom experienced the largest unbroken fall in GDP since 1945, the economy has grown consistently and without recession (Coates 2002; 2000). By the end of their first term in office, the number of registered unemployed had fallen by 550 000 to around 950 000, the lowest figure recorded since November 1975. On the government's preferred ILO measure, from the election in 1997 to March 2001 unemployment fell by 27 per cent (over 660 000) and employment levels rose by over 1 million. It was the continuing buoyancy of the labour market rather than their recourse to employability that explained the virtual elimination of long-term youth unemployment during New Labour's first term. The peculiar sensitivity of youth labour to changes in aggregate demand (see Chapter 3) ensured that young people were major beneficiaries of a relatively positive jobs environment, as youth unemployment in 2000, defined by the claimant count, dropped to its lowest level since 1974.

Further qualification comes with the realisation that unemployment had fallen more slowly during the first New Labour government, than it did under John Major; although with levels of aggregate employment so unusually high this was perhaps to be expected. Under New Labour too, the shift away from (full-time, high paid) jobs in manufacturing to (part-time, low paid) service sector employment continued, as the short-lived revival in manufacturing employment was reversed. With this shift came further confirmation of the longer-term trend towards a deterioration in the quality of work, as average manufacturing pay continued to flounder relative to the United Kingdom's major competitors; not least because of young people's exclusion from the full National Minimum Wage (see below). Under New Labour paid employment may have become more important as the means for young people's political reintegration, but as Levitas forcibly reminds us, 'the positions into which people are "integrated" through paid work are fundamentally unequal' (1996: 18).

A gateway opens?

Not that New Labour gave the young unemployed much choice in the terms of their reintegration. At the 1992 General Election, Labour had fought on a platform to reinstate benefits for unemployed 16 and 17 year olds and under Tony Blair's leadership the Party remained, for a while at least, opposed to compulsion and the Jobseekers Allowance. With plans for a New Deal announced in 1995, however, a conversion to the merits of the 'active benefits regime' was readily effected (see Chapter 4). By the time of the 1997 election, the party was promising that failure to start NDYP would lead in the first instance to a maximum of two weeks benefit sanctions, extended to four weeks for a subsequent refusal and a diminished role for hardship payments to cushion the impact on the most vulnerable. Internal Labour Party estimates suggested that as many as 40 000 young people could be affected. If more evidence of New Labour's conversion to the punitive benefits regime were needed, it came after two years when the government further expanded its power of sanction. With the passing of the Welfare Reform and Pensions Act 1999, penalties for persistent refusal to start NDYP were extended to six months and contingencies for the possible complete suspension of all hardship payments – whether or not a young person had caring responsibilities, a disability or dependent children – were made. Penalties for violating a Jobseekers Direction on dress code and inappropriate behaviour or self-presentation at interview were also strengthened to include the complete loss of benefits for 14 days. In using the benefits system to exclude the fifth 'option' of unemployment and to enforce compliance, the government's claim that it was balancing the greater rights embodied in NDYP with a series of more clearly defined responsibilities, was exposed as no more than a rhetorical device.

It is true that through the first term of government, these powers of compulsion and sanction were used sparingly. Sustained economic growth and steadily falling unemployment allowed the government to emphasise the 'carrots' on offer, rather than resort to a now mighty 'stick'. Added to this, the combined pressures of administering JSA meant that New Labour inherited a sizeable gap between the thrust of benefits policy and the detail of its 'street level' implementation (Powell 2001). This was probably just as well since these new and extended powers of sanction rarely achieved their aims. In opposition, New Labour had rightly argued that if government programmes for the young unemployed were worthy of the claims made on their behalf, then the 'active benefits regime' was at best a blunt instrument, at worst counter productive. It is something of a truism to reaffirm the fact that good schemes readily attract recruits. Once in power, however, such wise counsel was abandoned. Research by the ES into this new sanctions regime highlighted how tougher penalties failed to reach those they were aimed at, falling instead on those who had made considered judgements on the unsuitability of NDYP or simply because of a failure of communication (Britton 2002). What is more, among those most likely to face the toughest sanctions were those young people struggling to cope with a complex range of problems: drugs and alcohol, homelessness, poor health and perhaps a criminal record.

In spite of its proclaimed commitment to 'what works', the principles of NDYP were rapidly expanded into a more general programme of welfare to work without much convincing evidence of its practical value. In what constituted a major retreat from Labour's previous political commitment to inclusiveness, the government stated that its intention was now to 'rebuild the welfare state around work' (Department of Social Security 1998b: 23). Instead of the welfare state offering a means of protection from the market, however rudimentary this may have been, 'welfare to work' clearly expressed New Labour's belief that the more efficient use of market forces was the most effective means to meet the needs of the young. Within this generalised programme of 'welfare to work', a distinctive place for youth was retained. As New Deals were extended to the older unemployed (25 plus and 50 plus), communities, the disabled and lone parents, so too were the lives of unemployed young women brought more closely within its influence. Recognising the clearly gendered nature of NDYP – 70 per cent of all participants were young men – the Welfare Reform and Pensions Act 1999 also created a New Deal for Partners of the Unemployed (NDPU). Whereas previously it was the claiming partner who had to satisfy the conditions for the receipt of unemployment benefits – in 93 per cent of cases the male partner – after NDPU, both partners in an unemployed couple were required to satisfy the requirements of JSA.

Pressure on benefit dependent young women was further intensified under the New Deal for Lone Parents (NDLP). Although not explicitly directed at any particular age group or gender, NDLP's objective was the same group of young benefit dependent lone mothers who had so animated sections of the New Right (see Chapter 5). Launched in 1998 and initially voluntary in nature, NDLP extended an invitation to all lone parents to attend an interview with a personal caseworker as a means of discussing possible ways of getting into work. The government's justification for NDLP was that 90 per cent of lone parents wanted to work and that, once in work, they were notably better off. Both claims were tendentious, however, as the first was based upon research which generated the relatively uncontroversial finding that most lone parents wanted to work at some point in the future; leaving aside whether or not their short-term priority was caring for their children. And the second was based upon a small and unrepresentative sample that took no account of the fact that in-work costs – for instance, travel, food, new clothes, equipment and so on – make the reality of returning to work significantly less attractive (Levitas 1998). The government's intentions for this group were in any case clearly signalled by the controversial decision to carry through the cuts to benefits for lone parents, announced by John Major in 1996. Initially directed at lone parents with school age children (i.e. 5 years plus), NDLP was nevertheless extended in 2000 to those whose youngest child was 3 and, the following year, to all lone parents making a new claim. The increase in pressure derived in part from low rates of take up, with around 80 per cent of lone parents declining the invitation (Finn 2001), and from the government's belief in its value to participants. In the two years to the end of 2000, 116 000 lone parents had attended the interview, 90 per cent agreed to participate further, around 30 per cent went into jobs and around 8 per cent went into education and training.

As the influence of welfare to work grew, its more targeted approach was expanded into a general platform for all the young unemployed. Near to the end of New Labour's first term, in early 2000 a series of local pilots for the ONE service were launched, in which all newly unemployed people were required to attend an initial work-focused interview, with the possibility of subsequent recalls, as a condition for the receipt of benefit. The purpose of ONE was to reconstruct ES provision around the work of a Personal Adviser, whose brief included adjusting the aspirations of the unemployed in line with local employment opportunities. A new Working Age Agency announced in 2000, made up of the Employment Service and those parts of the Benefits Agency responsible for the unemployment benefits, also underlined the government's determination to apply technical solutions, such as the greater use of IT and other job-matching techniques, to the problem of integrating the unemployed back into jobs, education or training. This in turn reflected a growing confidence towards the end of the first Blair government that the problem of youth unemployment had to a large degree been resolved. In documents released by the Treasury, any remaining youth unemployed was explained away as a technical issue of matching the unemployed with available vacancies (Peck 2001).

Making work pay for the young: but who foots the bill?

As welfare to work exemplified New Labour's reconfiguration of youth within the pursuit of competitive efficiency, the bitter pill of low wage work was sugarcoated with in-work benefits. In what amounted to a tacit endorsement of British capitalism's inability to furnish the relatively high wage employment of the past, New Labour also moved to underpin the low wage economy for young people through a complex system of in-work benefits. The centrepiece of this was the Working Families Tax Credit, through which the worst consequences of low paid work could be partially off-set against a reduction in income tax liability. The attraction of in-work benefits is threefold. First, they help shore up a work ethic much dented by over two decades of mass unemployment, alleviating problems of social order on the way. Crime, delinquency and disorder are not such 'irrational' choices when the only jobs on offer are those unable to pay a living wage. Second, in socialising the costs of low wages they avoid a political confrontation with capital, since the cost is borne primarily by 'middle income' earners who have felt little benefit from the massive tax breaks to capital and the rich. The young working poor thus become recipients of a return to a Speenhamland-type system but without the vertical transfers of income that this had involved (Byrne 1999). Third, in-work benefits further solidify young people's place in the low wage economy, while at the same time cementing divisions between the young – middle and working class, black and white – and between the young and the old:

> ... the long term effect of these fiscal measures is that low pay will be even more institutionalised as an aspect of post-industrial capitalism, while the affluent who benefit as managers, service class workers, and owners of capital, will continue to enjoy the fruits of exploitation without paying much tax on them. Well, New Labour is definitely post-socialist. (*Ibid.*: 107)

We could perhaps add a fourth consideration. In-work subsidies have an additional, anti-inflationary value, since they provide a subsidy to low wages without adding to general pressures for wage increases.

For the young, the most significant aspect of this has been the National Minimum Wage (NMW). In what was presented as an antithesis to the Conservative's predilection for low wages, after gaining power New Labour moved quickly to honour its election commitment to establishing a NMW through the creation of a Low Pay Commission. The Commission's remit was to advise the government on the rate at which the NMW should be set and, reporting in 1998, advocated a general (adult) rate of £3.60 per hour, a separate Development Rate for young people aged 18 to 20 of £3.20 per hour and the exclusion of apprentices and school leavers (Low Pay Commission 1998). Endorsing the broad thrust of the Report the government nevertheless extended the Development Rate to 21 year olds and capped it at £3 per hour. In the run up to the 2001 General Election, the adult rate was subsequently adjusted upwards by ten pence and the Development Rate by 20 pence per hour, with further increases recommended for later in the year. For this reason, there is no denying the value of a NWM to some young workers. Their prevalence among the low paid was clearly recognised by the Commission and by the time of its third report they had estimated that around 105 000 18 to 21 year olds had benefited from its introduction (Low Pay Commission 2001). Moreover, whereas nearly three quarters of adults to benefit from the NMW were women, most of who were working part-time, its impact upon the young had been more evenly distributed across the genders.

At best, however, the NMW did little to bring about any significant modification to the pay of most young workers. At worst, and in all probability, it has most likely become a floor upon which the pay of young workers has settled. In coming to its final figure, the Low Pay Commission was mindful not to disturb the low wage equilibrium that defines the structure of wage inequalities for large numbers of workers, and trades unions demands for a general rate of £4 per hour were conspicuously ignored. As Edwards comments, 'the rate of £3 is around the level at which many employers were arguing that the effects would be manageable' (Edwards 1998: no page). For young people, the Development Rate was supposed to reflect the lower productivity and higher frequency of training that young workers were held to enjoy. This despite the majority of young workers having no access to formal off-the-job training (CESI 2002) and, in many cases, finding themselves working alongside others on the adult rate, doing the same tasks and with broadly comparable rates of productivity.

Education, education, education

A counterpart to welfare to work emerged in New Labour's restructuring of education. 'Education, education, education' was Tony Blair's clarion call at the 1996 Labour Party Conference – priorities which

John Major could endorse, if in a different order! – but as with NDYP, so the form of educational restructuring adopted by New Labour marked a significant retreat from its past. In its first term, New Labour did promise extra resources for education, providing they came from the pockets of individuals, were the product of efficiency savings or involved no tax increases. It also accepted that the pursuit of market forces alone would not bring about the 'world class' education system to which most recent British governments have aspired (Driver and Martel 1998). New Labour too may have acknowledged the importance of education in the maintenance and reproduction of social divisions. But during the first New Labour government, the importance attached to further educational restructuring was clearly driven by the political pursuit of competitive success.

For in New Labour's supply-side socialism, education became a euphemism for the best economic policy the nation possessed. Under New Labour, the quality of the nation's human capital was positioned as a method of investment decisive over that of money capital, equipment or materials in the global dash for jobs (Coates 2000; Thompson 1996). This was so because education was seen to constitute one of the few assets nationally anchored and therefore still open to government manipulation in the bid to attract international capital; preferably the sort offering high value-added and long-stay production facilities. Education also offered the possibility for a more palpable payback than in previous times. For in New Labour's vision of progressive competitiveness, flexible forms of learning and the training of young workers to, in effect, learn to learn, became a prerequisite for harnessing the competitive advantages offered by new technology. Lacking young workers capable of absorbing existing knowledge and an education system unable to foster the production of new ones, the competitive opportunities offered in the newly globalised economy were lost.

Without doubt, the outward plausibility of this vision is no more than a mark of its superficiality. As we saw in Chapters 2 and 3, the elevation of education and training to such a pivotal position in the modern economy – as a means of competitiveness and of securing jobs for all young people – was more significant in terms of the repudiation of Keynesian inclusiveness than as a practical solution to the problem of youth unemployment. Here too, this new role for education replicated in novel form the victim-blaming ideologies espoused by previous governments. Set within it was a view of education that clearly contrasted with its previous significance to Labour governments: from the intrinsic value of knowledge and learning for all, its potential to dissolve inequalities, as a means to foster a more inclusive youth, to promote social cohesion and so on. On the contrary, like employability before it, under New Labour education and training were repositioned as the means through which individuals could equip themselves with the ability to manage the ever-greater insecurities of modern capitalism. It was through a reconstituted and expanded education that an individual could be given the means to cope with the inevitable pressures of a global economy, by learning the new skills and competencies needed to move from task to task and job to job throughout their working lives (Ball 1999). Under New Labour efficiency thus became fairness and education the vehicle for its delivery.

A prime example was the government's resolve to remove as many 16 to 19 year olds from the labour market as possible and place them in full-time education and training (Mizen 2003b). One reason why young people were excluded from the NMW was the incentives this may have provided for school leavers to look for work. This was also a major impetus behind the government's determination to tackle those young people not in employment, education or training (SEU 1999), or so-called status zer0 youth (see Chapter 5). In ensuring that more young people were (re)connected with education or training, it was hoped that the corresponding investment in human capital would both diminish the personal and social costs of disengagement – unemployment, poverty, drug use, truancy, teenage conceptions, crime and delinquency and so on – and simultaneously enhance the supply of youth labour. For this reason, as well as those of cost, the government also ruled out reintroducing IS for unemployed 16 and 17 year olds, even though it represented the most effective and immediate initial measure for dealing with the problems of hard-pressed youth (COYPSS 1999). Instead, (re)engagement was attempted through measures like New Start in England, a programme of co-ordinated intervention for 14 to 17 year olds at risk of dropping out of full-time education. Alongside this, a careers service transformed into a semi-privatised Connexions agency, made up of elements of social services, the youth service and the private and voluntary sectors, became the front-line service for disaffected youth. Ostensibly a universal advice and placement service to aid progression at 16 plus, Connexions in effect spearheaded government attempts to cajole alienated 13 to 19 year olds to (re)engage with some form of education or training.

Connexions also formed an axis with the government's determination to breathe life into a moribund vocationalism. By adopting the broad framework for post-16 education and training bequeathed by the second Dearing review in 1996 (see Chapter 2), New Labour underscored the importance of separate vocational and academic routes through secondary and further education. In his review of qualifications for 16 to 19 year olds, Dearing confirmed the importance of a work-based route for 'non-academic' school students and, from 1998 onwards, schools were able under certain circumstances to deviate from the national curriculum in order to develop the wider use of work-related programmes of education and training. This was further formalised two years later by 'Curriculum 2000', which gave schools powers to set aside two core national curriculum subjects in an effort to boost their 'relevance' to groups of increasingly disaffected young people. Yet in taking this route, the second Dearing review also unintentionally revealed the problems that it would face. Changing the name of the by-now discredited youth training (YT) to youth traineeship (DfEE 1996), in the hope that it would increase its associations with apprentice training, not only reeked of desperate measures. It also emphatically underlined the lack of credibility to 'work-based' education and training brought about by over 20 years of what was passed off as vocationally oriented restructuring. Some genuine innovative practices notwithstanding (Coles 2000a), students already alienated from school were unlikely to find the prospect of an education made 'relevant' by the acquisition of low-level vocational information and generic competences an edifying prospect. Indeed, without addressing the pre-eminence of GCSEs and A levels, measured both in terms of their status and the reality of the employment and earnings outcomes that flowed from them, the 'parity of esteem' between the academic and vocational routes that Dearing aspired to, remained little more than an empty dream. Divisions of class and ethnicity were thus reanimated and reproduced.

Mores the pity, then, that New Labour enthusiastically embraced this vocationalism. Certainly the government's faith in Modern Apprenticeships (MApps), and the resources that followed it, was encouraging. Forty thousand new apprentices across the first Blair government certainly gave cause for celebration. But despite all the talk of investing in skills, MApps nevertheless remained a junior partner in the continuing emphasis on low skilled vocational preparation as the solution to the problems of youth unemployment and young people's detachment from school. The introduction of a Learning Gateway for 16 and 17 year olds in 1998, saw the reorganisation of provision for unemployed school leavers under the generic heading Work Based Training for Young People. In the main, this formalised existing differentials within youth training. The route to training at NVQ Level 2 was made clearer through another re-designation of National Traineeships (previously youth training) as Foundation Modern Apprenticeships, while the more remedial measures provided under the auspices of YT were re-grouped into the even less appealing category of Other Work Based Training for Young People. Re-branding training provision for school leavers in this way could not disguise New Labour's endorsement of a strategy that continued to confuse skill with competence, equate training with the acquisition of low-level vocational information and underwrote the re-composition of young people into a cheap and flexible source of labour.

Learning to New Labour

In schooling too, New Labour's pursuit of progressive competitiveness both accepted and developed the principles already well-established; qualified, of course, by the government's faith in the application of technical solutions to previous failure. The place of schooling was to be consolidated through the protection of playing fields from avaricious Boards of Governors and greedy property speculators, the average size of primary school classes for 5 to 7 year olds reduced to under 30 and teachers were to benefit from higher salaries through the introduction of performance-related pay. Notably, the government also fought the 1997 election on a pledge to phase out the Assisted Places Scheme (APS), with the monies saved going to help cut the size of primary school classes for 5 to 7 year olds. But as new resources were found to foster links between the private and state sector, the abolition of the APS was more important as a method for establishing clear (but certainly not red) water between New Labour and the Conservatives, rather than for its practical impact on schooling. New Labour's voluntary commitment to stay within the public expenditure constraints announced by the Conservatives in 1996 for the first two years of government, saw overall education spending in 1998 and 1999 as a percentage of GDP actually fall to its lowest level for 40 years (Coates 2002). The Treasury did manage to find £2.3 billion of new money for education from reserves and when stung by criticism for actually exceeding the cuts to education expenditure proposed by John Major, followed this in 1998 with the promise of £19 billion in extra funding. Headline grabbing as this figure was, it nonetheless disguised a much more modest increase in education expenditure which averaged

2.9 per cent per year across the life of the first Blair government (Hills 1998).

Welcome as these concessions were, the broad direction of educational restructuring remained the same. In opposition, New Labour had opposed the introduction of the national curriculum, the intensification of the examination process, league tables, selection, opt-outs from Local Education Authority (LEA) control and the Conservative's open hostility to LEAs. But once in government,

> there was an acceptance of the Conservative faith in choice and competition ... a continued rhetoric of 'raising standards' ... an adherence to the belief that all education institutions should be effectively managed along the lines of private business ... [and] a continued emphasis on the state regulation and control of the curriculum. (Tomlinson 2001: 85)

If the direction of change was a familiar one, the pace was unremitting. With the 1998 School Standards and Framework Act leading the way, the 'educational settlement' laid down by the 1988 Education and 1992 Further and Higher Education Acts was both deepened and consolidated. Education's role in differentiating between young people was strengthened, as the Act encouraged the development of specialisation and selection within the secondary school sector in the name of fostering healthy competition. In what amounted to, 'a clever re-labelling rather than an actual change of structure' (Tomlinson 2001: 96), the Act replaced school opt-outs from local authority control with a new hierarchy of fixed divisions through the creation of a new legal category of foundation and voluntary status schools, which effectively protected their privileged status. In a move that extended selection, specialist schools, later renamed colleges, were also further promoted. Developed by the Conservatives in 1993, a successful bid to become a specialist in technology, languages, sports or arts education permitted a school to select 10 per cent of its intake by 'aptitude', buttressed by extra funding from government and business. New Labour's own innovation of Beacon schools as shining lights of educational practice, further set school against school, LEA against LEA in the dash to secure the limited new funding on offer. By the end of their first term in office, Labour's historic support for universalism of provision and inclusiveness of schooling had become little more than a distant memory. After the 1998 Act, the government was supporting a hierarchy of 13 different types of schools, at whose apex was a stronger than ever private sector and whose base was the new Pupil Referral Units and Learning Support Centres to house the disaffected.

Changes to teaching and learning practices also further fostered division. Once in power, New Labour's earlier ambivalence to the national curriculum disappeared as centralised influence was extended downwards through the imposition of literacy, and later numeracy, hours in primary schools, in echoes of John Major's Victorian 'back to basics' campaign; and sideways through guidelines on homework. On the one hand, within the national curriculum the means to categorise students as non-academic was strengthened, as already noted, by the powers given to schools to set aside the provisions of the national curriculum for 'non-academic' students at age 14 plus. The Excellence in Cities proposal announced in 1999 to tackle inner city deprivation also provided the means for a limited dismantling of comprehensives. Its proposals smoothed the way for a return to setting students and the cessation of mixed ability teaching within those schools that remained comprehensive (Muschamp *et al.* 1999). On the other hand, new benefits were extended to the more 'academically able'. The same 1999 proposals sought the expansion of Beacon status and specialist schools to one quarter of all secondary schools by 2002, announced new opportunities for the most 'able' 5 to 10 per cent of students in the form of a National Academy for Gifted and Talented Youth, put in place a new 'world class' AS (advanced subsidiary) qualification from September 2000, advocated early examinations and fast-tracking for the most able students, while fortifying the means to segregate the most disruptive.

This strengthening of the means to segregate the most disruptive students contradicted earlier intentions. Certainty that education provided the most effective mechanism for overcoming young people's exclusion, by facilitating entry to paid work, occupational mobility, enhanced earnings capacity and a reduction in crime and delinquency, did lead initially to a more benign approach. Early in the first New Labour government, both the power of Head Teachers to exclude and the conditions upon which Appeals Panels could overturn such a decision were softened, and an SEU (1998) report appeared to commit the government to reducing exclusions by one third. Following vociferous criticism, however, this ambitious target was in effect jettisoned as new guidelines announced in 1999 relaxed the grounds upon which a Panel could refuse to uphold an appeal. Intentions on this matter were also clearly signalled by the strengthening of the Pupil Referral Units first established by the Conservatives in 1993. And in a further bid to manage the consequences of continuing high rates of school exclusion, in 1999 all schools were guaranteed access to newly created Learning Support Centres in which those school students most at risk of being excluded were to be housed.

No less important was the ostensible commitment to addressing less topical sources of educational exclusion. Announced by the 1998 School Standards and Framework Act, Education Action Zones (EAZ) appeared to mark something of a rediscovery of social background and inequality in the patterning of educational outcomes. They also brought within them a sizeable injection of resources for some of the most hard-pressed groups of students. EAZs, however, did not mark a return to a more inclusive notion of education expressed, for example, in the way that earlier we saw Educational Priority Areas of the 1960s sought to provide some degree of compensation for certain groups of working-class young people (see Chapter 2). Located in areas of considerable deprivation, EAZs gave the participating primary and secondary schools greater discretion over the curriculum – once again raising the spectre of a consolidated vocational or work-based route for disadvantaged and ethnic minority students – the structure of schooling, the terms and conditions of teachers and enhanced IT capacity. As significant was the introduction of a direct role for the private sector in the management and delivery of mainstream education. To make a successful bid, each zone required the development of partnerships with local businesses and the generation of £250 000 from the private sector. Given the lamentable record of private sector support for City Technology Colleges, also retained by New Labour, and the patent inability of the market to bring about some sort of meaningful renaissance in skills training for young people, the likely success of this was quickly placed in considerable doubt. From early on, EAZs were finding it difficult to raise even such modest amounts of cash and their overall impact on the education of some of the most deprived young people had been decidedly mute (Gerwitz 1999).

EAZs were also part of the Government's determination to force up educational standards in their drive for competitive efficiency. Promising unrelenting pressure on standards, the 1998 Act confirmed and extended the framework of competition enforced through key stage testing, the publishing of raw examination results, school 'league tables' and the 'naming and shaming' of failing schools (Kendall and Holloway 2001). The intent was signalled within a very short period after the 1997 election victory, when 18 'failing' and 100 of the bottom performing schools were 'named and shamed' by David Blunkett, then Secretary of State for Education and Employment, despite the vast majority struggling through in areas of considerable deprivation. This policy of publicly humiliating individual schools was, however, quietly dropped in 1998, perhaps in a tacit acknowledgement that simply closing down schools and resurrecting them under Fresh Start, with new senior management and some new resources, was not by itself sufficient to tackle the considerable problems that many faced. Then again, the government also set itself the more ambitious objective of holding LEAs to account in this respect. New powers gave greater central power over LEAs, as a rejuvenation of some planning functions was off-set by tighter control over expenditure activities and unprecedented moves to give the Secretary of State for Education the ability to intervene in their day-to-day running. Within a year of the 1998 Act, Hackney, Calderdale and Manchester LEAs had been publicly named as inadequate and, in measures that had been rejected by the Conservatives as too radical, the government also named 10 consortia willing to take the lead in any partial privatisation of state education (see also Hatcher and Hirtt 1999). Shortly after the first 'failing school' was turned over to private sector management and this was followed by the decision to allow Cambridge Education Associates to become the first private company to take over the day-to-day running of the education service in Islington, London. This, as Tomlinson (2001) notes, was despite the absence of any evidence to suggest that privatisation would solve the problems that these hard-pressed schools and LEAs faced.

Paying your way through higher education

Higher education was also brought within New Labour's strategy of progressive competitiveness. In what clearly served the interests of both major political parties, judgement on the looming crisis in higher education had been deferred to a third Dearing Report, the findings of which were conveniently due for publication two months after the 1997 election. Following a 'great' British tradition of public inquiries, the conclusions of the Report were pretty much known in advance but it did come as something of a surprise that on the same day as Dearing reported, the government announced its own arrangements for student support that went well beyond his recommendations (Naidoo and Callender 2000). Brought into law by the Teaching and Higher Education Act 1998, the government set about abolishing free higher education, phased out the student maintenance grants first introduced by the Conservatives in 1962, instigated loans as the main source of student support, introduced new methods of loan repayments and provided some limited financial help for part-time students. From 1998/99, new full-time entrants to universities were required to pay a £1000 contribution to tuition fees, adjusted each subsequent year according to inflation, subject to a means test of parental and spousal income. And from the same year, support for living costs was fully transferred to a system of loans (Dearing had recommended the retention of maintenance awards), the maximum value of which was partly means-tested and whose payment upon graduation was income contingent. Interest paid on these loans would be determined by the rate of inflation.

One of the justifications for opening up student support to market forces was that new funds would flow to higher education and, as a consequence, both students and the nation would benefit from the world-class universities that would follow. Some £1.1 billion of extra resources were indeed directed at the nation's universities during New Labour's first term, yet in what was becoming a familiar process of smoke and mirrors the Treasury emerged as the biggest beneficiary. From 1997, the key indicator of university well-being, funding per student, continued to fall until the last year of government when the first increase in real funding per student place bought levels back to virtual parity with the 1997 level. Throughout this time, new resources accruing to universities from student fees were pretty much off-set by a reduction in their direct grants. And in any case, new government expenditure on higher education was dwarfed by the considerable savings that amassed from the changes to student support. Some £2.1 billion were saved on the abolition of student grants between 1997/98 and 2000/01 and the £1.9 billion being paid out in student loans by the last year of government was money that would, in the main, eventually be repaid. For government, shifting the costs of higher education onto young people in this way meant that the introduction of fees and loans freed up around £4.1 billion of resources previously going to higher education in the first term of government alone.[4]

As is the case with market forces, the greatest burden of these new arrangements fell inevitably on the shoulders of the poorest. With some justification, the government argued that the 'value-added' by a higher education meant shifting a greater element of its cost to those who reaped the rewards was warranted. After all, by the end of their first term, data from the Labour Force Survey confirmed that unemployment rates for 20–34 year olds with university degrees was three times lower (2.7 per cent) than those with GCSEs (8.6 per cent). And that graduates aged 20–24 were earning on average 34 per cent more than those in the same age group whose highest qualification was GCSE, a difference that rose to a staggering 68.3 per cent by age 30–34 (CSU 2002). Yet the highly regressive effects of up-front fees and loans were quick to emerge. Young people from the middle class had always had their higher education funded by their parents – indeed a university education often proved far cheaper than the fees paid to support their children's private education – and this had become proportionately easier to fund as government set about redistributing wealth from the poor to the rich (see Chapter 5). Research quickly established that those struggling under the heaviest debt burden came from the lowest socio-economic groups (Callender and Kemp 2000). Unsurprisingly, these same categories of students also proved the most 'debt averse' so that, rather than building access as the government claimed it would, increased student debt proved a major disincentive, particularly for the working class, mature students and lone parents. More surprisingly, the attractive interest rates for state bankrolled student loans, relative to those on offer in the private sector, had led 10 per cent of students to take out loans not for living expenses but because it offered themselves or their parents a cheap or tax-efficient source of credit. Thus, in the universities, as elsewhere in education,

> while New Labour was preaching inclusiveness and developing new palliatives to mitigate disadvantage, market and selective forces were demonstrably excluding large sections of the working and non-working class, plus many ethnic minority children and those with learning difficulties, from the more desirable schools and universities. (Tomlinson 2001: 86)

Numbers of undergraduate students actually fell between 1996/97 and 2000/01 by nearly 50 000, reaching a nadir in 1997/98 and then rising only very slowly. Deterred by cost, the decline in student : staff ratios, a crumbling infrastructure, the need to combine paid employment with study and with the prospect of graduating with a five figure debt, government ambitions to get half of all young people under 30 years old into some form of higher education by 2010, equivalent of 60 000 new students per year, were looking hugely over-optimistic. Stung by criticism, a broader use of Access funds for poorer and part-time students, means-tested bursaries, support for child care costs and a tweaking of the social security regulations to make study more attractive for mature students were all announced. But by the end of their first term, and with the abolition of tuition fees and a more sympathetic system of student support erected in Scotland, and moves in the same direction in Wales, New Labour went to the polls again in 2001 with its policy for higher education in England under mounting pressure.

Four years' hard labour

Just as the restructuring of welfare to work, training and education sought to tie the lives of the young more closely to the pursuit of progressive competitiveness, so too was this the case for youth justice. On coming to power, New Labour placed much stress on the cost of youth crime, for individuals, communities and the nation as a whole, as young lives were ruined, communities broken and valuable national resources squandered in the pursuit of law and order. 'Tough on the causes of crime' was one half of another of Tony Blair's (in)famous sound bites, this time when Shadow Home Secretary. In what represented a notable and significant change of tone, New Labour appeared willing to revive an understanding of the social, and the patterns of inequality that flowed from this, in influencing young offending. What is more, in government it quickly substantiated this with important innovations as early interventions through schooling and in the community, more 'relevant' schooling, welfare to work measures, the promotion of employability and new resources for rehabilitation and counselling, were all packaged as measures that would tackle youth offending at root cause. More ominously, however, Tony Blair's rediscovery of the social was predicated in more familiar tones that pledged the government to get tough on young criminals. For those who proved incapable or unwilling to avail themselves of the opportunities that New Labour was prepared to put their way, the government pledged to enforce young people's 'responsibilities' through 'a marked expansion of the legal means through which young people's behaviour can be circumscribed' (Muncie 1999: 169).

Any expectations that New Labour's strategy for youth justice would constitute a return to a more inclusive politics were therefore quickly countermanded. This was particularly unfortunate, given that the government inherited the steady and continuing decline in rates of youth offending after 1994. Acknowledging that youth offending is the product of social, economic and even political forces was certainly an important advance. But this was ultimately confined within an understanding of youth offending as the product of broken community, the inability to choose between right and wrong and, most importantly, a deficit of parenting. For the capacity of parent's to control their children became a progressively more important legitimating theme of governing policy, as the complex basis of youth offending was collapsed back into the ideological convenience of 'irregular' families, poor child-rearing practices and weak parental control (Drakeford and McCarthy 2000). In this respect, New Labour's approach reproduced important elements of explanations developed by previous Labour administrations, resting as they did on the conservatism of working class family practices (see Chapter 6). This time, however, there was no parallel commitment to addressing the welfare of young offenders and to resurrecting a more politicised notion of need. Instead, the huge expansion in both the reach of the law and the machinery of youth justice that New Labour brought about during its first term of government, was characterised by an interventionism that took its cue from correction, punishment and deterrence; an emphasis on individual responsibility and accountability; and one that actually placed more young people at ever greater risk from damage caused by early contact with the law. In short, 'it is an interventionism that promotes prosecution, violates rights, and, in the final analysis, will only serve to criminalise the most structurally vulnerable children' (Goldson 2000: 52).

Using the law as the principle means of containing the anti-social and criminal behaviour of young people, also marked important continuities with the practical developments of the 1990s. 'But what distinguishes [New Labour's] ... legislation from its Conservative predecessors is the centrality afforded to notions of early intervention and prevention as the most efficient and cost-effective means of combating crime' (Muncie 2000: 148; see also Pitts 2000). This concern to address the potential to offend at the earliest possible age was dominant in New Labour's centrepiece legislation, the 1998 Crime and Disorder Act. Going where the Conservatives had aspired to tread but never dared, under the pretence of young people's welfare the Act removed the right of children and young people to protection from the full weight of the criminal law by abolishing *doli incapax* (i.e. incapable of evil) for 10 to 14 year olds (Goldson 2000).

The Act also further extended 'zero tolerance' which, as we have already seen, so impressed Conservative Home Secretaries. Through the introduction of Anti-Social Behaviour Orders minor incivilities were no longer to be tolerated, in what amounted to the effective criminalisation of moral indiscretions and the transgression of socially condoned modes of behaviour. Drawn widely, the definition of anti-social behaviour as conduct causing or likely to cause alarm or distress looked set to draw more young people within the influence of the criminal justice system, via petty forms of conduct such as low-level offending, disorderly behaviour or simply being out of place. The offensive against young people's incivility was further supported by the extension of the power of curfews. Curfew as a tool of youth justice policy was by itself not a new development, although it was a rarely used tool. What marked the 1998 Act out, however, was its broadening of these provisions to children under 10 years old on the one hand, and their availability on the basis of presumption rather than confirmation of guilt on the other. In a marked escalation of the power of supervision, a high 'risk' of offending rather than clear proof of a criminal act now opened up the prospects of curfew.

In line with the belief that parents were usually a prime source of their children's errant behaviour, the 1998 Act also sought to shore up the family's policing function. Again there was little new in the principle that parents were to some degree culpable for their children's criminal actions and should thus be held to account. The 1998 Act, however, was aimed explicitly at strengthening the connections between parental supervision and young offending, with parents vulnerable to criminal sanction for their children's breach of curfew and children open to the possibility of safety orders. The addition of a Parenting Order to enforce compliance required parents of anti-social or criminal young people to undergo compulsory counselling or guidance sessions, as well as comply with any other directions stipulated by the court such as ensuring their child's attendance at school. For a government apparently committed to upholding the centrality of the family, this tough line on parental responsibility actually represented as much a risk to the stability of the family as a solution to the problem of youth crime. Making parents already unable to cope with the offending behaviour of their children take on the additional pressures brought about by court appearances and the need to intimately supervise their children's physical movements was, at best a myopic move. At worst, instead of providing these families with the assistance they urgently required, it threatened to further stigmatise and hasten the process of family disintegration. Thus, 'while the new legislation marks a return to the interventionist politics of the 1960s and 1970s it does so with a totally different tone, one which is repressive, coercive and has no regard to how wider social contexts impinge on the lives of parents' (Drakeford and McCarthy 2000: 102).

As the means for legal intervention into the lives of the young was both extended and enforced onto younger and younger children, so too did New Labour set about extending the repertoire of punishment for its transgression. More resources for targeted education initiatives, welfare to work and treatment programmes, for drugs, management of anger and anti-social behaviour, certainly offered some element of genuine assistance to young offenders struggling with a host of personal and social problems. The creation of local Youth Offending Teams to bring some measure of 'joined-up' practice to these various strands was also a significant innovation. In this respect at least, some principles of welfare and rehabilitation survived New Labour's conversion to the rule of law. But in the main these initiatives remained modest in scale and aspiration, and their influence was generally submerged under the government's resort to punishment. In fact, the 1998 Act strengthened the punitive mood of youth justice. Extending the reach and intensity of so-called punishment in the community, the 1998 Act extended electronic tagging of 10 to 15 year olds as a means of enforcing supervision orders and curfews, despite clear and convincing evidence that rates of compliance with such measures are lowest among the young (Muncie 2000). The much-vaunted policy of cautioning young offenders as a means of diversion was also jettisoned in favour of a new system of reprimands and final warnings. Heavily prescriptive, reprimands were to be imposed in cases of clear guilt, with a mandatory warning for repeat or more serious offending. In what amounted to a ratcheting up of the potential for contact with the police and criminal justice system (Goldson 2000), the issue of a warning would produce an obligatory referral to a locally constituted Youth Offending Team, itself a product of the 1998 Act, followed by the probability of some form of intervention.

New Labour also persevered with the pivotal role of custody for more serious young offenders, despite both its ineffectiveness and the destructive consequences that follows incarceration. As Muncie astutely notes, 'New Labour, it seems, is only prepared to sanction inclusion as long as exclusion is retained for particular groups of offenders' (2000: 27). Generally hostile to the Conservative's obtuse 'prison works' regime when in opposition, once in power New Labour presided over its consolidation. A new Detention and Training Order for 12–17 year olds rationalised the means of imposing a custodial sentence upon the young. The second 'boot camp' for 'hardcore' young offenders, established in 1997, was closed down reluctantly only on the ground of cost (around £850 per week compared to the £250 per week in other young offender institutions), while the first, opened the year before, was retained. Plans for secure training centres for persistent and serious offenders under the age of 15, announced in 1994, were also brought to fruition. No new centres had been constructed by the time of the 1997 General Election but shortly afterwards the new Home Secretary, Jack Straw, gave the go-ahead and the following year the first was opened at a cost of £2500 per young person per week. Justifying its decision, the government placed great stress on the centres' educational functions and the need to honour signed contracts. Four new centres were subsequently announced.

'As with so many other retrogressive and divisive social and economic policies inherited from the Conservatives, Labour has left youth custody in place' (Muncie 1999: 168). For a government seemingly committed to 'what works' in shaping the content and direction of policy, this marked a startling leap of faith. The confidence of Home Secretaries Jack Straw and David Blunkett in 'boot camps', with their harsh corrective regimes, belied the absence of any serious evidence of their efficacy, as rates of re-offending within two years of a young person leaving custody ran between 70 and 90 per cent (Moore 2000). By any gauge a costly step to take, New Labour seemed to have forgotten that youth custody allows few opportunities for rehabilitation, is insignificant as a deterrent and continuing high rates of youth offending mean its value as a mode of incapacitation is negligible. The greater use of custody places even greater pressure on already strained family relations and once detained, a young person is likely to be subject to a regime defined by crime and abuse. Drug offences, physical and sexual abuse, assault, theft, extortion, physical and psychological abuse, and racism are all routine aspects of a young person's life 'in-side'. It is therefore no wonder that even Her Majesty's Inspector of Prisons, in a review of Feltham Young Offender Institution in 1997, was forced to conclude: 'I do not believe that children under 18 should be held in prison ... More damage is done to immature adolescents than to any other type of prisoner, by current conditions' (quoted in Moore 2000: 120).

Conclusion

Far from hastening its demise, under the first New Labour government youth assumed a new political importance. At one level, this was simply a matter of rhetoric, as the relative youth of its leadership became a means to help Tony Blair's Labour Party politically distance itself from the failed and unpopular programmes of both its Conservative predecessors and past Labour governments alike. In this respect, New Labour's youthfulness was central to its ability to portray itself as a party of national renewal, one that could break free from the disastrous years of Conservative mismanagement and give force to its ambition to bring about the rejuvenation of British society. But New Labour also proved distinctively youthful in other, more substantive ways. Under the first Blair government, youth assumed a coherence perhaps not previously evident in previous government practice. Despite the pronouncements of some, New Labour showed no inclination to curtail the importance of age as a means of politically organising the lives of the young. Indeed, the first New Labour government presided over the intensification of state influence over the lives of the young, as government set its sights on many of the problems that have come to define contemporary youth.

At its clearest, this youthfulness was evident in the work of the newly created Social Exclusion Unit (SEU), with its mandate to think the unthinkable and develop 'joined-up solutions' to 'joined-up problems'. Yet what came to dominate the work of the Unit work was not so much the need to tackle the problems faced by some groups of young people in ways that may have been sympathetic to their needs. Rather, the SEU was more concerned with the familiar themes of labour discipline and social order. By the end of the first Blair government, the considerable activity on the part of the SEU, at least measured in terms of the number of reports published, had done little to alter the overall balance of political and administrative interests when it came to the question of youth (Mizen 2003a). Indeed, when all is said and done, throughout the first New Labour government, the impact of the SEU upon policy formation and development was considerably overshadowed by the continuing and growing influence of those more traditional sources of 'youth policy': those government departments responsible for public expenditure (Treasury), law and order (Home Office), work and unemployment (Department for Work and Pensions) and education (Department of Education and Skills). What is more, whatever the merits of having Cabinet-level representation of the interests of youth, as New Labour tentatively sought to do (Coles 2000a), it was the interests of these departments that continued to dominate.

Caveats like these do not mean that there has been no substance to New Labour's youthfulness. On the contrary, this chapter has argued that the level of government activity directed at the young underwent a notable intensification after 1997 and, in this respect, New Labour was good to its word. In work and unemployment, social security and training, the re-regulation of the labour market, at all levels of post-primary education and in relation to the exercise of the law, New Labour was active in the development of policies that had a marked affect on the lives of the young. Some of these were to be welcomed. Few could object to the new resources made available to the young, however prudent the basis upon which this was done. Much was also to be welcomed in those distinctive attempts to engage with the young, either through more meaningful forms of guidance and coun-selling for the unemployed, the disaffected or the delinquent. But, taken in sum, it is difficult to escape the conclusion that the driving force of New Labour's restructuring programme for youth was not so much motivated by genuine attempts to support young people's tran-sitions to adult life, whatever the rhetoric of government and policy-makers, if this is understood to be a defining characteristic of 'youth policy'. Rather, the intention was to reorganise the lives of the young more fully according to the dictates of New Labour's political strategy of 'progressive competitiveness'.

We see this in the importance of youth to New Labour's faith in technocratic solutions to the problems engendered by the pursuit of naked market forces. New Labour did not enter power simply trying to ape the exclusionary politics of youth evident in the monetarist strat-egy of restructuring and, in this respect, the government was gen-uinely novel. But neither in the first New Labour government did we find a return to Labour's traditional strategy of inclusiveness. Rather, the significance that New Labour attached to youth is to be found in its subordination to a political programme that stressed the more effi-cient management of market forces. It has been in relation to this strategy of 'progressive competitiveness', that the restructuring of edu-cation continued apace as education and training achieved a hitherto unrealised political importance, expressed in terms of both the secu-rity and success of individual young people but also in New Labour's vision of a prosperous and internationally competitive society. And it is in relation to the inefficiency, waste and disruption caused by social decay, crime and delinquency that the terms of New Labour's engage-ment with youth has been decided, mainly through the further enforcement of the rule of law. For this reason, the sparkle of New Labour's youthfulness loses much of its lustre, as age and youth have become, once again, reduced to a more familiar place in the restructuring programme of governments. As with the monetarist process of restructuring, age in youth continued to provide New Labour with the means to politically reintegrate young people into the development of capitalist social relations, this time pursued through the imperatives of efficiency, effectiveness and economy embodied in the Third Way. Fundamentally therefore, the first New Labour continued the process of withdrawing young people's access to and rights over key sources of social support that began a generation earlier.

Conclusion: Youth in a New State?

In setting out to explore the changing state of youth across the last quarter or so of the twentieth century, this book addressed two interrelated themes. The first considered the political significance of youth, not so much in terms of the more familiar preoccupation with youth's discursive importance; of how politicians, policy-makers, academics, the media and other moral entrepreneurs construct our understanding of youth through they ways they talk and write about the young. Our purpose has been to consider the political significance of youth by examining young people's relationship to the state and how this has changed over time. The second theme is closely related. In seeking to explore the changing state of youth our objective has also been to consider the ways in which youth has become a much more costly 'state' to be, at least for most young people.

Consideration of youth's practical relationship to the state took us to the political importance of age. A curious feature of recent trends in 'youth studies' has been the failure to address the political importance of age, an omission that is in many respects a surprising one given that even a cursory glance at the structure of modern societies reveals that age criteria provide one of the most conspicuous means through which states relate to and organise the lives of the young. Indeed, when we pause and start to think about the politics of age three distinctive issues emerge. The first is that age provides an important means of division, one which allows governments to manage social relations in ways that obscure or deny those forces which are ultimately responsible for determining the structure of contemporary social life. Seen from a perspective that stresses youth's significance as a means of 'growing up' socially, the undoubted importance attributed to age as a way of allocating the rights and responsibilities of formal citizenship may display little coherence or fail to show any neat or logical chronology to how young people are integrated as full social members. But such inconsistencies matter little when age is viewed as a source of division because the apparent and sometimes arbitrary organisation of the formal entitlements that come with particular ages, nevertheless do have a practical value as a means of dividing young people from their families and communities: through education and schooling, the family, welfare, the labour market, the criminal justice system and the law, and much further beyond.

The second point to emphasise is that the age also reveals the substance of claims on youth as a universal condition. Rightly, many remain suspicious of universalistic notions of youth and point to the inability of theories of adolescence to explain what is ultimately a socially determined phenomenon. Such uncertainties are further strengthened by the ease with which these accounts render opaque those sources of social power that are ultimately responsible for dividing young people from one another and from the central institutions of the societies in which they live. But as we have often stressed, like all the most powerful ideologies, however distorted the visions they create, claims to youth's universalism have as their basis the practical and concrete organisation of social life. Whatever the other sources of division, the possession of a certain age does give young people's lives a real measure of equivalence whereby all must be schooled, are excluded from participation in formal democratic structures, are marginalised from access to important sources of social power and so on. Moreover, to assert the real unifying presence of age is not to obscure those divisions which are central to the lives of the young, so much as to bring into sharper relief the means through which they are reproduced. In relating to young people primarily in terms of age – rather than their class, gender, ethnicity, sexuality, disability and so on – the universalism that age gives to the lives of the young, also provides a medium through which these sources of inequality can be reproduced and, in more recent times, given new life and meaning.

The third point to stress is that age also establishes the terms upon which states integrate young people into social life. Being a certain age not only involves a young person's removal from their families and communities and their placement into specific institutions or relationships, but in the process of being separated in these ways, young people are also exposed in no uncertain terms to the broader political strategies that states adopt in their attempts to manage social relations. Not only does age therefore divide young people off into specific institutions, like schools and training schemes, and organise their lives according to particular sets of social relations, like students and trainees, in doing so age also provides the means through which young people can be (re)integrated into social life on terms dictated by the state.

Our consideration of the changing state of youth has thus also been an examination of the political construction of youth and how this has been subject to profound restructuring in recent years. In seeking to make this process intelligible, the political construction and reconstruction of youth was examined in terms of the crisis of the Keynesian state and its 'resolution' on terms expressed through monetarism. Under the former, age assumed a new political importance as youth was elevated into a key site in the broader Keynesian strategy and its attempts to manage the contradictory development of social relations through a strategy of inclusion and concession. The subsequent crisis of the Keynesian welfare state and the emergence of money and the market as key agents of restructuring, saw the terms of young people's relationship to the state undergo a far-reaching process of change.

Under these new conditions, the terms of young people's relationship to the state was inverted. More precisely, it was the inclusiveness of the Keynesian state that now explained the crisis engulfing the young. Comprehensive schools lowered standards, produced ill-disciplined students, encouraged a growing 'gap' between school and work and ultimately turned out school leavers 'deficient' in those qualities that employers were now demanding; the commitment to 'jobs for all' had priced young people out of work, institutionalised labour market inflexibility and eroded incentives to greater productivity; a more inclusive welfare state had featherbedded the young to the point where the work ethic had been corrupted, new cultures of dependency produced and a subsidy to indolent living created; and treating the young offender as in need rather than simply bad or immoral eroded respect for authority, presided over an explosion in rates of youth crime and threatened the very existence of the rule of law. Without doubt profoundly ideological, the considerable power of this emerging critique nevertheless drew its strength from a series of deeper political forces which had seen governments, from the middle of the 1970s onwards, lurch from crisis to crisis. It was in response to the political problems this posed, as much as any underlying economic ones, that saw governments increasingly look to politically disengage themselves from the previous direct responsibilities they had assumed, by turning to money and the market as their agents of restructuring.

The crisis of the Keynesian welfare state was therefore simultaneously expressed as a crisis of youth and its subsequent restructuring transformed the lives of the young. Beyond the anti-state rhetoric, throughout the 1980s and 1990s governments presided over a massive expansion of the state's influence over the young, as existing age criteria were consolidated, others extended and new ones put in place. Under the process of monetarist restructuring pursued by successive governments, age was reconstituted as a means to limit social security and housing benefit entitlements and redistribute resources away from the young. New age criteria were established in the name of 'targeting', as welfare benefits were removed and lower rates introduced for certain age groups. Similar divisions of age were replicated in the 'active benefits regime', as young people found themselves at the sharpest point of the ever-more intensive efforts to confine their aspirations for work more closely to what employers and the market were prepared to offer. Young people's relation to the family was similarly transformed, as dependent young people bore the brunt of the redistribution of income in regressive ways and their aspirations for independent living were made much more contingent on the market and access to money. In relation to law and order too, new age categories were introduced in relation to the disposal, sentencing, monitoring, punishment and confinement of young offenders.

Previously the object of new resources, in the turn to money and the market the previous inclusiveness of youth was progressively redefined. Provision for young people became the specific object of cuts in public expenditure, as young people lost out in the scramble to compete for those available resources. Moreover, in those institutions and social relations which the young were now forced to inhabit, young people found their lives aggressively reconstituted in terms dictated by market forces. In education, the experience of being young was reconstructed in terms of greater selection, competitive 'league tables', a centralised curriculum, a more intensive system of examination and the introduction of student fees. Training and work experience programmes were dominated by the 'needs' of employers, driven by the requirements of vocationalism, training credits and further marketisation in the form of initiatives like Training and Enterprise Councils (TECs). Being unemployed now meant narrower benefit entitlements, stiffer availability for work tests, lower benefit levels and the requirement that some job-search or training activity be undertaken. Young people's access to an income was tied to low-level training allowances and low wages, confined within wage ceiling measures, the abolition of wages councils and the generalisation of part-time working. Aspirations for independent living were recomposed in terms of narrow entitlements to support housing costs, the marketisation of rents and the promotion of the private sector. And for those young people transgressing the law, the consequence was redefined in more 'exclusive' terms as governments looked to the rule of law to manage offending behaviour.

Across the final quarter of the twentieth century, governments thus reconstructed youth in fundamental ways. The new state of youth that emerged from this, in many respects, reconstructed the condition of being young into a much more costly 'state' to be. For sure, for a notable minority these changes opened up the possibility of obtaining benefits and rewards that were perhaps previously unimaginable. For a few of those middle class young people still monopolising the elite universities, for example, the rewards from this new state of youth have already been remarkable: university and college sponsorship deals, recruitment incentives and 'golden hellos', generous starting salaries that increase exponentially and a degree of security and prosperity throughout their working lives that many others can only dream about. For these young people, even the increased cost that has come with the protracted dependence upon the family and the destruction of a system of higher education free at the point of demand, have been more than off-set by the massive transfer of wealth and income from the poor to the rich that took place throughout the last decades of the twentieth century. For many more, however, the price of this changing state of youth has been a considerable one, as large numbers of young people contemplate their lives from a position of hardship and austerity, unemployment, insecure and part-time working, protracted dependence upon their families, insecurity, a marked intensification of their lives at school and in work, the institutionalisation of low wages and significant increases to the costs involved in securing some reasonable degree of independent living. From their perspective, the conditions of being young has become a much more arduous state to be.

Added to these costs has been a further one: the price of failure. When judged against its predecessor, the monetarist process of restructuring and the new age of austerity that it ushered in has been even less successful than the failed Keynesian strategy it systematically destroyed. Despite the promise of jobs, youth unemployment has remained at unprecedented levels for unprecedented periods of time. Its recent decline to a rate more akin to those of a quarter of a century ago has only been achieved at the further cost of removing large numbers of young people from the labour market, first through work experience and training schemes and subsequently through the expansion of further and higher education. These same levels of youth unemployment also reveal the failure of the turn to education and training as the monetarists' prime 'solution' to the change in the demand for youth labour. Longer periods of education, the relentless pursuit of qualifications, the intensification of schooling and examination, and the generalisation of training to ever-greater numbers of young people, on their own have failed to create the jobs and prosperity that a generation of young people have been promised. The removal of universal entitlements from welfare benefits, the promotion of means-testing augmented by stricter eligibility criteria, lower benefit levels and the requirement to undertake some reciprocal activity have similarly failed to end young people's dependence upon the state, as state support in the form of welfare benefits or tax credits remain more important than ever to the lives of the young. Despite the emphasis on the family, pressures of unemployment, insecurity and the withdrawal of state provision have produced an unprecedented increase in child poverty, the deferment of young people's capacity to live independently and sustain stable family lives for themselves, and have led to a crisis in housing and homelessness. And despite the turn to law and order, governments have presided over a mounting wave of youth offending.

Without doubt this is a bleak assessment. Its premise is the massive political defeat of the socialist movement and the capitulation of the Labour Party at the end of the 1960s and first half of the 1970s, in the face of very real and intense global pressures. In recoiling from any meaningful engagement with capital and the market, as we have argued at some length, Labour set in motion the progressive destruction of those state forms that had given the Keynesian commitment to an inclusive youth some practical substance. In doing so, Labour governments of the 1970s disarmed many of those forces that could have provided the basis for a meaningful opposition to powerful demands for the imposition of austerity measures, thus paving the way for the development of these new political forms of youth. The genuinely progressive possibilities contained within the social democratic commitment to the reform of market relations, however submerged, were abandoned as Labour governments responded by shifting responsibility for the deepening crisis away from the actual sources of failure and onto the those least able to offer meaningful sources of resistance.

Labour in government may have encouraged this changing state of youth but it was the Conservative governments of the 1980s and 1990s that gave it coherence and focus. Slow to begin with, early years of Conservative rule did little more than continue along a trajectory similar to the one that Labour had already set in motion, although this time pursued with much greater ideological conviction and a greater willingness to confront any sources of opposition that dared to stand in its way. It was not until the late 1980s, however, that a genuinely ambitious programme of restructuring emerged. In all aspects of young people's lives, by the turn of the 1990s, the Conservatives had set in place a more coherent and focused programme for the root and branch reconstruction of what it meant to be young. By the time of Labour's election to government once again in 1997, the lives of the young had been transformed.

As a political construction this changed state of youth can, of course, be deconstructed. But the signs that this will happen are not encouraging. The return to governing power of the Labour Party in 1997 after such a prolonged period of opposition, seemed to offer up new possibilities for confronting this new and austere state of youth. New Labour's avowedly youthful focus, its apparent ability to communicate with young people and to tap into their aspirations and anxieties, its concern with the plight of large numbers of young people excluded from meaningful ways of participating in society, its avowed determination to address the multiple and complex sets of problems experienced by more and more young people, seemed to many – welfare professionals, academics, the young themselves – to add up to a genuine 'new deal' for the young.

The substance, however, has been more disappointing. What has emerged from Blair's New Labour has been a reluctance to do much to initiate this deconstruction in ways that could extend to the young some of the practical and substantive sources of support that may have laid the foundations for a meaningful alternative. Of course there is no going back to the past, even if this were a desirable road to take (which it is not). But New Labour's repudiation of monetarism in favour of its own modernising agenda has provided, at best, no more than a pale version of the previous inclusiveness contained within the Party's historic commitment to social democracy. At worst, it represents little more than a humanised version of the monetarist strategy that had seemingly been discarded. Behind the 'Third Way', the politics of 'progressive competitiveness' has so far offered little more than a strategy for the further erosion of young people's rights to and claims upon the resources that could perhaps bring about a more benign and responsive state of youth: the guarantee of a job or alternative source of income, an education genuinely geared to the needs of the young, high quality training or the right to support for independent living determined by need. Without such a strategy, the government's hope that its state sanctioned process of productive efficiency, investment and social effectiveness as the platform for attracting globally mobile capital, will most likely mean further damaging changes to the terms of young people's lives. For the future, at least the immediate one, most young people look set to face a situation defined by the push for a more intensive and selective schooling, the strengthening of employer-led training, a more thoroughly re-regulated labour market, a further lessening of their substantive claims upon the welfare state and even greater resort to the rule of law.

What is certain is that the importance of young people to New Labour's restructuring programme means that talk of youth's demise is certainly premature. In all probability it is most likely mistaken. The background to the expansion of 'youth studies' over the past two or three decades was the need to make sense of the transformations that have overtake the lives of the young during a period in which the post-war world was turned literally up-side down. As we have seen, the 'state' of youth has been transformed beyond recognition but to read these developments as 'the individualisation of young people's biographies and situations' (Roberts 1995: 120), or in a more extreme form as the 'de-centring' of youth into its post-modern fragments (Wallace and Kovatcheva 1998), is to seriously misunderstand the continuing importance of youth and age to the political management of capitalist societies. On the one hand, to equate the proliferation of new institutional contexts for youth with its fragmentation is to ignore that these are, in the main, political (re)constructions that reaffirm the systemic influence of the state and the social relations of production. On the other hand, within the changing state of youth there remains a powerful force of homogenisation as, in many respects, age has become a more important criterion. From the schooling of students, labour market participation and the boundaries of parental responsibility through to the operation of youth justice and the administration of social welfare, the political importance of age and youth is as never before.

What is also certain is that when all is said and done the fortunes of the young will remain inextricably linked, as they did in the past, to that of their bothers and sisters, parents, grandparents and the communities in which they live. Thus to reconstruct a new state of youth in ways more responsive to the needs of the young, one starting point is the urgency of overcoming the arbitrary impositions of age and its value as a source of division. New Labour may offer young people and the problems they face new governmental structures, ministerial-level representation and dedicated committees and units to back these up. But beyond the rhetoric of welfare and development, it is doubtful that they will do much to defend the interests of the young in the face the wider political pressures that governments are facing. In all probability, the new administrative importance attached to youth and age in recent years will become the basis for young people's more effective subordination to the imperatives of New Labour's more general strategy for regeneration. If they do extend meaningful reforms to the young, it will only be at expense of others like children or the elderly, and the increased prominence of age as a principle of social administration will most likely only provide solutions for young people by exporting their problems to others. A starting point for any alternative is therefore one that refuses to mimic the political imposition of divisions through age and the arbitrary separation of the fortunes of young people from those of their families and communities. Only then we will no longer continue to misspend our youth.

Notes

Chapter 1 The Changing State of Youth

1. See the exchange between Bryan Turner and Sarah Irwin in *British Journal of Sociology*, Vol. 49, No. 2.
2. For Marx the social relations of production did not refer to the immediate labour process. Rather Marx argued that 'the relations of production in their totality constitute what are called the social relations, society, and specifically, society at a definite stage of historical development' (1977: 256). As far as the state is concerned, this position has been most fully developed in the 'state debate' conducted under the auspices of the Conference of Socialist Economists. An excellent introduction and critical assessment can be found in Clarke (1991).

Chapter 2 The Changing State of Education

1. Although at times guilty of post-Fordist excesses, Pat Ainley's work is indispensable for an understanding of the trajectory of recent education change. This chapter unashamedly uses his work freely, together with Brian Simon's (1991) definitive history of education covering the 40 years after the Second World War.
2. This was a trend repeated throughout the industrialised world although Britain's historical legacy of relatively low rates of participation in post-compulsory education and training and higher education has persisted (OECD 2000).
3. Further testimony to this is the increased numbers of school leavers who, by the beginning of the 1990s, were simply 'dropping out'. See Chapter 5.

Chapter 3 The Changing State of Work

1. Unless otherwise stated, the figures used here are the seasonally adjusted claimant count, provided by the Office for National Statistics, which take account of past discontinuities (discussed below) in order to be consistent with current definitions.
2. Young people were also targeted under the 1983 Enterprise Allowance Scheme, which provided an allowance of £40 per week for up to 12 months,

for those wanting to start their own businesses and who possessed start-up capital of £1000 (see MacDonald and Coffield 1991).

Chapter 4 The Changing State of Social Security

1. Consideration of social security is limited here to provision for the young unemployed.
2. The cost implications of uprating insurance and means-tested benefits and of fulfilling Beveridge's commitments to properly funded state pensions did, however, cause considerable controversy throughout the period.
3. These points draw upon an email posted by Paul Spicker to the social policy mail base discussion group (social-policy-request@mailbase.ac.uk) on 05/08/98.

Chapter 5 The Changing State of the Family

1. The term status zer0 was derived from how this category of school leaver was classified by the careers service. The term was later sanitised by re-designating these young people as neither in employment, education or training (NEET).

Chapter 6 The Changing State of Law and Order

1. The term 'young offender' has no legal status but is used here to refer a person between 10 and 20 years old who has been found guilty of an offence.
2. The general rule is that Youth Courts will hear criminal cases against all young offenders, aged 10–17 years old.

Chapter 7 A New State of Youth?

1. The remit of the SEU did not stretch to the other regions of the United Kingdom.
2. A 'sixth option' of self-employment under New Deal was subsequently introduced but the mandatory nature of the programme still remains.
3. Reported in the *Guardian*, 28 February 2002.
4. *Times Higher Education Supplement*, 11 May 2001.

Bibliography

Abel Smith, B. and Townsend, P. (1965), *The Poor and the Poorest*, London, Bell and Sons

Addison, P. (1977), *The Road to 1945*, London, Quartet Books

Ainley, P. (1988), *From School to YTS*, Milton Keynes, Open University Press

Ainley, P. (1999a), 'Towards a Learning Society or Towards Learningfare?', May, M., Brunsdon, E. and Craig, G. (eds), *Social Policy Review 9*, London, Social Policy Association

Ainley, P. (1999b), *Learning Policy: Towards a Certified Society*, Basingstoke, Macmillan

Alcock, P. (1999), 'Poverty and Social Security', Page, R. and Silburn, R. (eds), *British Social Welfare in the Twentieth Century*, Basingstoke, Macmillan

Allen, S. (1968), 'Some Theoretical Problems in the Study of Youth', *Sociological Review*, Vol. 16, No. 3

Allen, I. and Bourke Dowling, S. (1998), *Teenage Mothers, Decisions and Outcomes* London, Policy Studies Institute

Anderson, I. (1999), 'Young Single People and Access to Social Housing', Rugg, J. (ed.), *Young People, Housing and Social Policy*, London, Routledge

Andrews, K. and Jacobs, J. (1990), *Punishing the Poor*, London, Macmillan

Ashton, D. (1986), *Unemployment under Capitalism: The Sociology of British and American Labour Markets*, London, Wheatsheaf Books

Ashton, D. and Green, F. (1996), *Education, Training and the Global Economy*, Cheltenham, Edward Elgar

Auld, J., Dorn, N. and South, N. (1986), 'Irregular Work, Irregular Pleasures: Heroin in the 1980s', Mathews, R. and Young, J. (eds), *Confronting Crime*, London, Sage

Bacon, R. and Eltis, W. (1976), *Britain's Economic Problems: Too Few Producers*, London, Macmillan

Balding, J. (2000), *Young People and Illegal Drugs into 2000*, Exeter University, Schools Health Education Unit

Ball, L. (1989), 'What Future YTS?', *Unemployment Bulletin*, London, Unemployment Unit, No. 30, Summer

Ball, S.J. (1993), 'Education Markets, Choice and Social Class: The Market as a Class Strategy in the UK and the US', *British Journal of Sociology of Education*, Vol. 14. No. 1

Ball, S.J. (1998), 'Education Policy', Ellison, N. and Pierson, C. (ed), *Developments in British Social Policy*, Basingstoke, Macmillan

Ball, S.J. (1999), 'Labour, Learning and the Economy: A "Policy Sociology" Perspective', *Cambridge Journal of Education*, Vol. 29, No. 2

Banks, M. and Bryn Davies, J. (1990), *Motivation, Unemployment and Employment Department Programmes*, London, Department of Employment, Research Paper No. 80

Banks, M., Bates, I., Breakwell, G., Bynner, J., Emler, N., Jamieson, L. and Roberts, K. (1992), *Careers and Identities*, Milton Keynes, Open University Press

Barnett, C. (1986), *The Audit of War*, London, Macmillan

Bates, I. and Riseborough, G. (eds) (1993), *Youth and Inequality*, Milton Keynes, Open University Press

Benn, C. and Fairley, J. (1988), 'Introduction: Towards an Alternative Policy for Jobs, Training and Education', Benn, C. and Fairley, J. (eds), *Challenging the MSC: On Jobs, Education and Training*, London, Pluto Press

Bivand, P. (1998), 'Employment Service Annual Report', *Working Brief*, London, Unemployment Unit/Youthaid, Issue 98, October

Bivand, P. (2000), 'Outside Education and Work: Do the Numbers Add Up?', *Working Brief*, London, Unemployment Unit/Youthaid, Issue 119, January

Bivand, P. (2002a), 'New Deal Causes "Surprise" Fall in Claimant Count', *Working Brief*, London, Centre for Social Inclusion, Issue 133, April

Bivand, P. (2002b), 'New Deal for Lone Parents Proves Most Cost Effective', *Working Brief*, London, Centre for Economic and Social Inclusion, Issue 131, February

Bonefeld, W., Gunn, R. and Psychopedis, K. (1992) (eds), *Open Marxism: Volume 1*, Basingstoke, Macmillan.

Bonefeld, W., Brown, A. and Burnham, P. (1995), *A Major Crisis? The Politics of Economic Policy in Britain in the 1990s*, Aldershot, Dartmouth Publishing

Bosanquet, N. (1983), *After the New Right*, London, Heineman

Boulton, A. (1990), 'Youth Homelessness and Health Care', Fisher, K. and Collins, J. (eds), *Homelessness, Health Care and Welfare Provision*, London, Routledge

Bowles, S. and Gintis, H. (1976), *Schooling in Capitalist America*, London, Routledge

Box, S. (1987), *Recession, Crime and Punishment*, Basingstoke, Macmillan

Britton, L. (2002), 'Sanctions and the Hard to Help', *Working Brief*, London, Centre for Economic and Social Inclusion, Issue 130, January

Brewer, M. and Gregg, P. (2002), *Eradicating Child Poverty in Britain, Welfare Reform and Children since 1997*, Working Paper 01/08, London, Institute for Fiscal Studies

Brown, S. (1998), *Understanding Youth and Crime*, Milton Keynes, Open University Press

Brown, P. and Lauder, H. (1996), 'Education, Globalisation and Economic Development', *Journal of Education Policy*, Vol. 11, No. 2

Brown, P. and Lauder, H. (2000), *Capitalism and Social Progress*, Basingstoke, Palgrave

Bryson, A. and Jacobs, J. (1992), *Policing the Workshy*, Avebury, Aldershot

Burnham, P. (1999), 'The Politics of Economic Management in the 1990s', *New Economy*, Vol. 4, No. 1.

Burnham, P. (2001), 'New Labour and the Politics of Depoliticisation', *The British Journal of Politics and International Relations*, Vol. 3, No. 2

Bynner, J., Ferris, E. and Shephered, P. (1997), *Twenty Something in the 1990s*, Aldershot, Ashgate

Byrne, D. (1999), *Social Exclusion*, Milton Keynes, Open University Press

Callender, C. and Kemp, M. (2000), *Changing Student Finances: Income, Expenditure and the Take-Up of Student Loans*, London, Department for Education and Employment

Campbell, A. (1981), *Delinquent Girls*, Oxford, Blackwell

Carlen, P. (1996), *Jigsaw: A Political Criminology of Youth Homelessness*, Milton Keynes, Open University Press

Carlen, P., Gleeson, D., and Wardhaugh, J. (1992), *Truancy: The Politics of Compulsory Schooling*, Buckingham, Open University Press

Carter, M. (1966), *Into Work*, London, Pelican

Casey, B. and Smith, D. (1995), *Truancy and Youth Transitions*, Sheffield, Employment Department

Centre for Contemporary Cultural Studies (1978), *Unpopular Education: Schooling and Education in Britain since 1945*, London, Hutchinson

CESI (2002), 'Little Change in Work Training', *Working Brief*, London, Centre for Economic and Social Inclusion, Issue 133, April

Clarke, S. (1987), 'Capitalist Crisis and the Rise of Monetarism', Panitch, L. and Miliband, R. (eds), *The Socialist Register*, London, Merlin Press

Clarke, S. (1990), 'Crisis of Socialism or Crisis of the State?', *Capital and Class*, No. 42, Winter

Clarke, S. (1991), 'The State Debate', S. Clarke (ed.), *The State Debate*, Basingstoke, Macmillan

Clarke, J. and Willis, P. (1984), 'Introduction', Bates, I., Clarke, J., Cohen, P., Finn, D., Moore, R. and Willis, P. (eds), *Schooling for the Dole: The New Vocationalism*, Basingstoke, Macmillan

Clarke, J. and Langan, M. (1993), 'Restructuring British Welfare: The British Welfare Regime in the 1990s', Cochrane, A. and Clarke, J. (eds), *Comparing Welfare States: Britain in International Context*, London, Sage

Coates, D. (2000), *Models of Capitalism: Growth and Stagnation in the Modern Era*, Cambridge, Polity Press

Coates, D. (2002), 'New Labour and the Pursuit of International Competitiveness', Paper presented to the *International Studies Association Annual Convention*, New Orleans, United States, March

Cockburn, C. (1988), *Two-Track Training: Sex Inequalities and the YTS*, Basingstoke, Macmillan

Coffield, F. and Grafton, L. (1994), *Drugs and Young People*, London, Institute for Public Policy Research

Cohen, P. (1997), *Rethinking the Youth Question*, Basingstoke, Macmillan

Cohen, P. and Ainley, P. (2000), 'In the Country of the Blind?: Youth Studies and Cultural Studies in Britain', *Journal of Youth Studies*, Vol. 3, No. 1

Coleman, J. and Hendry, L. (1991), *The Nature of Adolescence*, London, Routledge

Coles, B. (1995), *Youth and Social Policy: Youth, Citizenship and Young Careers*, London, UCL Press

Coles, B. (2000a), *Joined-Up Youth Research, Policy and Practice: A New Agenda for Change?*, Leicester, Youth Work Press

Coles, B. (2000b), 'Slouching Towards Bethlehem: Youth Policy and the Work of the Social Exclusion Unit', Dean, H., Sykes, R. and Woods, R. (eds), *Social Policy Review 12*, London, Social Policy Association

Convery, P. (1998), 'Allowances for Trainees and the Unemployed', *Working Brief*, London, Unemployment Unit/Youthaid, Issue 94, June

Corrigan, P. (1977), *Schooling the Smash Street Kids*, London, Macmillan

COYPSS (1999), *Sort it Out! Reforming the Benefit System for 16 and 17 Year Olds*, London, Coalition of Young People and Social Security

Cregan, C. (2002), 'Are Things Really Getting Better? The Labour Market Experience of Black and Female Youth at the Start of the Twentieth Century', *Capital and Class*, No. 77, Summer

Crow, I., Richardson, P., Riddington, C. and Simon, F. (1989), *Unemployment, Crime and Offenders*, London, Routledge

CSU (2002), *Graduate Market Trends*, Spring, www.prospects.ac.uk/student/cidd/

Cutler, T. (1992), 'Vocational Training and British Economic Performance: Another Instalment of the British Labour Problem', *Work, Employment and Society*, Vol. 6, No. 2

Dale, R. (1989), *The State and Education Policy*, Milton Keynes, Open University Press

Daniel, P. and Ivatts, J. (1998), *Children and Social Policy*, Basingstoke, Macmillan

David, M. (1993), *Parents, Gender and Education Reform*, Cambridge, Polity Press

Davies, B. (1986), *Threatening Youth: Towards a National Youth Policy*, Milton Keynes, Open University Press

Deacon, A. (1997), 'Welfare to Work: Options and Issues', May, M., Brunsdon, E. and Craig, G. (eds), *Social Policy Review 9*, London, Social Policy Association

Deakin, B.M. (1996), *The Youth Labour Market in Britain: The Role of Intervention*, Cambridge, Cambridge University Press

Deakin, S. and Wilkinson, F. (1991), 'Labour Law, Social Security and Economic Inequality', *Cambridge Journal of Economics*, Vol. 15, No. 2

Dean, H. and Taylor Gooby, P. (1992), *Dependency Culture: The Explosion of a Myth*, London, Harvester Wheatsheaf

Dean, H. and Melrose, M. (1999), 'Unravelling Citizenship', *Critical Social Policy*, No. 48

Department for Education and Employment (1995), *Youth Training Leavers Survey*, London, Department for Education and Employment

Department for Education and Employment (1996), *Learning to Compete: Education and Training for 14 to 19 Year Olds*, Cm 3486, London, Stationery Office

Department for Education and Employment (1997), *Careers Service Activity Survey*, London, Department for Education and Employment

Department for Education and Employment (2000), *Statistics of Education: Schools in England*, London, The Stationery Office

Department of Employment (1981), *The New Training Initiative: An Agenda for Action*, Cmnd 8450, London, HMSO

Department of Employment (1988a), *Employment for the 1990s*, Cm 540, London, HMSO

Department of Employment (1988b), *Training for Employment*, Cm 316, London, HMSO

Department of Employment (1994), *Jobseeker's Allowance*, Cm 2687, London, HMSO

Department of Social Security (1992), *Social Security Statistics*, London, HMSO

Department of Social Security (1998a), *New Ambitions for Our Country: A New Contract for Welfare*, Cmnd 3805, London, Stationery Office

Department of Social Security (1998b), *A New Contract for Welfare: New Ambitions for Our Country*, Cm 3805, London, The Stationery Office

Diaz, R. and Coleman, B. (1997), *Who Says There's No Housing Problem?*, London, Shelter

Downes, D. and Rock, P. (1995), *Understanding Deviance: A Guide to the Sociology of Crime and Rule Breaking*, Oxford, Clarendon Press

Drakeford, M. and McCarthy, K. (2000), 'Parents, Responsibility and the New Youth Justice', Goldson, B. (ed.), *The New Youth Justice*, Lyme Regis, Russell House Publishing

Driver, S. and Martel, L. (1998), *New Labour: Politics After Thatcherism*, Cambridge, Polity Press

Durning, J.M., Johnson, S.W., Shaw, J.L. and Lancer, P. (1990), *Efficiency Scrutiny: Take Up of Employment Department Programmes*, London, Employment Department

Dutton, P. (1987), *The Impact of YTS on Engineering Apprenticeships: A Local Labour Market Study*, Coventry, Institute for Employment Research, University of Warwick

Economist (2001), *Survey of Illegal Drugs*, London, Economist, 28 July 2001

Education Group (1981), *Unpopular Education: Schooling and Social Democracy in England since 1944*, London, Hutchinson

Edwards, P. (1998), 'Minimum Pay', *European Industrial Relations Observatory On-line*, eiroline, www.eiro.eurofound.ie/1998/07/Feature/UK9807135F.html

Eisenstadt, S.N. (1956), *From Generation to Generation: Age Groups and Social Structure*, New York, The Free Press

Ermisch, J. (1990), *Fewer Babies, Longer Lives*, London, Joseph Rowntree Foundation

Etzioni, A. (1993), *The Spirit of Community: The Reinvention of American Society*, New York, Touchstone

Evans, M. (1998), 'Social Security: Dismantling the Pyramids?', H. Glennerster and Hills, J. (eds), *The State of Welfare: The Economics of Social Spending*, Second Edition, Basingstoke, Macmillan

Farrington, D.P. (1992), 'Trends in English Juvenile Delinquency and their Explanation', *International Journal of Comparative and Applied Criminal Justice*, Vol. 16, No. 2

Field, F. (1996), 'Stakeholder Welfare', A. Deacon (ed.), *Stakeholder Welfare*, London, Institute for Economic Affairs

Field, F. (1997), 'Re-inventing Welfare: A Response to Lawrence Mead', L. Mead (ed.), *From Welfare to Work: Lessons from America*, London, Institute for Economic Affairs

Finegold, D. and Soskice, D. (1988), 'The Failure of Training in Britain: Analysis and Prescriptions', *Oxford Review of Economic Policy*, Vol. 4, No. 3

Finn, D. (1982), 'Whose Needs? Schooling and the "Needs" of Industry', Rees, T.L. and Atkinson, P. (eds), *Youth Unemployment and State Intervention*, London, Routledge and Kegan Paul Ltd

Finn, D. (1987), *Training Without Jobs: New Deals and Broken Promises*, Basingstoke, Macmillan

Finn, D. (1988), 'Training and Employment Schemes for the Long-Term Unemployed: British Government Policy for the 1990s', *Work, Employment and Society*, Vol. 2, No. 4

Finn, D. (1998), 'Labour's New Deal for the Unemployed and the Stricter Benefits Regime', Brunsdon, E., Dean, H. and Woods, R. (eds), *Social Policy Review 10*, London, Social Policy Association

Finn, D. (2001), 'Welfare to Work? New Labour and the Unemployed', Savage, S.P. and Atkinson, R. (eds), *Public Policy under Blair*, Basingstoke, Palgrave

Flood-Page, C., Campbell, S., Harrington, V. and Miller, J. (2000), *Youth Lifestyles Survey*, London, Home Office, Research Study 209

France, A. (1996), 'Youth and Citizenship in the 1990s', *Youth and Policy*, No. 53.

Frith, S. (1980), 'Education, Training and the Labour Process', Cole, M. and Skelton, B. (eds), *Blind Alley: Youth in a Crisis of Capital*, Ormskirk, G.W. and A. Hesketh

Frith, S. (1984), *The Sociology of Youth*, Ormskirk, Causeway Press

Furlong, A. and Cartmel, F. (1997), *Young People and Social Change: Individualisation and Risk in Late Modernity*, Milton Keynes, Open University Press

Gabriel, Y. (1988), *Working Lives in Catering*, London, Routledge

Gerwitz, S. (1999), 'Education Action Zones: Emblems of the Third Way' Dean, H. and Woods, R. (eds), *Social Policy Review 11*, London, Social Policy Association

Giddens, A. (1998), *The Third Way*, Cambridge, Polity Press

Gilchrist, R. and Jeffs, T. (1995), 'Foyers: Housing Solution or Folly', *Youth and Policy*, No. 50

Gilroy, P. (1987), *There Ain't No Black in the Union Jack*, London, Routledge

Ginsburg, N. (1979), *Class, Capital and Social Policy*, London, Macmillan

Gleeson, D. and McLean, M. (1994), 'Whatever Happened to TVEI? TVEI, Curriculum and Schooling', *Journal of Education Policy*, Vol. 9, No. 3

Glennerster, H. (1998), 'Education: Reaping the Harvest?', Glennerster, H. and Hills, J. (eds), *The State of Welfare: The Economics of Social Spending*, Oxford, Oxford University Press

Glover, C. and Stewart, J. (2000), 'Modernizing Social Security? Labour and its Welfare-to-Work Strategy', *Social Policy and Administration*, Vol. 34, No. 3

Glynn, S. (1991), *No Alternative? Unemployment in Britain*, London, Faber and Faber

Glynn, S. and Booth, A. (1996), *Modern Britain: An Economic and Social History*, London, Routledge

Goldson, B. (1997a), 'Children, Crime, Policy and Practice: Neither Welfare Nor Justice', *Children and Society*, Vol. 11

Goldson, B. (1997b), 'Children in Trouble: State Responses to Juvenile Justice', P. Scraton (ed.), *Childhood in Crisis*, London, UCL Press

Goldson, B. (2000), 'Wither Diversion? Interventionism and the New Youth Justice', Goldson, B. (ed.), *The New Youth Justice*, Lyme Regis, Russell House Publishing

Gough, I. (1979), *The Political Economy of Welfare*, London, Macmillan

Graham, J. and Bowling, B. (1995), *Young People and Crime*, London, Home Office, Research Study 145

Gray, D. and King, S. (1986), *The Youth Training Scheme: The First Three Years*, Sheffield, Manpower Services Commission

Griffin, C. (1992), *Representations of Youth*, Cambridge, Polity Press

Haines, K. and Drakeford, M. (1998), *Young People and Youth Justice*, Basingstoke, Macmillan

Hall, S. and Jefferson, T. (eds) (1976), *Resistance Through Rituals: Youth Subcultures in Post-War Britain*, London, Harper Collins

Hall, S., Critcher, C., Jefferson, T., Clarke, J. and Roberts, B. (1978), *Policing the Crisis: Mugging, the State and Law and Order*, London, Macmillan

Hall, T., Williamson, H. and Coffey, A. (1998), 'Conceptualising Citizenship: Young People and the Transition to Adulthood', *Journal of Education Policy*, Vol. 13, No. 3

Halsey, A.H. (2000), 'Further and Higher Education', A.H. and Webb, J. (eds), *Twentieth Century British Social Trends*, Basingstoke, Macmillan

Halsey, A.H. and Young, M. (1997), 'The Family and Social Justice', in A.H. Halsey, H. Lauder, P. Brown and A. Stuart Wells (eds), *Education: Culture, Economy, Society*, Oxford, Oxford University Press

Harris, N. (1988), 'Social Security and the Transition to Adulthood', *Journal of Social Policy*, Vol. 17, No. 4

Hasluck, C. (2001), 'Lessons from the New Deal: Finding Work, Promoting Employability', *New Economy*, Vol. 8, No. 4

Hatcher, R. and Hirtt, N. (1999), 'The Business Agenda Behind Labour's Education Policy', Allen, M., Benn, C., Chitty, C., Cole, M., Hatcher, R.,

Hirtt, N. and Rikowski, G., *Business, Business, Business: New Labour's Education Policy*, London, The Tufnell Press

Hay, C. (1999), *The Political Economy of New Labour*, Manchester, Manchester University Press

Hebdige, D. (1988), *Hiding in the Light: On Images and Things*, London, Comedia Books

Hill, M. (1991), *Social Security Policy in Britain*, Aldershot, Edward Elgar

Hills, J. (1995), *Inquiry into Income and Wealth*, York, Joseph Rowntree Foundation

Hills, J. (1998), *Thatcherism, New Labour and the Welfare State*, London, Centre for the Analysis of Social Exclusion, London School of Economics, CASE Paper 13, August

Hobbs, S., Lindsay, S. and McKechnie, J. (1996), 'The Extent of Child Employment in Britain', *British Journal of Education and Work*, Vol. 9, No. 1

Hobsbawm, E. (1994), *Age of Extremes: The Short History of the Twentieth Century*, London, Michael Joseph

Holloway, J. (1992), 'The State and Everyday Struggle', S. Clarke (ed.), *The State Debate*, Basingstoke, Macmillan

Holloway, J. and Picciotto, S. (1978), *State and Capital: A Marxist Debate*, London, Arnold

Home Office (1998), *Drug Misuse Declared in 1998: Latest Results from the British Crime Survey*, London, Home Office, Research Study 197

Home Office (1999), *Criminal Statistics: England and Wales*, London, Office for National Statistics

Home Office (2000), *Statistics on Race and the Criminal Justice System*, London, Home Office

Horn, P. (1994), *Children's Work and Welfare 1780–1890*, Cambridge, Cambridge University Press

Howard, M., Garnham, A., Fimister, F. and Veit-Wilson, J. (2001), *Poverty, the Facts*, London, CPAG

Humphries, S. (1990), *Hooligans or Rebels?*, Oxford, Blackwell

Hutson, S. and Liddiard, M. (1994), *Youth Homelessness, the Construction of a Social Issue*, London, Macmillan

Irwin, S. (1995), *Rights of Passage: Social Change and the Transition from Youth to Adulthood*, London, UCL Press

Jones, C. and Novak, T. (1999), *Poverty, Welfare and the Disciplinary State*, London, Routledge

Jones, G. (1988), 'Integrating Process and Structure in the Concept of Youth: A Case for Secondary Analysis', *Sociological Review*, Vol. 36, No. 4

Jones, G. and Wallace, C. (1992), *Youth, Family and Citizenship*, Milton Keynes, Open University Press

Kalra, V.S., Fieldhouse, E.A. and Alam, S. (2001), 'Avoiding the New Deal', *Youth and Policy*, No. 72

Kendall, I. and Holloway, D. (2001), 'Education Policy', Savage, S.P. and Atkinson, R. (eds), *Public Policy under Thatcher*, Basingstoke, Palgrave

Kettle, M. (1983), 'The Drift to Law and Order', Hall, S. and Jacques, M. (eds), *The Politics of Thatcherism*, London, Lawrence and Wishart

Kettle, M. and Hodges, L. (1982), *Uprising*, London, Paladin

Kiernan, K., Land, H. and Lewis, J. (1998) *Lone Motherhood in Twentieth Century Britain: From Footnote to Front Page*, Oxford, Clarendon Press

King, D. (1995), *Actively Seeking Work?*, Chicago, Chicago University Press

Kumar, V. (1993), *Poverty and Inequality in the UK: The Effects on Children*, London, National Children's Bureau

Langan, M. (1996), 'The Crumbling Bridges Between Childhood and Adulthood', Brannen, J. and O'Brien, M. (eds), *Children in Families: Research and Policy*, London, Falmer Press

Lavallette, M. (1995), *Child Employment in the Capitalist Labour Market*, Aldershot, Avebury

Layard, R. (1997), 'Preventing Long-Term Unemployment: An Economic Analysis', Snower, D. and de la Dehesa, G. (eds), *Unemployment Policy: Government Options for the Labour Market*, Cambridge, Cambridge University Press

Lea, J. and Young, J. (1984), *What is to be Done About Law and Order?*, Harmondsworth, Penguin

Lee, D. and Wrench, J. (1983), *Skill Seekers*, Leicester, National Youth Bureau

Lee, D., Marsden, D., Rickman, P. and Duncombe, J. (1990), *Scheming for Youth: A Study of YTS in the Enterprise Culture*, Milton Keynes, Open University Press

Levitas, R. (1996), 'The Concept of Social Exclusion and the New Durkheimian Hegemony', *Critical Social Policy*, Vol. 16, No. 46

Levitas, R. (1998), *The Inclusive Society? Social Exclusion and New Labour*, Basingstoke, Macmillan

Lindley, R.M. (1983), 'Active Manpower Policy', Bain, G.S. (ed.), *Industrial Relations in Britain*, Oxford, Basil Blackwell

London Edinburgh Weekend Return Group (1980), *In and Against the State*, London, Pluto Press

Low Pay Commission (1998), *The National Minimum Wage: First Report of the Low Pay Commission*, Cm 3976, London, Stationery Office

Low Pay Commission (2001), *The National Minimum Wage: Making a Difference*, Third Report of the Low Pay Commission, Cm 5075, London, Stationery Office

Lucas, R. (1997), 'Youth, Gender and Part-Time Work, Students in the Labour Process', *Work, Employment and Society*, Vol. 11, No. 4

Lund, B. (2000), 'Work and Need', Dean, H., Sykes, R. and Woods. R. (eds), *Social Policy Review 12*, London, Social Policy Association

MacDonald, R. (1997), *Youth, The 'Underclass' and Social Exclusion*, London, Routledge

MacDonald, R. and Coffield, F. (1991), *A Risky Business? Youth and The Enterprise Culture*, London, Falmer Press

MacKinnon, D. and Statham, J., with Hales, M. (1996), *Education in the UK: Facts and Figures*, London, Hodder and Stoughton

Maclagan, I. (1997), *Out of Credit: A Report on the Impact of Youth Credits*, London, Youthaid

Maguire, M. (1991), 'British Labour Market Trends', Ashton, D. and Lowe, G. (eds), *Making their Way: Education, Training and the Labour Market in Britain and Canada*, Milton Keynes, Open University Press

Maguire, M. (1997), 'Crime Statistics, Patterns and Trends: Changing Perceptions and their Implications', M. Maguire, R. Morgan and R. Reiner (eds), *The Oxford Handbook of Criminology*, Oxford, Oxford University Press

Maguire, S. and Maguire, M. (1996), 'Young People and the Labour Market', MacDonald, R. (ed.), *Youth, the Underclass and Social Exclusion*, London, Routledge

Marsland, D. (1996), *Welfare or Welfare State?*, Basingstoke, Macmillan

Marx, K. (1977), 'Wage Labour and Capital', G. McLellan (ed.), *Karl Marx: Selected Writings*, Oxford, Oxford University Press

Mays, J.B. (1972), *Juvenile Delinquency, the Family and Social Group*, London, Longman

McIlroy, R. (2000), 'How is the New Deal for Young People Working?', *European Industrial Relations Observatory On-line*, eiroline, www.eiro.eurofound.i.e./print/2000/02/feature/UK0002155F.html

McKay, G. (1996), *Senseless Acts of Beauty: Cultures of Resistance since the Sixties*, London, Verso

McRobbie, A. (1995), *Post-Modernism and Popular Culture*, London, Routledge

Measham, F., Newcombe, R. and Parker, T. (1994), 'The Normalisation of Recreational Drug Use Among Young People in the North West of England', *British Journal of Sociology*, Vol. 45, No. 2

Meiksins Wood, E. (1995), *Democracy Against Capitalism*, Cambridge, Cambridge University Press

Middleton, S. Ashworth, K. and Braithwaite, I. (1997), *Small Fortunes, Spending on Children, Childhood Poverty and Parental Sacrifice*, York, Joseph Rowntree Foundation

Middleton, S. and Loumidis, J. (2001), 'Young People, Poverty and Part-time Work', Mizen, P., Pole, C. and Bolton, A. (eds), *Hidden Hands, International Perspectives on Children's Work and Labour*, London, RoutledgeFalmer

Milner, J. and Blythe, E. (1999), *Improving School Attendance*, London, Routledge

Minford, P. (1985), *Unemployment: Cause and Cure*, Oxford, Basil Blackwell

Mizen, P. (1990), 'Race Equality in London's Youth Training Schemes', *Unemployment Bulletin*, No. 32, Spring

Mizen, P. (1995), *Young People, Training and the State: In and Against the Training State*, London, Mansell

Mizen, P. (2003a), 'The Best Days of Your Life? Youth, Policy and Blair's New Labour', *Youth and Policy*, No. 42.

Mizen, P. (2003b), 'Tomorrow's Future or Signs of a Misspent Youth? Youth, Policy and the First Blair Government', *Critical Social Policy*.

Mizen, P., Pole, C. and Bolton, A. (1999), 'School Age Workers, The Paid Employment of Children in Britain', *Work, Employment and Society*, Vol. 13, No. 3

Mizen, P., Pole, C. and Bolton, A. (eds) (2001), *Hidden Hands, International Perspectives on Children's Work and Labour*, London, RoutledgeFalmer

Moore, S. (2000), 'Children, Incarceration and the New Youth Justice', Goldson, B. (ed.), *The New Youth Justice*, Lyme Regis, Russell House Publishing

Morgan, R. (1997), 'Imprisonment: Current Concerns and a Brief History since 1945', Maguire, M., Morgan, R. and Reiner, R. (eds), *The Oxford Handbook of Criminology*, Oxford, Oxford University Press

Morris, L. and Llewellyn, T. (1991), *Social Security Provision for the Unemployed: A Report for the Social Security Advisory Committee*, London, HMSO, Social Security Advisory Committee, Research Paper No. 3

Morrow, V. (1994), 'Responsible Children? Aspects of Children's Work and Employment Outside School in Contemporary UK', B. Mayall (ed.), *Children's Childhoods, Observed and Experienced*, London, Falmer Press

Muncie, J. (1997), *Youth and Crime*, London, Sage

Muncie, J. (1999), 'Institutionalised Intolerance: Youth Justice and the 1998 Crime and Disorder Act', *Critical Social Policy*, Vol. 19, No. 2

Muncie, J. (2000), 'Pragmatic Realism? Searching for Criminology in the New Youth Justice', Goldson, B. (ed.), *The New Youth Justice*, Lyme Regis, Russell House Publishing

Mungham, G. (1982), 'Workless Youth as a "Moral Panic"', Rees, T.L. and Atkinson, R. (ed.), *Youth Unemployment and State Intervention*, London, Routledge and Kegan Paul

Murray, C. (1990), *The Underclass in Britain*, London, Institute for Economic Affairs

Murray, C. (1992), *The Emerging British Underclass*, London, Institute for Economic Affairs

Murray, I. (1996), 'Compulsion is Not Working', *Working Brief*, London, Unemployment Unit, Issue 71, February

Murray, I. (1997), 'Employment Service Targets Under Review', *Working Brief*, Unemployment Unit, London, Issue 88, October

Muschamp, Y., Jamieson, I. and Lauder, H. (1999), 'Education, Education, Education', Powell, M. (ed.), *New Labour, New Welfare State? The Third Way in British Politics*, Bristol, Policy Press

NACAB (1994), *In Search of Work: CAB Evidence on Employment and Training Programmes for Unemployed People*, London, National Association of Citizen's Advice Bureaus

NACRO (2000), *Youth Crime: Fact Sheet*, London, NACRO

Naidoo, R. and Callender, C. (2000), 'Towards a More Inclusive System? Contemporary Policy Reform in Higher Education', Dean, H., Sykes, R. and Woods, R. (eds), *Social Policy Review 12*, London, Social Policy Association

Newburn, T. (1996), *Crime and Criminal Justice Policy*, London, Longmans

Newburn, T. (1997), 'Youth, Crime and Justice', Maguire, M., Morgan, R. and Reiner, R. (eds), *The Oxford Handbook of Criminology*, Oxford, Oxford University Press

Newburn, T. and Stanko, E. (eds) (1994), *Just Boys Doing the Business*, London, Routledge

Novak, T. (1997), 'Hounding Delinquents: The Introduction of the Jobseeker's Allowance', *Critical Social Policy*, Vol. 17, No. 1

Novak, T. (1998), 'Young People, Class and Poverty', Jones, H. (ed.), *Towards a Classless Society?*, London, Routledge

OECD (1996), 'Growing into Work: Youth and the Labour Market Over the 1980s and 1990s', *Economic Outlook*, Paris, Organisation for Economic Co-Operation and Development

OECD (2000), *Giving Young People a Good Start: The Experience of OECD Countries*, London, OECD Minister's Conference on Youth Employment

Office for National Statistics (1996), *Social Trends 26*, London, The Stationery Office

Office for National Statistics (1998), *Social Trends 28*, London, Office for National Statistics

O'Higgins, N. (2001), *Employment and Unemployment Policy*, Geneva, International Labour Office

O'Keefe, D. (1993), *Truancy in English Secondary Schools*, London, HMSO

Oppenheim, C. and Harker, L. (1996), *Poverty: The Facts*, London, Child Poverty Action Group

Osler, A. and Hill, J. (1999), 'Exclusion From School and Racial Equality', *Cambridge Journal of Education*, Vol. 29, No. 1

Parker, H. (1998), *Illegal Pleasures*, London, Routledge

Parsons, C. (1998), *Education, Exclusion and Citizenship*, London, Routledge

Parsons, T. (1942), 'Age and Sex in the Social Structure of the United States', *American Sociological Review*, No. 7

Pearson, G. (1987), *Young People and Heroin*, Aldershot, Gower

Pearson, G. (1991), *Hooligan: A History of Respectable Fears*, Basingstoke, Macmillan

Peck, J. (1991), 'Letting the Market Decide (with public money): Training and Enterprise Councils and the Future of Labour Market Programmes', *Critical Social Policy*, Vol. 11, No. 1

Peck, J. (2001), 'Job Alert! Spins and Statistics in Welfare to Work Policy', *Benefits*, Issue 30, January/February

Phoenix, A. (1991), *Young Mothers?*, Cambridge, Polity Press

Pierson, C. (1991), *Beyond the Welfare State?*, Cambridge, Polity Press

Pitts, J. (1988), *The Politics of Juvenile Crime*, London, Sage

Pitts, J. (1996), 'The Politics and Practice of Youth Justice', E. McLaughlin and J. Muncie (eds), *Controlling Crime*, London, Sage

Pitts, J. (2000), 'The New Youth Justice and the Politics of Electoral Anxiety', Goldson, B. (ed.), *The New Youth Justice*, Lyme Regis, Russell House Publishing

Please, N. and Quilgars, D. (1999), 'Youth Homelessness', Rugg, J. (ed.), *Young People, Housing and Social Policy*, London, Routledge

Pollert, A. (1988), 'The "Flexible Firm": Fixation or Fact?', *Work, Employment and Society*, Vol. 2, No. 3

Pollert, A. (1996), 'Gender and Class Revisited; or, the Poverty of "Patriarchy"', *Sociology*, Vol. 30, No. 4

Powell, M. (2001), 'Mind the Gap: Exploring the Implementation Deficit in the Administration of the Stricter Benefits Regime', *Social Policy and Administration*, Vol. 35, No. 2

Power, A. and Tunstall, R. (1997), *Dangerous Disorder: Riots and Violent Disturbances in 13 Areas of Britatin 1991–92*, York, Joseph Rowntree Foundation

Pullinger, J. and Summerfield, C. (eds) (1998), *Social Focus on the Unemployed*, London, The Stationery Office

Quilgars, D. and Please, N. (1999), 'Housing and Support Services for Young People', Rugg, J. (ed.), *Young People, Housing and Social Policy*, London, Routledge

Raffe, D. (1983), 'Can There be an Effective Youth Unemployment Policy', Fiddy, R. (ed.), *In Place of Work?*, Brighton, The Falmer Press

Redhead, S. (1993), 'The Politics of Ecstasy', S. Redhead (ed.), *Rave Off*, Aldershot, Avebury

Reid, R. (1999), *Truancy in Schools*, London, Routledge

Reiner, R. (1989), 'Race and Criminal Justice', *New Community*, Vol. 16, No. 1, October

Riley, R. and Young, G. (1999), *The Macroeconomic Impact of the New Deal for Young People*, Discussion Paper 184, London, National Institute for Economic Research

Roberts, K. (1995), *Youth and Employment in Modern Britain*, Oxford, Oxford University Press

Rolfe, H. (1996), *The Effectiveness of TECs in Achieving Jobs or Qualifications for Disadvantaged Groups*, London, HMSO

Rugg, J. (1999), 'The Use and "Abuse" of Private Renting and Help with Rental Costs', Rugg, J. (ed.), *Young People, Housing and Social Policy*, London, Routledge

Selman, P. (1996), 'Teenage Motherhood Then and Now: A Comparison of the Pattern and Outcomes of Teenage Pregnancy in England and Wales in the 1960s and 1980s', Jones, G. and Millar, J. (eds), *The Politics of the Family*, Aldershot, Avebury

Shiner, M. and Newburn, T. (1997), 'Definitely, Maybe Not? The Normalisation of Recreational Drug Use Amongst Young People', *Sociology*, Vol. 31, No. 3

Shire, D. (1997), *Half Truths, Half Measures: Hidden Statistics on Black Unemployment*, London, Black Employment Institute

Simon, B. (1988), *Bending the Rules: The Baker 'Reform' of Education*, London, Lawrence and Wishart

Simon, B. (1991), *Education and the Social Order*, London, Lawrence and Wishart

Sinfield, A. and Showler, B. (1981), 'Unemployment and the Unemployed in 1980', Showler, B. and Sinfield, A. (eds), *The Workless State*, London, Martin Robinson

Skellington, R. (1992), *'Race' in Britain Today*, London, Sage

Smith, D. (1983), 'Structural Functionalist Accounts of Youth', *Youth and Policy*, Vol. 1, No. 3

Smith, G. (2000), 'Schools', Halsey, A.H. and Webb, J. (eds), *Twentieth Century British Social Trends*, Basingstoke, Macmillan

Smith, J. (1997), 'The Ideology of "Family and Community": New Labour Abandons the Welfare State', Miliband, R. and Pantich, L. (eds), *Socialist Register*, London, Merlin Press

Smith, J.D. (1995), 'Youth Crime and Conduct Disorders', Rutter, M. and Smith, J.D. (eds), *Psychosocial Disorders in Youth*, Chichester, Wiley

Smith, J.D. (1997), 'Ethnic Origins, Crime and Criminal Justice', Maguire, M., Morgan, R. and Reiner, R. (eds), *The Oxford Handbook of Criminology*, Oxford, Oxford University Press

Social Exclusion Unit (1998a), *Rough Sleeping*, Cm 4008, London, Stationery Office

Social Exclusion Unit (1998b), *Truancy and Exclusion*, Cm 3957, London, Stationery Office

Social Exclusion Unit (1999a), *Bridging the Gap: New Opportunities for 16–18 Year Olds Not in Education, Employment or Training*, Cm 4405, London, Stationery Office

Social Exclusion Unit (1999b), *Teenage Pregnancy*, Cm 4342, London, Stationery Office

Solomos, J. (1988), *Black Youth, Racism and the State*, Cambridge, Cambridge University Press

South, N. (1997), 'Drugs, Use, Crime and Control', M. Maguire *et al.* (eds), *Oxford Handbook of Criminology*, Oxford, Oxford University Press

Stafford, A. (1981), 'Learning Not to Labour', *Capital and Class*, No. 15. Autumn

Standing, G. (1997), 'Globalisation, Labour Flexibility and Insecurity: The Era of Market Regulation', *European Journal of Industrial Relations*, Vol. 3, No. 1

Steinberg, L.D., Greenberger, E., Vaux, A. and Ruggiero, M. (1981), 'Early Work Experience: Effects on Adolescent Occupational Socialisation', *Youth and Society*, Vol. 12, No. 4

Taylor, A. (1993), *Women Drug Users*, Oxford, Clarendon Press

Taylor Gooby, P. (1992), 'The New Educational Settlement: National Curriculum and Local Management', Taylor Gooby, P. and Lawson, R. (eds), *Markets and Managers*, Buckingham, Open University Press

TEN (1997), *Earning and Learning: Education, Training and Employment for the 21st Century*, London, Training and Enterprise Network

Thompson, N. (1996), 'Supply-side Socialism: The Political Economy of New Labour', *New Left Review*, 216

Titmus, R.M. (1958), *Essays on the Welfare State*, London, Allen and Unwin

Titmus, R.M. (1968), *Commitment to Welfare*, London, Allen and Unwin

Tomlinson, S. (2001), *Education in Post-Welfare Society*, Milton Keynes, Open University Press

Troyna, B. (1993), *Racism and Education*, Buckingham, Open University Press

Unemployment Unit (1994), *Turning Up the Heat*, London, Unemployment Unit

Ungerson, C. (1994), 'Housing, Need, Equity, Ownership and the Economy', George, V. and Miller, S. (eds), *Social Policy Towards 2000*, London, Routledge

Usher, G. (1990), 'Employment Training: Britain's New Bantustans', *Race and Class*, Vol. 32, No. 1

Wallace, C. and Kovatcheva, S. (1998), *Youth in Society*, Basingstoke, Macmillan

Webster, D. (1997), 'Welfare to Work: Why the Theories Behind the Policies Don't Work', *Working Brief*, London, Unemployment Unit, Issue 85, June

Weiner, G., Arnot, A. and David, M. (1997), 'Is the Future Female? Female Success, Male Disadvantage and Changing Patterns of Education', Halsey, A.H., Lauder, H., Brown, P. and Stuart Wells, A. (eds), *Education: Culture, Economy and Society*, Oxford, Oxford University Press

Wells, W. (1983), *The Relative Pay and Employment of Young People*, Research Paper No. 42, London, Department of Employment

West, D.J. and Farrington, D.P. (1977), *The Delinquent Way of Life*, London, Heineman

Whiteside, N. (1991), *Hard Times: Unemployment in British Social and Political History*, London, Faber and Faber

Whitty, G. (1989), 'The New Right and the National Curriculum: State Control or Market Forces', *Journal of Education Policy*, Vol. 4, No. 4

Williams, F. (1989), *Social Policy: A Critical Introduction*, Cambridge, Polity Press

Williamson, H. (1996), 'Status Zer0, Youth and the Underclass: Some Considerations', MacDonald, R. (ed.), *Youth, The 'Underclass' and Social Exclusion*, London, Routledge

Willis, P. (1977), *Learning to Labour: How Working Class Kids Get Working Class Jobs*, London, Saxon House

Willis, P. (1990), *Common Culture*, Milton Keynes, Open University Press.

Wilson, E. (1977), *Women and Welfare*, London, Tavistock

Wilson, E. (1987), 'Thatcherism and Women: Seven Years After', Miliband, R. and Saville, J. (eds), *Socialist Register*, London, Merlin Press

Winn, S. (1997) 'Student Loans: Are the Policy Objectives Being Achieved?', *Higher Education Quarterly*, Vol. 51, No. 2

Worrall, A. (1997), *Punishment in the Community: The Future of Criminal Justice*, Harlow, Addison, Wesley, Longman

Wyn, J. and White, R. (1997), *Rethinking Youth*, London, Sage

Young, J. (1999), *The Exclusive Society*, London, Sage

Index